T0329896

HOW WE COOPERATE

How We Cooperate

A Theory of
Kantian Optimization

JOHN E. ROEMER

Yale

UNIVERSITY PRESS

NEW HAVEN AND LONDON

Published with assistance from the foundation established in memory of
Amasa Stone Mather of the Class of 1907, Yale College.

Yale University Press books may be purchased in quantity for educational, business,
or promotional use. For information, please e-mail sales.press@yale.edu (US office)
or sales@yaleup.co.uk (UK office).

Set in Electra type by Newgen North America.
Printed in the United States of America.

Library of Congress Control Number: 2018952545
ISBN 978-0-300-23333-9 (hardcover : alk. paper)

A catalogue record for this book is available from the British Library.

This paper meets the requirements of ANSI/NISO Z39.48-1992
(Permanence of Paper).

10 9 8 7 6 5 4 3 2 1

CONTENTS

Economic theory, I argue, has focused almost entirely on how economic agents compete with each other, in market economies and in games. But competition does not exhaust our economic behavior: humans cooperate in many economic situations, and they often achieve better results than they could through competition. Although game theorists have attempted to incorporate cooperative behavior into their standard template (namely, by explaining cooperation as the Nash equilibrium of a multistage game), I believe that this explanation of cooperation is unconvincing. More recently, behavioral economists have rebelled against such an explanation and have argued that explaining cooperation requires dropping the standard assumption of economic theory, that economic agents are self-interested or self-regarding. The behavioral economists' explanation of cooperation, while replacing self-regarding preferences with ones that include as arguments the welfare of others or a conception of fairness, still relies upon the main tool of conventional game theory: Nash equilibrium.

I do not believe that cooperation is usually achieved in a way that is properly modeled as the Nash equilibrium of a game—with either conventional self-regarding preferences or nonstandard preferences that incorporate more exotic arguments. In Nash equilibrium, each player treats all other players' actions *parametrically*, that is, as part of his or her environment. How do we define Nash optimization? *Taking the actions of the others as fixed*, what is the best action for me? I think a model of cooperation should show explicitly how each individual in the group contemplates how others will coordinate with him or her—others should be viewed, not as part of the environment, but as *part of the action*. This means that optimization must be done in a non-Nash way.

Defining an equilibrium of a game requires two kinds of data: the preferences of the players and the manner in which they optimize. The disagreement between neoclassical and behavioral economists, up until now, has focused only upon the first component of this duo, but agrees upon the manner of optimizing. I believe that we can more intuitively explain cooperation by assuming that players optimize in a different way from when they play competitively. In simple games (symmetric ones), a player in a cooperative situation asks himself, "What is the strategy I would like all of us to play?" I call this Kantian optimization, because it seems like a natural interpretation of Immanuel Kant's categorical or hypothetical imperative: take those actions that you would will be universalized.

Those of us schooled in game theory will, at least initially, say that such optimizing behavior is irrational. We have come to understand Nash optimization as the uniquely rational way to optimize in a game. To explain cooperation, neoclassical economists must construct rather complicated games (with many stages). My approach is much simpler; it is achieved not with the architecture of multistage games but by reconceptualizing optimization as *itself* a cooperative venture.

The simplest maxim that summarizes the motivation for Kantian optimization, at least in situations of symmetry, is "We must, indeed, all hang together, or most assuredly we shall all hang separately." This wonderful aphorism depends, of course, on the double meaning in English of the verb "to hang." I do not know if other languages have as pithy a summary of the motivation for cooperation. Benjamin Franklin was apparently the first to utter this phrase, when trying to stimulate solidarity among those men who were debating whether to sign the Declaration of Independence, and it later became a staple of the labor movement in the United States. It is difficult to call a kind of behavior irrational if, somehow, people are convinced to behave in the prescribed manner and the results are better for them than if they did not.

I have been thinking about this problem for twenty years and actively working on it for less than a decade. I have not kept a list of all those with whom I have discussed the approach, but I would like at least to acknowledge the following people, each of whom has provided me with either written comments or extended discussion upon versions of this work: Wolfgang Buckholtz, Bart Campéau, Luis Corchon, Giacomo Corneo, Steven Darwall, Herbert Gintis, Philip Kitcher, David Levine, Humberto Llavador, François Maniquet, Andreu Mas-Colell, Juan Moreno-Ternero, Joseph Ostroy, Roman Pancs, Stefan Penczynski, Ariel Rubinstein, Larry Samuelson, Carsten Schröder, Joaquim Silvestre, Joel Sobel, Stephen Stearns, Roberto Veneziani, Alain Trannoy, Burak Ünveren, Karine Van der Straeten, and Ebonya Washington. I am deeply grateful to all of them. Naturally, I remain responsible for the errors—important conceptual ones and more straightforward mathematical ones, both kinds of which doubtless remain.

HOW WE COOPERATE

ONE

Introduction

Cooperation, Altruism, and Economic Theory

1.1 A Cooperative Species

It is frequently said that *Homo sapiens* is a cooperative species. We are clearly not unique in this regard: ants and bees cooperate, and perhaps other mammalian species do, too. But the evolutionary psychologist and linguist Michael Tomasello (2014a, 2014b, 2016) argues that the only cooperative species among the five great apes (chimpanzees, bonobos, gorillas, orangutans, and humans) is our own.[1] Tomasello believes that the tendency to cooperate with other humans is inborn. He offers a number of examples of our features and behavior that are unique to humans among the five great apes. Here are three: (1) among the great apes, humans are the only beings with sclera (the whites of the eyes); (2) only humans point and mime; (3) only humans have language. Each of these features, Tomasello argues, evolved for cooperation. Sclera, for example, are useful because they enable you to see what I am looking at. If I am looking at an animal that would make a good meal, and if you and I cooperate in hunting, it is useful for me that you can see the prey that I see, because then we can catch and consume it together. Were you and I only competitors, it would not be useful for me that you see the object of my gaze, because we would then fight over who gets the animal. Thus, one would expect the mutation of sclera to be selected in a cooperative species but not to be selected in a competitive one.[2] Miming and pointing also probably emerged in hunting and were useful for members of a species who cooperated in hunting. Chimpanzees, which do not cooperate in hunting, do not mime or point[3]—either with other chimpanzees or with humans. Miming and pointing are the predecessors of language. Complex organs like the eye and complex systems like language must have evolved incrementally as the result of selection from among many random mutations. Tomasello argues that language would not be useful, and therefore would not evolve, in a species that did not already have cooperative behavior. If you and I are simply competitors, why should you believe anything I tell you? I am only out for myself, and must be trying to mislead you, because cooperation is not something in our toolkit. So language, should primitive forms of it emerge in a noncooperative species, would die out for lack of utility.

Tomasello has conducted experiments in which he compares human infants to chimpanzees, who are set with a task in which cooperation would be useful. The general outcome of these experiments is that human infants (ten months or older) cooperate immediately, whereas chimpanzees do not. Often, the cooperative project that Tomasello designs in the lab involves working together to acquire food, which then must be shared. If chimpanzees initially cooperate in acquiring the food, they find that they cannot share it peacefully but fight over it, and hence they do not cooperate the next time the project is proposed to them, because they know that the end would be a fight, which is not worth the value of the food that might be acquired. Human infants, however, succeed immediately and repeatedly in cooperating in both acquiring and eating the food.[4]

There are, of course, a myriad of examples of human cooperation, involving projects infinitely more complex than hunting or acquiring a piece of food that is difficult to get. Humans have evolved complex societies, in which people live together, cheek by jowl, in huge cities, and do so relatively peacefully. We organize complex projects, including states and taxation, the provision of public goods, large firms and other social organizations, and intricate social conventions, which are sustained only because most of those who participate do so cooperatively—that is, they participate, not because of the fear of penalties should they fail to do so, but because they understand the value of contributing to the cooperative venture. (This may seem vague at this point but will be made more precise below.) We often explain these human achievements by the high intelligence that we uniquely possess. But intelligence does not suffice as an explanation. The tendency to cooperate, whether inborn or learned, is surely necessary. If we are persuaded by Tomasello, then that tendency is inborn and was necessary for the development of the huge and complex cooperative projects that humans undertake.

Of course, Tomasello's claim (that humans are extremely cooperative great apes) does not fall if cooperation is learned through culture rather than transmitted genetically. In the former case, cooperation would be a meme, passed down in all successful human societies.

It is even possible that the large brains that differentiate humans from the other great apes evolved as a result of the cooperative tendency. Why? Because large brains are useful for complex projects—initially, complex projects that would further the fitness of the members of the species. From an evolutionary viewpoint, it might not be efficient to spend the resources to produce a large brain if complex projects were not necessary. Such projects would not be feasible without cooperation: complexity here, by definition, means that the projects are too difficult to be carried out by an individual and require coordinated effort. If humans did not already have a tendency to cooperate, then a mutation that enlarged the brain would not perhaps be selected, because it would not be useful. So not only language, but intelligence generally, may be the evolutionary product of a prior selection of the cooperative "gene." See Dunbar (2009) for further elaboration of this hypothesis.

Readers, especially economists, may object: cooperation, they might say, is fairly rare among humans, who are mainly characterized by competitive behavior. Indeed, what seems to be the case is that cooperation evolves in small groups—families, tribes—but that these groups are often at war with one another. Stone Age New Guinea, which was observable up until around the middle of the twentieth century, was home to thousands of tribes (with thousands of languages) that fought one another; within each tribe, however, cooperation flourished. (One very important aspect of intratribal cooperation among young men was participating in warfare against other tribes. See Bowles and Gintis [2011], who attribute the participation of young men in warring parties against other tribes to their altruism toward cotribals. I am skeptical that altruism rather than cooperation is the key here.) Indeed, up until the present, human society has been characterized by increasingly complex states, within which cooperative behavior is pervasive but between which there is lack of trust. Sharp competition between states (war) has been pervasive. So the human tendency to cooperate is, so it appears, not unlimited, but generally, as history has progressed, the social units within which cooperation is practiced have become increasingly large, now sometimes encompassing more than a billion humans.

1.2 Cooperation versus Altruism

For members of a group to cooperate means that they "work together, act in conjunction with one another, for an end or purpose" (*Oxford English Dictionary*). There is no supposition that the individuals care about each other. Cooperation may be the only means of satisfying *one's own self-interested preferences*. You and I build a house together so that we may each live in it. We cooperate, not because of an interest in the other's welfare, but because cooperative production is the only way of providing *any* domicile. The same thing is true of the early hunters I described above: without cooperation, neither of us could capture that deer, which, when caught by our joint effort, will feed both of us. In particular, I cooperate with you because the deer will feed *me*. It is not necessary that I ascribe any value to the fact that it will feed you, too.

Solidarity is defined as "a union of purpose, sympathies, or interests among the members of a group" (*American Heritage Dictionary*). The writer H. G. Wells is quoted there as saying, "A downtrodden class . . . will never be able to make an effective protest until it achieves solidarity." Solidarity, so construed, is not the cooperative action that the individuals take but rather a characterization of their objective situation: namely, that all are in the same boat and understand that fact. I take "a union of interests" to mean that we are all in the same situation and have common preferences. It does not mean we are altruistic toward each other. Granted, one might interpret "a union of . . . sympathies" to mean altruism, but I focus rather on "a union of purpose or interests." The statement by Wells clearly indicates the distinction between the joint action and the state of solidarity, because the action *proceeds* from the solidaristic state.

Of course, people may become increasingly sophisticated with respect to their ability to understand that they have a union of interests with other people. Benjamin Franklin's oft-quoted remark, "We must all hang together, or most assuredly we will each hang separately," urges everyone to see that they do, indeed, have similar interests to others and, hence, that it may be logical to act cooperatively. Notice that Franklin's statement appeals, not to our altruism, but to our self-interest, and to the solidaristic state in which we find ourselves.

My claim is that the ability to cooperate for reasons of self-interest is less demanding than the prescription to care about others. I believe that it is easier to explain the many examples of human cooperation from an assumption that people learn that cooperation can further their own interests than to explain those examples by altruism. For this reason, I separate the discussion of cooperation among self-interested individuals from cooperation among altruistic ones (altruism will not be addressed until chapter 5).

Altruism and *cooperation* are frequently confounded in the literature. I do not mean the example I gave from Samuel Bowles and Herbert Gintis, who in their book *A Cooperative Species: Human Reciprocity and Its Evolution* explicitly view altruism as the characteristic that induces young men to undertake dangerous combat for their community. If they are right, this is a case in which altruism engenders cooperative action. I mean that writers often seem not to see a distinction between altruism and cooperation. The key point is that cooperation of an extensive kind can be undertaken because it is in the interest of *each*, not because each cares about others. I am skeptical that humans can, on a mass scale, have deep concern for others whom they have not even met, and so to base grand humanitarian projects on such a psychological propensity is risky. I do, however, believe that humans quite generally have common interests and that it is natural to pursue these cooperatively. (One can hardly avoid thinking of the control of global greenhouse gas emissions as a leading such issue at present.) It seems that the safer *general* strategy is to rely on the underlying motive of self-interest, active in cooperation, rather than on love for others, active in altruism.

The necessary conditions for cooperation are solidarity (in the sense of our all being in the same boat) and trust—trust that if I take the cooperative action, so will enough others to advance our common interest. Solidarity comes in different degrees—recall the famous statement by Martin Niemöller, who because of his opposition to Hitler spent the last seven years of Nazi rule in a concentration camp: "First they came for the Socialists, and I did not speak out—Because I was not a Socialist. . . . Then they came for the Jews, and I did not speak out—Because I was not a Jew. Then they came for me—and there was no one left to speak for me." The listener is being urged, here, to see that "we are all in the same boat," even if superficial differences among us may frustrate that understanding. Trust usually must be built by past experience of cooperation with the individuals concerned. Trust may be distributed in a somewhat continuous way in a population: some people are unconditional cooperators, who will cooperate regardless of the participation of others; some will cooperate when a certain threshold is reached (say, 20 percent of others are cooperating); and some will never cooperate, even if all else are doing so. The common name we have for persons of the first kind is *saint*.

1.3 Cooperation and Economic Theory

Economic theory has focused not on our cooperative tendencies but on our competitive ones. Indeed, the two great theoretical contributions of microeconomics are both models of competition: the theory of competitive or Walrasian equilibrium, and game theory, with its associated stability concept, Nash equilibrium. It is clear that cooperation does not exist in the everyday meaning of the word in these theories. There is indeed nothing that can be thought of as social action. The kind of reasoning, or optimization, that individuals engage in in these theories is *autarkic*: other humans' actions are treated as parameters of the individual's problem, not as part of the action.

In general equilibrium theory, at least its most popular Walrasian version, individuals do not even observe what other people are *doing*: they simply observe the price vector and optimize against prices.[5] Prices summarize all the relevant information about what others are doing, and so it is superfluous for the individual to have specific information about others' actions. This indeed is usually championed as one of the beauties of the model—its ability to decentralize economic activity in the sense that each person need only know information about itself (preferences for humans, technologies for firms) and prices for Pareto efficiency to be achieved. To be precise, the "achievement" of efficiency is an incomplete story because it lacks dynamics: we know only that *if* an equilibrium is reached, it will be Pareto efficient, and the theory of dynamics remains incomplete. (The first theorem of welfare economics, which states that a competitive equilibrium is Pareto efficient, holds only under stringent and unrealistic conditions: economic problems that require cooperation, such as the financing of public goods and the regulation of public bads, are stipulated not to exist.) In the Nash equilibrium of a game each player treats his competitors as inert: he imagines a counterfactual in which he alone changes his strategy while the others hold theirs fixed. A Nash equilibrium is a strategy profile such that each person's strategy is optimal (for himself) given the inertness of others' strategies. One can say that a Nash optimizer treats others as parameters of the environment rather than as persons such as herself.

There is no doubt that general equilibrium and game theory are beautiful ideas; they are the culmination of what is probably the deepest thinking in the social sciences over the past several centuries. But they are not designed to deal with that aspect of behavior that is so distinctive of humans (among the great apes): our ability to cooperate with one another.

Economic theory, though it does not entirely ignore cooperation, attempts to fit it into the procrustean bed of the competitive model. Until behavioral economics came along, the main way of explaining cooperation—which here can be defined as the overcoming of the Pareto inefficient Nash equilibria that standardly occur in games—was to view cooperation as a *Nash* equilibrium of a complex game with many stages. (See Kandori 1992.) Think of a game such as the prisoner's dilemma, in which there is a cooperative strategy and a noncooperative one. These strategies inherit their names from the fact that if both players play the cooperative strategy, each does better than if both play the noncooperative one. In this well-known game, the unique Nash equilibrium is for both players to play the noncooperative strategy. The complex stage game in which the one-shot prisoner's dilemma can be embedded stipulates that if a player fails to cooperate at stage t, then she is punished at stage $t + 1$ by another player. However, punishment, being costly for the enforcer, is carried out only against noncooperators in stage t if there is a stage $t + 2$ in which those enforcers who fail to punish are themselves punished. The game must have an infinite number of stages, or at least an *unknown* number of stages, for this approach to support a cooperative equilibrium. For if it were known that the game had only three stages, say, then enforcers in the third stage would not punish the lazy enforcers who failed to punish in the second stage, because nobody would be around to punish *them* for failing to do so (there being no fourth stage). So those who are charged with punishing in the second stage will not do so (punishing being costly), and thus a player can play the noncooperative strategy in the first stage without fear of punishment. Therefore, with a known, finite number of stages, the good equilibrium (with cooperation) unravels.

But is this really the explanation of why people cooperate? The influential economist Mancur Olson (1965) argued that it is. Workers join strikes only because they will be punished by other workers if they do not; they join unions not in recognition of their solidaristic situation, but because they are offered side payments to do so.

Communities that suffer from the so-called free-rider problem in the provision of public goods often do adopt punishment strategies to induce members to cooperate. Fishers must often control the total amount of fishing to preserve the fishery. Absent cooperation, common-pool resources such as fisheries are overexploited. Maine lobstermen apparently had a sequence of increasing punishments for those who deviated from the prescribed rules. If a lobsterman put out too many nets, the first step was for others to place a warning note on the buoys of the offending nets. If that didn't work, a committee visited him. If that failed, his nets were destroyed. Now consider the optimization problem of those who were appointed to do these acts of warning and punishment. If they failed in their duty, there must be another group who was charged with punishing them—or perhaps this would be accomplished simply by social ostracism. But is it credible that the whole system was maintained even though *everyone* was in fact optimizing in the autarkic Nash way, carrying out his duty to punish only because of a fear of punishment should he shirk in this duty? I am skeptical. It is perhaps more likely that there were many who were committed to implementing the cooperative solution, many who did not require the threat of punishment to take the cooperative action, at any stage of the game. The complex equilibrium in which cooperation is maintained by an elaborate chain of punishments is, I think, too fragile to explain the real thing. The explanation is Ptolemaic, an effort to fit an observed phenomenon into a theory that cannot explain it in a simple way.

Social and political theorist Jon Elster (2017) introduces useful distinctions. A *social norm* is a behavior that is enforced by punishment of those who deviate from it; those who observe the deviation and fail to punish the deviator are themselves punished by others who observe this. A social norm is thus a Nash equilibrium of a game with stages, in which those who fail to cooperate are punished, and so on and on. A person obeys a social norm because he is afraid of *being seen* if he fails to, and hence punished by the observer. In contrast, a *quasi-moral norm* is one that is motivated by wanting to do the right thing. But the "right thing" is defined in large part by what others do. If I observe that most others are recycling their trash, and therefore I recycle, I am behaving according to a quasi-moral norm. In this case, I cooperate not because I am afraid of being seen should I fail to; rather, I cooperate because I *see others* taking the cooperative action. A *moral norm* is, in contrast, unconditional. I take the cooperative action regardless of what others are doing. The Kantian categorical and hypothetical imperatives are moral norms. The behavior of the lobstermen described above could be a social norm or a quasi-moral norm. It is unlikely that it constitutes a moral norm. Because I believe that trust is a necessary condition, I view cooperation as a quasi-moral norm, for trust is established by observing that others are taking the cooperative action or have taken similarly cooperative actions in the past.

The second place where we find cooperation addressed in neoclassical economic theory is in the theory of cooperative games. A cooperative game with a player set N is a function v mapping the subsets of N into the real numbers. Each subset $S \in 2^N$ is a coalition of players, and the number $v(S)$ is interpreted as the total utility (let us say) that S's members can achieve by cooperation among themselves. A solution to a cooperative game is way of assigning utility to the members of N that satisfies the constraint that total utility cannot exceed $v(N)$. For instance, the *core* is the set of "imputations" or utility allocations such that no coalition can do better for itself by internal cooperation. If $(x^1, \ldots, x^n)$ is a utility imputation in the core, then the following inequality must hold:

$$(\forall S \in 2^N)(v(S) \leq \sum_{i \in S} x^i) . \tag{1.1}$$

Although cooperation is invoked to explain what coalitions can achieve on their own, the core itself is a competitive notion: the values $v(S)$ are backstops that determine the nature of competition among the player set as a whole. It is therefore somewhat of a misnomer to call this approach "cooperative." Indeed, Andreu Mas-Colell (1987, 659) writes: "The typical starting point [of cooperative game theory] is the hypothesis that, in principle, any subgroup of economic agents (or perhaps some distinguished subgroups) has a clear picture of the possibilities of joint action and that its members can communicate freely before the formal play starts. Obviously, what is left out of cooperative theory is very substantial." Indeed!

Behavioral economists have challenged this unlikely rationalization of cooperative behavior as a Nash equilibrium of a complex game with punishments by altering the standard assumption of self-interested preferences. There are many versions, but they share in common the move of putting new and "exotic" arguments into preferences—arguments such as a concern with fairness (Fehr and Schmidt 1999 and Rabin 2003) or of giving gifts to one's opponent (Akerlof 1982) or of seeking a warm glow (Andreoni 1990). Once preferences have been so altered, then the cooperative outcome can be achieved as a *Nash* equilibrium of the new game. Punishments may indeed be inflicted by such players against others who fail to cooperate, but it is no longer necessarily costly for the enforcer to punish, because his sense of fairness has been offended or a social norm has been broken that he values. Or he may even get a warm glow from punishing the deviator! I will discuss these approaches more below. My immediate reaction to them is that they are too easy—in the sense of being nonfalsifiable. The invention of the concept of a preference order is extremely important, but one must exercise a certain discipline in using it. Just as econometricians are not free to mine the data, so theorists should not allow everything ("the kitchen sink") to be an argument of preferences. It is, of course, a personal judgment to draw the line as I have suggested it be drawn.

If the undisciplined use of preferences were my only critique of behavioral economics, it might be minimized. A more formidable critique, I think, is that the trick of modifying preferences only works—in the sense of producing the "good" or cooperative Nash equilibrium—when the problem is pretty simple. ("Simple" usually means that a player has only a few strategies and that the "cooperative" strategy is obvious to everyone. This is true in most 2×2 matrix games. In laboratory games involving the voluntary contribution to a public good, and in ultimatum and dictator games, there are many strategies, but it is nevertheless clear what the cooperative action is.) If we consider, however, the general problem of the tragedy of the commons in common-pool resource games, the cooperative strategy profile—in which each player plays her part of a Pareto-efficient solution—is not obvious. Either some kind of *decentralization of cooperation* is needed or cooperation must be organized by a central authority.

Just as the Walrasian equilibrium of a market economy is not obvious to anyone and requires decentralization, so does cooperation with any degree of complexity. Although we have many examples of cooperation that are organized by a central authority, it is surely the case that the vast majority of cases of cooperation in human experience are not centrally organized. An ordinary person encounters hundreds of situations a year in which cooperation would be profitable but is not centrally organized. How, then, do people manage to cooperate in these cases?

I do not believe that the strategy of behavioral economics supplies *microfoundations for cooperation* of a general kind. And if cooperation is a major part of what makes us human, we should be looking for its general microfoundations.

1.4 Simple Kantian Optimization

In this book I will offer a partial solution to the problem of specifying micro-foundations for cooperation, which I call Kantian optimization, with its concomitant concept of Kantian equilibrium. The new move is, instead of altering preferences from classical, self-interested ones, to alter *how people optimize*. In the simplest case, consider a symmetric game. A two-person game is symmetric if the payoff matrix is symmetric, as in the prisoner's dilemma of table 1.1.

Table 1.1 **The payoff matrix of a prisoner's dilemma game; the first number in parentheses is the payoff to the row player, and the second number is the payoff to the column player**

	A	B
A	(1,1)	(−1,2)
B	(2,−1)	(0,0)

A symmetric game is one in which players are identically situated: they are all in the same boat. In the game of table 1.1, a Nash optimizer asks himself, "Given the strategy chosen by my opponent, what is the best strategy for me?" The answer, regardless of the opponent's choice, is that I should play *B*. *B* is a "dominant strategy," in the language of game theory. But a Kantian optimizer—so I propose—asks, "What is the strategy I would like both of us to play?" Clearly the answer is *A*, because I do better if we both play *A* than if we both play *B*. It is not relevant to me that *you* also do better when we both play *A*—altruism is not my motivation. It is, however, important that I understand the symmetry of the game and, hence, know that the answer to the proposed question is the same for both of us.

The symmetry of the situation naturally suggests that we ask the Kantian question. Tomasello argues that the ability to cooperate is founded in our ability to form "joint intentionality." My interpretation of this concept is that we each think, "What would I like each of us to do?" and *if* we trust each other, we understand that each of us is thinking in this way and will behave in the way the answer instructs. I will elaborate on this in chapter 2.

DEFINITION 1.1 In a symmetric game, the strategy that *each* would prefer *all* to play is a *simple Kantian equilibrium* (SKE).[6]

I invoke Immanuel Kant here because of his categorical and hypothetical imperatives, which state that one should take those actions one would like to see universalized.[7] I understand that it would be more precise to call this "quasi-moral optimization," because Kant's imperatives are unconditional, whereas mine is not. I opt, however, for the more imprecise "Kantian" nomenclature because there is a history of using it in economics, as I will review in section 2.7, and because it is aptly described by Kant's phrase, "Take those actions you would will be universalized," even if Kant meant this in an unconditional way.

The concept of Kantian equilibrium will later be generalized beyond the case of symmetric games, but it is useful to consider these games first, because they are the simplest. Many laboratory experiments in economics involve symmetric games, and it is in symmetric games that Kantian optimization takes its simplest and most compelling form.

It is important to note that the Kantian optimizer asks what common strategy (played by all) would be *best for him*: he is not altruistic, in thinking about the payoffs of others. To calculate the strategy he would like everyone to play, he need only know his own preferences. But to invoke joint intentionality, he must also know that others are similarly situated—that is, that the game is symmetric. This implies that the common strategy that is best for him is also best for others, a fact that does not appeal to his perhaps non-existent altruism but motivates his expectation that others will act in like manner. That expectation, however, must also be engendered by trust or an experience of past cooperation.

What I emphasize is that cooperation, in this view, is achieved, not by inserting a new argument into preferences, such as altruism or a warm glow, but by conceptualizing the optimizing process in a different way. These are diverse ways of modeling the problem—one involves altering preferences but keeping the Nash optimization protocol, and the other involves keeping preferences classical but altering the optimization protocol. Despite the conceptual distinction, it may be difficult to test which model better explains the reality of cooperation, a problem to which we will return.

A quite *different* question, to which I have no complete answer, is when, in a game, do players choose to invoke the Kantian protocol and when the Nash protocol? Often, I believe, this depends on the degree of trust in the other players. Of course, trust is irrelevant for a Nash optimizer.

1.5 Some Examples

I conclude this chapter with several examples of what I believe to be Kantian optimization in real life.

A. *Recycling*. In many cities, many or most people recycle their trash. There is no penalty for failing to do so. Often, others do not observe if one does not recycle. The cost of recycling may be nontrivial—certainly greater than the marginal benefit in terms of the public good of a clean environment that one's participation engenders. James Andreoni's (1990) view, that one cooperates in order to receive a "warm glow," is an example of explaining recycling by inserting an exotic argument into preferences. I think this puts the cart before the horse: one may indeed enjoy a warm glow, but that's *because* one has done the right thing—that is, taken the action one would like all to take. The warm glow is an unintended by-product of the action, not its cause. Suppose that I help my child with her algebra homework: she masters the quadratic formula. I feel a warm glow. But seeking that glow was not my motivation: it was to teach her algebra, and the warm glow follows, unintendedly, as a consequence of success in that project. While recycling may be a quasi-moral norm, teaching my daughter algebra is probably due to altruism. In either case, I find the "warm glow" to be no explanation at all.

B. *"Doing one's bit" in Britain in World War II.* This was a popular expression for something voluntary and extra that one did for the war effort. Is it best explained by seeking the respect or approval of others or by doing what one wished everyone to do? For some, this could be a social norm, punished, if

14

avoided, by ostracism. For others, it was a quasi-moral norm, done because it was the right thing to do, as evidenced by what others were doing.

C. *Soldiers protecting comrades in battle.* This can be a Kantian equilibrium but also could be induced by altruism. One becomes close to others in one's unit. In this case, the Kantian equilibrium is also an instance of the golden rule—"Do unto others what you would have them do unto you." Golden-rule optimization is a special case of simple Kantian equilibrium.

D. *Voting.* The voting paradox is not one from the Kantian viewpoint: I vote because I'd like everyone to vote, rather than not to vote, to contribute to the public good of democracy. A somewhat different form is that I vote because I would like everyone *similarly situated* to me (that is, sharing my politics) to vote.

E. *Paying taxes.* It has often been observed that the probability of being caught for tax evasion and the penalties assessed for doing so are far too small to explain the relatively small degree of tax evasion in most advanced countries. In most countries (though not all), tax cheaters are not publicly identified, so shame (an exotic argument in preferences) is not an issue. Elster (2017), however, points out that in Norway, everyone's tax payment is published on the internet, and this increases compliance. A caveat to the example is that the practice of withholding tax owed minimizes the possibility of evasion.

F. *Tipping.* A practice viewed by some as a paradox (Gambetta 2015) is not one from the Kantian viewpoint: here, there is an altruistic element, but it is not the interesting part of the behavior. The thought process is that I tip what I would like each to tip. I understand what I think it's proper to tip by observing what the custom is—hence the quasi-moral nature of the behavior.

G. *Charity.* The Nash equilibrium is often not to donate, even if I value the public good produced. There is a Kantian and a Rawlsian explanation of charity: the Kantian gives what he'd

like all others (like him) to give. For the Rawlsian, charity is
the random dictator game: behind the veil of ignorance, who
will be the donor and who the recipient of charity? These
two ways of looking at the problem generate different levels
of charity (I may give much more in the so-called Rawlsian
version). My conjecture is that the so-called Kantian thought
process is more prevalent.[8]

I have organized the book as follows. Part I, comprising chapters 2 through
10, studies Kantian optimization in games. The main result is that in many
cases, Kantian optimization solves the two major problems that afflict Nash
equilibrium: the inefficiency of equilibrium in the presence of congestion
externalities, known as the *tragedy of the commons*, and the inefficiency of
equilibrium in the presence of public goods or positive externalities, known
as *the free-rider problem*. In two important classes of games—those with
positive and negative externalities—Kantian equilibrium is Pareto efficient.
Moreover, we will see that in such games, Nash equilibrium is *always* Pareto inefficient. So Kantian optimization "solves" what must appear as the
two greatest failures of Nash optimization, from the viewpoint of human
welfare.

In Part II, chapters 11 through 14, I apply Kantian optimization to market economies: that is, I embed cooperation in general equilibrium models.
These four chapters present six such examples, which include showing how
the problem of controlling global carbon emissions can be decentralized by
using a cap-and-trade regime, as a "unanimity equilibrium"; how Kantian
optimization in the labor-supply decision by workers in a "market-socialist"
economy produces Pareto-efficient equilibria with any desired degree of
income redistribution, which is to say that the equity-efficiency trade-off
dissolves; how public goods can be produced efficiently in a market economy; and how an economy consisting of worker-owned firms can achieve
efficient equilibria, again with many degrees of freedom in the distribution of income, using Kantian optimization. Chapter 15 offers some final
reflections.

PART ONE

Kantian Optimization in Games

Simple Kantian Equilibrium

2.1 To Cooperate or Not?

Consider the prisoner's dilemma of table 1.1. I propose that there are two ways for a self-interested player to decide what to do when playing this game.

Method One. A player thinks: no matter which strategy the other player chooses, my payoff is greater if I play B. Therefore, I should play B.

Method Two. Assume that it is common knowledge that the payoff matrix is symmetric and that my opponent and I have equal capacities and reasoning power. Hence, due to the symmetry of the game, I assume that whatever strategy I decide upon will also be decided upon by my opponent. It follows that I must only consider strategy profiles (x,x) as ones that might occur, where $x \in \{A, B\}$. I therefore should choose the strategy x that maximizes my payoff, if (x,x) is played by my opponent and me. That is strategy A. My opponent will choose the same action, because he will reason this way as well, and of this I am confident, because of the common-knowledge assumption and our equal reasoning powers.

Obviously, Method One is Nash optimization and Method Two is Kantian optimization: the first is aptly called noncooperative, the second cooperative. Method One engenders a Nash equilibrium (NE), and Method Two engenders a simple Kantian equilibrium (SKE). The second method involves more assumptions about the environment: to wit, it is common knowledge that the players reason identically and the game is symmetric. Method One is particularly simple for the prisoner's dilemma, because B is a dominant strategy.

Various philosophers have written about what is called *joint intentionality*: this group includes Margaret Gilbert (1990), Michael Bratman (1992), Stephen Darwall (2009), Philip Kitcher (2011), and the evolutionary psychologist Michael Tomasello (2016). They have somewhat different definitions of the concept; none seems exactly like the cooperative protocol in Method Two, but I think the common thread of this literature shows that many believe that a cooperative protocol exists and that it differs from the Nash protocol. None of these authors explains cooperation, when it occurs, as a Nash equilibrium of a game with many stages, involving punishment of those who deviate from the cooperative strategy, which is the most common way for (nonbehavioral) economists to explain cooperation.

One often thinks of trust as key in cooperative situations: trust is necessary for cooperation because the strategy profile (A,A) is not a Nash equilibrium (that is, one player could defect against the other and gain personally). A Nash theorist says that (A,A) is unstable. I think of trust as induced by the assumptions of common knowledge and common capacity. We know that, in reality, racial, ethnic, and linguistic heterogeneity tend to weaken trust: this is because these kinds of heterogeneity weaken the plausibility of the common knowledge and common capacity assumptions. In particular, it is not because homogeneity induces altruism that like people cooperate but because homogeneity makes the common-knowledge assumption credible. Conversely, if you and I are in different tribes, I am not confident that you will reason as I do.

Trust is conventionally defined as the belief that my opponent will play cooperatively. I am suggesting an explanation of trust. If it is common knowledge that the game is symmetric and that all players are equally capable and think in the same way, then (my argument says) they will limit their domain of admissible strategy profiles to ones in which all players take the same action, and (to continue my argument) that must therefore be the action that is best for each, about which unanimity prevails (assuming there is a unique such action). Thus, the microfoundation of trust, and hence cooperation, is common knowledge of the game's symmetry and equality of capability of the players.

Tomasello (2016) speaks of *common ground* in early societies—the common experiences and expectations and knowledge that members of the group have. It is common ground that gives rise to the common knowledge assumption. Common ground, for Tomasello, includes knowledge of "how we do things," which we could formalize as, among other things, the strategies we play in gamelike situations with each other. Tomasello does not state any protocol as abstract as Method Two.

What I have described as Method Two of optimizing, some would protest, is too thin a conception of cooperation. In particular, Darwall (2013) emphasizes what he calls second-personal protest. If I play strategy A and you play B in the prisoner's dilemma, I will protest: you have not done what is the "right thing" in our society, which is to play A. Darwall's discussion applies to projects that the two of us have agreed to undertake, and attendant with that is an agreement for us each to do the right thing, which Tomasello would say is part of the common ground assumption. This is not necessarily the situation I posed, of a prisoner's dilemma, which may be a situation we find ourselves in together, willy-nilly, but not a project with a goal that we have formulated. Certainly, forming a joint project may entail an obligation that we each carry out our expected roles, and each may protest against a partner who fails to do the right thing; nor is it surprising that a partner could be deterred from failing in his obligation for fear of the protest that would follow.

However, Darwall's justification of second-personal protest could apply as well to prisoner's dilemma situations that are not joint projects but situations we find ourselves in, willy-nilly. For if we are from the same cultural group, then there may well be an expectation that when members of our group are thrown together in a prisoner's dilemma, we each play strategy A. The obligation to do so comes, not from a prior agreement between us specifically to carry out a project, but from the agreement among our cultural group to play strategy A when such situations come up. This kind of agreement is a social norm and, I do not think, *at this stage* is modeled as the outcome of individual optimizing.

In chapter 1, I discussed how Jon Elster (2017) distinguishes among social norms, moral norms, and quasi-moral norms. Elster (1989a, 1989b, 2017) has also written about magical thinking: I take an action because I believe that it will cause people similar to me to take a similar action. Surely magical thinking, if present, can induce Kantian optimization. I take the action that I would like all others to take, believing that my taking the action will induce them to do so; and therefore magical thinking can induce Kantian optimization in the absence of an ethical commitment to behave morally. The thought process I describe as Method Two above is not magical thinking, although it may have the same consequence.

Darwall and Tomasello may be correct that cooperation (and morality) evolved as social norms, instructing people how to behave in a variety of situations. But unless there is a general rule of behavior, then cooperation must require a catalog of what the right behaviors are in every possible situation one might encounter with others. What I propose is that the general rule that always finds the cooperative solution in symmetric games is "Choose the strategy I would like all to choose." This *defines* the "right thing to do." Once a person discovers this rule inductively, then looking up the right social (or moral) norm for the situation at hand in the culture's catalog can be replaced with optimization. Moreover, the rule can be applied to cases that are omitted from the catalog.

In proposing Method Two, I am not proposing to describe how cooperation evolved historically among humans. Cooperation may well have come about in the manner Tomasello describes, from a catalog instructing members of a group how they are to behave in a variety of situations, where deviations from that behavior would have been punished by others. My claim is that there is an underlying logic to the rules of behavior and, moreover, that many humans must have learned to understand it. Indeed, every religion has a general rule along the lines of "Do unto others as you would have them do unto you," a special case of Kantian optimization. People who learned to understand the general rule (Method Two) had no further need of the cultural catalog of behavior. The advent of morality may be described as learning the general rule, no longer having to rely on the catalog.

As an ironic comment on the plausibility of simple Kantian equilibrium, let me remind the reader of a scene in the movie *A Beautiful Mind*, the biopic about the mathematician John Nash. In the film, Nash proposes to his two buddies how the three of them should approach four women (three brunettes and a blonde) who have entered a bar: purportedly, he is describing a Nash equilibrium of the implicit game among the four men.[1] His proposal, that each man approach one of the brunettes, however, is not a Nash equilibrium but a simple Kantian equilibrium (where the strategies are "approach a brunette" and "approach the blonde"). If two of the three men approach a brunette, the third should deviate to the blonde, according to Nash optimization, given the preferences of the men, who are assumed to prefer blondes!

2.2 Monotonicity and Pareto Efficiency

We consider games in which all players have a common strategy space S of real numbers. A game with n players is defined by the payoff functions $V^i : S^n \to \Re$ for $i = 1,\ldots,n$. Call this the game **V**.

DEFINITION 2.1 A game **V** is *(strictly) monotone increasing* if, for each i, V^i is (strictly) increasing in the strategies of the other players $j \neq i$. In like manner, a game is *(strictly) monotone decreasing* if, for each i, V^i is (strictly) decreasing in the strategies of the other players $j \neq i$. A game is *(strictly) monotone* if it is either (strictly) monotone increasing or decreasing.

A game has a *common diagonal* if the payoff functions of all players coincide on the diagonal, $\{(p,p,\ldots,p) \in S^n \mid p \in S\}$—or, in ordinal language, if each player orders the elements on the main diagonal in the same way. This condition is weaker than saying that the game is symmetric. (For a two-person game, symmetry means that for all $p,q \in S$, $V^1(p,q) = V^2(q,p)$.) It is immediate that if a game has a common diagonal, then it possesses a simple Kantian equilibrium.

PROPOSITION 2.1

*a. If a game **V** possesses a common diagonal, then an SKE exists.*

b. In a strictly monotone game, any SKE is Pareto efficient.

PROOF OF PART *b*. Let the game be strictly monotone decreasing. Let $(p^*, p^*, \ldots, p^*)$ be an SKE, and suppose that it is Pareto dominated by $(p^1, \ldots, p^n)$, so:

$$(\forall i)(V^i(p^1,\ldots,p^n) \geq V^i(p^*,\ldots,p^*)),$$

with at least one inequality strict. Obviously the $\{p^i\}$ are not all equal, for this would contradict the fact that p^* is an SKE. Let $\underline{p} = \min_i p^i$. Let j be an index such that $p^j = \underline{p}$. Then:

$$V^i(\underline{p},\ldots,\underline{p}) > V^i(p^1,\ldots,p^n) \geq V^i(p^*,\ldots,p^*),$$

where the first inequality follows by the strict monotone-decreasing property of the game, invoked for the jth player. But this inequality contradicts the premise that p^* is an SKE: player j would prefer the vector $(p,p,\ldots,p)$.

An analogous argument establishes the result if the game is strictly monotone increasing. ∎

The case of monotone decreasing games is the standard case in which the *tragedy of the commons* afflicts the Nash equilibrium. In this case, each person's action imposes a negative externality on other players. The lake upon which we all fish becomes congested if we all fish too much, and everyone's productivity declines. The case of monotone increasing games is one in which each person's action increases the welfare of others: it is the classical case of a group's contributions to a public good. This is the classical case in which *the free-rider problem* afflicts Nash equilibrium.

The tragedy of the commons and the free-rider problem are the two most noted pathologies of Nash reasoning in monotone games—pathologies in the sense that Nash reasoning produces a Pareto-inefficient outcome. Proposition 2.1 establishes that in symmetric games of either type, Kantian reasoning resolves them both.[2]

2.3 Two-Person Symmetric Games

As we noted above, a two-person symmetric game has a common diagonal, and so Proposition 2.1 applies.

The general prisoner's dilemma is given by the payoff matrix of table 2.1. In the discrete version of the game, call "Defect" strategy 0 and "Cooperate" strategy 1. Then the game is strictly monotone increasing, and so the simple Kantian equilibrium, which is (Cooperate, Cooperate), is Pareto efficient (by Proposition 2.1). If we move to mixed strategies, where the strategy space is $S = [0,1]$ for each player, then the equilibrium depends on the payoff matrix, which is, in general form:[3]

Table 2.1 The prisoner's dilemma game, with $0 < b < c$

	Cooperate	Defect
Cooperate	(0,0)	(−c,1)
Defect	(1,−c)	(−b,−b)

The payoff function of the row player is:

$$V^{PD}(p,q) = -p(1-q)c + (1-p)q - b(1-p)(1-q),$$

where $p(q)$ is the probability that the row (column) player plays Cooperate. The game is symmetric (thus, the payoff function of the column player is $V^{PD}(q,p)$). Recall that in the mixed-strategy game, Pareto efficiency is defined in terms of expected utility (that is, ex ante efficiency).

The prisoner's dilemma game is strictly monotone increasing: just note that:

$$\frac{\partial V^{PD}(p,q)}{\partial q} = pc + (1-p)(1+b) > 0.$$

It follows immediately from Proposition 2.1 that the simple Kantian equilibrium of the mixed-strategy prisoner's dilemma (PD) game is Pareto efficient.

PROPOSITION 2.2

   a. The SKE of the PD game is Pareto efficient.
   b. If $1 \le c \le 1 + b$, the SKE of the PD game is $(p^*, p^*) = (1,1)$.
   c. If $c < 1$, the SKE of the PD game is $p^* = \dfrac{2b+1-c}{2(1+b-c)}$ and $0 < p^* < 1$.
   d. If $1 + b < c$, the SKE of the PD game is $p^* = 1$.

PROOF. Part *a* follows from Proposition 2.1 because the PD game is strictly monotone increasing.

The function $V(p,p)$ is concave if and only if $c - b \le 1$. In this case, the first-order condition $\dfrac{d}{dp}V^{PD}(p,p) = 0$ gives the SKE. If $1 \le c$, the solution is a corner one, at $p^* = 1$ (part *b*). If $c < 1$, the solution is interior, and given by part *c*. If $c - b > 1$, the function $V^{PD}(p,p)$ is convex, and hence the SKE occurs at either $p = 0$ or $p = 1$. The value is higher at $p = 1$, giving part *d*. ∎

It is interesting that in the case of part *c*, although the simple Kantian equilibrium is Pareto efficient, it entails less than full cooperation. The intuition here is that the payoff to defecting against a cooperator (which is unity) is high, and so it may be optimal for both players not to cooperate fully. This shows that cooperation, in the Kantian sense, does not always deliver what we might intuitively consider to be "ideal" cooperative behavior.

Parts b and c of the proposition establish that, if $c > 1$, then the simple Kantian equilibrium entails full cooperation.

We next consider the game of chicken, also known as the hawk-dove game, which we take as the names of the strategies. The payoff matrix is given in table 2.2.

Table 2.2 **The game of chicken, with** $1 > c > b > 0$

	Dove	Hawk
Dove	(c,c)	$(b,1)$
Hawk	$(1,b)$	$(0,0)$

The payoff function is $V^{HD}(p,q) = cpq + bp(1-q) + q(1-p)$, where $p(q)$ is the probability that the row (column) player plays Dove. We immediately verify that hawk-dove is a strictly monotone increasing game, and so the simple Kantian equilibrium is Pareto efficient. The simple Kantian equilibrium is given by:

$$p^* = \begin{cases} 1, \text{ if } c \geq \dfrac{1+b}{2} \\ \dfrac{1+b}{2(1+b-c)}, \text{ if } c < \dfrac{1+b}{2}. \end{cases}$$

Thus, peace reigns if c is sufficiently large; otherwise, there is a positive probability that peace reigns, although it is not assured. There are three Nash equilibria to hawk-dove: $(1,0)$, $(0,1)$, and $(\dfrac{b}{1+b-c}, \dfrac{b}{1+b-c})$. The simple Kantian equilibrium Pareto dominates the symmetric Nash equilibrium.

We next consider the battle of the sexes game. For the game to be symmetric (that is, for $V^{Row}(p,q) = V^{Col}(q,p)$), we must write the payoff matrix unconventionally, as in table 2.3.

Table 2.3 **The battle of the sexes: unconventional version,** $0 < b < a < 1$

	Dance	Box
Box	(b,b)	$(1,a)$
Dance	$(a,1)$	$(0,0)$

That is, the *first* strategy for the row player (He) is the event he prefers, and the *first* strategy for the column player (She) is the event she prefers. The payoff function for the row player is $V^{BS}(p,q) = bpq + p(1 - q) + aq(1 - p)$, and the column player's payoff is $V^{BS}(q,p)$. The simple Kantian equilibrium in pure strategies is (Box, Dance). It is not Pareto efficient, being dominated by both (Dance, Dance) and (Box, Box).

The reader can check that the battle of the sexes (BS) game in mixed strategies is not a monotone game. We have:

PROPOSITION 2.3

a. The SKE of the 2 × 2 mixed-strategy BS game of table 2.3 is
$(p^*,p^*) = \dfrac{1+a}{2(1+a-b)}$, *and* $0 < p^* < 1$.

b. There are BS games in which the SKE is not Pareto efficient.

c. The NE of the mixed-strategy BS game is $\hat{p} = \hat{q} = \dfrac{1}{1+a-b}$. *It is strictly Pareto dominated by the SKE.*

d. $p^* < \hat{p}$.

PROOF. Compute that $V^{BS}(p,p) = (b - (1 + a))p^2 + p(a + 1)$, which is a strictly concave function of p. Hence the first-order condition gives us the SKE, which is $p^* = \dfrac{1+a}{2(1+a-b)}$. It is easy to compute that p^* is interior in $[0,1]$. Compute that $V^{BS}(p^*,p^*) = \dfrac{(a+1)^2}{4(a+1-b)}$. Let $a = 0.75, b = 0.01, p = 0$, $q = 0.6$. Then $V^{BS}(p^*,p^*) = 0.4400$, $V^{BS}(p,q) = 0.45$, $V^{BS}(q,p) = 0.6$, and so (p^*, p^*) is Pareto-dominated by (p,q).

The NE of the mixed-strategy BS game is computed from the first-order conditions for NE. Write $V^{BS}(p,q) = p(bq + 1 - q - aq) + aq$. Therefore, Row's best response to q is:

$$p = \begin{cases} 1, & \text{if } bq+1-q-aq > 0 \\ 0, & \text{if } bq+1-q-aq < 0 \\ [0,1], & \text{if } bq+1-q-aq = 0. \end{cases}$$

It follows that (1,1) is not an NE, because if $q = 1$, the best response of Row is 0. Likewise (0,0) is not an NE, because if $q = 0$, the best response of Row is 1. The only NE occurs in the third case, when $p = q = \dfrac{1}{1+a-b}$. ∎

27

In other words, simple Kantian optimization does not generally deliver Pareto efficiency in the BS game, although the simple Kantian equilibrium always dominates the Nash equilibrium of the game. From part *d*, we have that in the simple Kantian equilibrium, both She and He offer to attend their favorite event with lower probability than in the Nash equilibrium: in other words, they *compromise more* in simple Kantian equilibrium than in Nash equilibrium.

More generally, we must have that, in any game with a common diagonal, the simple Kantian equilibrium Pareto dominates the symmetric Nash equilibrium, as long as the two equilibria are not the same, because the symmetric Nash equilibrium is of the form (p,p) and the simple Kantian equilibrium maximizes the payoff of the players on the diagonal of strategy space S^2.

For Nash equilibrium, it does not matter in which order we write the strategies. But for Kantian equilibrium it does, because Kantian optimization requires a conception of which strategies are the "same" for the two players. In the above formulation, of the battle of the sexes, we identified the first strategy for the two players as the event that He or She preferred. In contrast, we can write the payoff matrix in its traditional form, as in table 2.4.

Table 2.4 **The battle of the sexes: conventional version, $0 < b < a < 1$**

	Box	Dance
Box	$(1,a)$	(b,b)
Dance	$(0,0)$	$(a,1)$

The game in this form lacks a common diagonal. We cannot suppose that a simple Kantian equilibrium exists, and in fact one does not exist. His payoff function is now $\hat{V}(p,q) = pq + bp(1-q) + (1-p)(1-q)a$, and $\hat{V}(p,p)$ is maximized at $p = 1$. Her payoff function is maximized at $q = 0$, and so a simple Kantian equilibrium, indeed, does not exist.

Finally, we examine the stag hunt game, the payoff matrix of which is shown in table 2.5.

Table 2.5 The stag hunt, with $a < 0 < b < 1$

	Cooperate (Share)	Defect (Grab)
Cooperate (Share)	(1,1)	(a,b)
Defect (Grab)	(b,a)	(0,0)

The story behind the game is as follows. We can cooperate in trying to catch a deer, which requires two hunters. Or each of us may defect and go after a hare, which can be caught by one hunter but provides less meat than the deer would provide for each of us. If Row cooperates but Column defects, then Column's payoff is surely less than 1(b), and Row will have wasted her time hunting the deer alone (so $a < 0$). The game is strictly monotone increasing and so the simple Kantian equilibrium is Pareto efficient.

Another story modeled by this game, perhaps important from an evolutionary viewpoint, is the following, played between two individuals who are prospective mates. Should I Grab all the meat available, or Share it with my prospective mate? Unlike the prisoner's dilemma game, Grab is not a dominant strategy: in fact, (Share, Share) is a Nash equilibrium. The reason neither player will defect from (Share, Share) is that each values having a prospective mate who is well nourished (hence $b < 1$). In addition to this Nash equilibrium, there are two others: (0,0) is one, and there is a mixed-strategy Nash equilibrium. (For the details, see chapter 8.) However, the unique simple Kantian equilibrium is (Share, Share). This is an important game, as it will be shown in chapter 8 that Kantian players have an evolutionary advantage over Nash players in stag hunts.

The stag hunt has been studied by philosopher Brian Skyrms (2004), who focuses on signals that Nash players could send each other to attempt to coordinate on the good Nash equilibrium, (Share, Share). If players reason in the Kantian manner, no signaling is necessary, as the SKE is uniquely (Share, Share). Perhaps one could interpret Skyrms as thinking that signaling between players could create common knowledge in the sense needed for cooperation, but his approach seems more closely wedded to thinking of cooperation as a particular refinement of Nash equilibrium in the stag hunt.

2.4 Some Simple Asymmetric Games

Besides the 2×2 games, three other simple games about which much has been written are the dictator, ultimatum, and trust games. I will assume classical preferences: a player's von Neumann–Morgenstern utility is some strictly concave increasing function of the monetary prize, u, normalized so that $u(0) = 0$ and $u(1) = 1$. The second player's von Neumann–Morgenstern utility function is v, similarly normalized. The *stochastic dictator* game begins with Nature's choosing one of two players to be the dictator, who then assigns a division of a dollar between herself and the other player. Thus, assuming that each player is chosen to be the dictator with probability one-half, the expected utility of the first player, if she keeps x, and of the second player, who, if chosen, decides to keep y, is $\frac{1}{2}(u(x) + u(1-y))$. In a simple Kantian equilibrium, the first player chooses x to maximize $\frac{1}{2}(u(x) + u(1-x))$, the solution to which is $x = \frac{1}{2}$. Clearly, the second player also chooses $x = \frac{1}{2}$. Strict concavity is necessary to generate this result.

The standard dictator game is asymmetric, because it begins *after* Nature has chosen the dictator. We render the game symmetric by beginning it before Nature moves.

We render the standard ultimatum game symmetric in the same fashion. In the stochastic ultimatum game, a player's strategy consists of an ordered pair (x,z), where x is what he will give to the other player, should he be chosen to be the decision maker, and z is the minimum that he will accept, should the other player be chosen to be the decision maker. The game has three stages: first, Nature chooses the ultimator; second, the ultimator presents an offer; third, the other player either accepts or rejects the offer. The unique subgame perfect NE is $(x,z) = (1,0)$.

It is not obvious how to model cooperation in the ultimatum game. This is the first time we have encountered a game where the strategy is multidimensional. It seems to me that a Kantian should think as follows. If I were chosen to be the ultimator, and were to propose to keep x, this must be the amount I would also like the other person to keep, were she chosen to be the ultimator, and hence I must accept any amount from her that is at least

$1 - x$. Therefore, $z \leq 1 - x$. Consequently, the simple Kantian solution is the solution to the program:

$$\max \frac{1}{2}u(x) + \frac{1}{2}u(z)$$
$$\text{subj. to}$$
$$z \leq 1 - x \quad .$$

The unique solution, if u is strictly concave, is $(x, z) = (\frac{1}{2}, \frac{1}{2})$.

Arguably, the simple Kantian equilibria, in these two games, are closer to what is often observed in experiments than the Nash equilibrium. Moreover, we have established this result without recourse to including a sense of fairness in the utility function. Granted, in the ultimatum game, players who reject offers of less than 0.25 may say that they do so because the offers were unfair. My claim is that those offers are considered unfair *because these are not the offers a person should make* if he recognizes the arbitrariness of being chosen the ultimator. Thus, one uses the Kantian protocol because the situation strongly suggests that "we are all in the same boat"— Nature is just flipping a coin to choose the ultimator. In the more conventional explanation, it is a social norm to share in situations of solidarity, and deviators are punished by norm followers. The same explanation applies in the dictator game, even though no retaliation is possible against a stingy dictator. I prefer to say that the arbitrariness that Nature's choice induces in players suggests that the right (moral) thing to do is to view the game as symmetric, and use of the Kantian protocol (cooperation) is called for. The morality, however, enters in the instruction to optimize in a certain way, not as altruism toward the other player or, more generally, as an additional argument of preferences.

These games demonstrate what is a general feature of Kantian optimization in stage games. *The notion of subgame perfection does not apply.* Fairness enters, not as an argument of preferences, but as the realization that Nature could have chosen either player to be the first. Thus, a Kantian optimizer in these games asks, "How would I like each of us to play if each of us could be chosen to be the first player?"

Last, I discuss the trust game, a public-good game. There are two players, who draw lots to determine who moves first. Each player is endowed with M units of value. Player One chooses an amount, x, to give to Player Two.

Player Two, however, receives ax units of value, where $a > 1$ is a constant known to both. Then Player Two returns some amount, y, to Player One, which is again multiplied by the experimenter to become ay, and the game is over. It is played only once.

I present four ways of modeling the trust game.

1. Conventionally, the game is modeled as a stage game, in which each player's payoff is the amount of money she ends up with. The game has three stages: first, Nature chooses the order of players; second, the first player moves; third, the second player moves. The unique *subgame perfect Nash equilibrium* is $x = y = 0$ if the players have self-interested preferences.

2. We next model this as a game where players are Kantian. Suppose that a player's von Neumann–Morgenstern utility function for money lotteries is u. Unlike in subgame-perfect analysis, each player calculates before Nature moves. Before the game begins, her expected utility is $\frac{1}{2}u(M - x + ay) + \frac{1}{2}u(M + ax - y)$. She chooses a strategy (x,y) that she would like both players to choose, which is the one that maximizes her expected utility:

$$\max \frac{1}{2}u(M - x + ay) + \frac{1}{2}u(M + ax - y)$$

s.t.

$$0 \leq x \leq M \quad (\lambda)$$
$$0 \leq y \leq M + ax$$

.

We look for a solution of this program where the first constraint binds and the second constraint is slack. The Kuhn-Tucker conditions are:

$$(\partial x) \quad -u'(M - x + ay) + au'(M + ax - y) = \lambda \geq 0$$
$$(\partial y) \quad au'(M - x + ay) = u'(M + ax - y)$$

$$x = M.$$

Substituting from the (∂y) condition into the (∂x) condition, we have:

$$(a^2 - 1)u'(M - ax + y) \geq 0,$$

which is surely true, since $a > 1$. Now the (∂y) condition implies that

$$M - x + ay > M + ax - y,$$

because u' is a decreasing function, and hence it follows that $x < y$ and so, $y > M$. We should also expect that $y < (1 + a)M$, if $u'(0)$ is large. In sum, at the simple Kantian equilibrium of this game we have:

$$x = M, \quad M < y < (1 + a)M.$$

3. In this version, each player maximizes total wealth: that is, each player's payoff is the utilitarian social welfare function. We examine the subgame-perfect Nash equilibrium by backward induction. The second player will have an endowment $M + ax$ when she must move; her problem is to choose y to

maximize $M + x + y + ay$ subject to $y \leq M + ax$.

The solution is $y = M + ax$. Knowing this, the first player chooses x to

maximize $M - x + M + ax + 0$,

whose solution is $x = M$. Thus, the equilibrium is:

$$x = M, y = M(1 + a).$$

Total wealth is maximized over all feasible allocations, at $a(1 + a)M$. However, the allocation is very unequal: the entire wealth goes to the first player.

4. In this version, each player maximizes the minimum payoff to both players. The payoff function for each is the egalitarian social welfare function. We examine the subgame-perfect Nash equilibrium. When Player Two moves, she has wealth $M + ax$. She chooses y such that $ay = M + ax - y$, for this equalizes the two wealths. Thus, $y = \dfrac{M + ax}{1 + a}$. Knowing this, Player One chooses x to maximize $\min(M - x + a\left(\dfrac{M + ax}{1 + a}\right), M + ax - \dfrac{M + ax}{1 + a})$. The solution is:

$$x = M, y = M,$$

and each player ends up with wealth aM.

James Cox and colleagues (2009) performed the trust game with students and reported their results. Thirty-four games were played, where $M = 10$ and $a = 3$. From fig. 1 of their paper, we see that in six of these games, the play was consistent only with the simple Kantian equilibrium—that is, the second model described above, or $x = 10$ and $10 < y < 40$. (Cox et al. 2009 do not call it that: I am imposing my interpretation on the results.)

In another three of these games, the play was that of the model where each player is a maximinner: $x = y = M$. In four of the thirty-four games, the classical Nash equilibrium was played: $x = y = 0$. There are no games in which version (3) was played, in which both players possess a utilitarian payoff function. In most of the remaining games, both players gave less than M to the opponent, but did give some positive amount. In eleven out of thirty-four games, Player One transferred his entire endowment to Player Two: this shows trust and is consistent with three of the four above models of the game.

Little interpretive gloss on the results is provided in Cox et al. (2009); however, James Walker and Elinor Ostrom (2009) do provide an interesting gloss on the results of the earlier paper. The authors discuss the results of experiments with three games: the trust game of Cox et al. (2009), another public-good game, and a common-pool resource game. They write that each of these games are instances of "social dilemmas": "Social dilemmas characterize settings where a divergence exists between expected outcomes from individuals pursuing strategies based on narrow self-interests versus groups pursuing strategies based on the interests of the group as a whole. . . . Individuals make decisions based on individual gains rather than group gains or losses; and environments that do not create incentives for internalizing group gains or losses into individuals' decision calculus" (92).

From my viewpoint, these authors are confounding cooperation with altruism. As I showed, the fully cooperative solution is attained by a Kantian optimizer who has no concern for others, *as such*: her morality consists not in caring explicitly about the payoff accruing to other players but rather in playing the strategy she would like all to play. Saying that the problem in social dilemmas is based on "a divergence between . . . narrow self-interest versus . . . strategies based on the interests of the group as a whole" is, I think, a gratuitous interpretation of the thought process. (If we interpret this phrase as saying that each player is utilitarian, then there is no evidence for the claim in their experiment.) Playing the strategy that one would like everyone to play is, for me, motivated by the common knowledge assumption (Method Two) and trust, not by a concern for the welfare of the group as a whole. It entails a recognition that cooperation can make *me* better off (incidentally, it makes all of us better off). But that parenthetical fact is not or *need not be* the motivation for my playing "cooperatively." The fact that these games were played only once by a team shows that building a reputation was not an issue.

My interpretation of the Cox et al. (2009) results for the trust-game experiment is that about one-third of the players chosen to be first movers were playing (their part) of the simple Kantian equilibrium, because they had trust in their opponents/partners. About 54 percent of their partners responded by playing (their part) of the Kantian equilibrium (that is, six out of eleven). Another 33 percent of the second players in these matches equalized the payoffs of the two players. Only one of the second players in these matches played the Nash solution in the subgame that she faced (that is, returning nothing to the first player). Only four out of thirty-four pairs played the Nash equilibrium, each contributing nothing to their partner. I cannot reject the hypothesis that a significant number of individuals are Kantian optimizers. It is difficult to distinguish between models (2) (Kantian) and (4) (equalize the payoffs). Maximization of team payoffs is not observed.

2.5 Economies with Production

We now introduce more complex games, associated with simple production economies, which are more complex than simple matrix games. The goal is to study, here, simple Kantian equilibrium in the games that are induced in these economies.

There are n producers, each with a concave utility function u^i defined over consumption (x) and effort (E). Effort is measured in efficiency units (if s is a person's skill level and he exerts E units of efficiency effort, then his labor time is E / s). Production is defined by a concave function mapping total units of efficiency labor into total output. Defining $E^S = \sum E^i$, then total output at the effort vector $\mathbf{E} = (E^1,\ldots,E^n)$ is $G(E^S)$.

An *allocation rule* $\mathbf{X} = (X^1,\ldots,X^n)$ assigns output to each individual as a function of the vector of efforts: thus, $X^i(E^1,\ldots,E^n) = x^i$ is i's share of the output when the effort vector is $\mathbf{E} = (E^1,\ldots,E^n)$.

Suppose that we consider a fishing economy: fishers fish on a lake, and there are decreasing returns to scale in labor expended fishing, due to congestion effects. Formally, we say that the production function G is concave. The allocation rule is that each fisher keeps his catch. This yields the *proportional rule*:

$$x^i = X^{Pr,i}(E^1,...,E^n) = \frac{E^i}{E^S} G(E^S);$$

that is, except for random variation, the fish caught by a fisher will be proportional to the labor in efficiency units he expends. Traditionally, this allocation rule has been used in fishing communities. Given preferences, technology, and the allocation rule, a game is defined in which the payoff function for fisher i at an effort allocation is given by:

$$V^i(E^1,E^2,...,E^n) = u^i(\frac{E^i}{E^S} G(E^S),E^i). \tag{2.1}$$

In this chapter, we assume homogeneous preferences, and so $u^i = u$ for all i.

It is well known that, if G is strictly concave, then the Nash equilibrium of this game is Pareto inefficient. Fishers fish too much: each does not take into account the fact that his labor contributes to a public bad, the reduction of the productivity of the lake. The Nash equilibrium of the game $\{V^i\}$ is given by:

$$(\forall i) \quad -\frac{u_2[i]}{u_1[i]} = \frac{E^i}{E^S} G'(E^S) + (1 - \frac{E^i}{E^S}) \frac{G(E^S)}{E^S}, \tag{2.2}$$

where $u_j[i]$ is the jth partial derivative of u evaluated at the consumption bundle of individual i. Equation (2.2) says that the marginal rate of substitution for each player is equal to a convex combination of the marginal product $(G'(E^S))$ and the average product $(\frac{G(E^S)}{E^S})$. But the condition for Pareto efficiency at an interior solution is:

$$(\forall i) \; MRS^i \equiv -\frac{u_2[i]}{u_1[i]} = MRT = G'(E^S). \tag{2.3}$$

Only in the case where G is linear (and so the average and marginal products are equal) does (2.2) reduce to (2.3). In general, the MRS^i is greater than the MRT (because the marginal product is less than the average product for strictly concave G), and each fisher could benefit from a reduction in the effort of all players. This example is the simplest form of the "tragedy of the commons" (Hardin 1968).

The game defined by (2.1) is strictly monotone decreasing: if another player increases her fishing time, then ceteris paribus, my payoff falls, because the productivity of the lake has decreased. Therefore, the simple Kantian equilibrium, which exists under the hypothesis that all preferences are identical, is Pareto efficient *in the game* by Proposition 2.1.

Why do I italicize these three words? Because the game defined by (2.1) considers only *proportional* allocations of fish and effort: in other words, Proposition 2.1 tells us that, restricted to the set of allocations in which fish received is proportional to effort expended, the simple Kantian equilibrium is Pareto efficient. We now ask: Is it the case that the simple Kantian equilibrium is Pareto efficient *in the economic environment?* Might there be, in other words, some nonproportional allocation of fish and labor that Pareto dominates it?

Let's compute the simple Kantian equilibrium for this game. Each fisher solves the problem:

$$\max_{E} u(\frac{E}{nE}G(nE),E);\qquad(2.4)$$

the first-order condition is:

$$u_1[i]G'(nE)\frac{n}{n}+u_2[i]=0 \text{ or } -\frac{u_2[i]}{u_1[i]}=G'(nE),\qquad(2.5)$$

and so the simple Kantian equilibrium is Pareto efficient in the economy. Thus, Kantian reasoning overcomes the commons's tragedy in a strong way. It is doubly Pareto efficient.

In contrast, the Nash equilibrium of the game is doubly Pareto inefficient. We've noted above that it fails to be Pareto efficient in the economy. But it is not Pareto efficient in the game either, because it is Pareto dominated by the simple Kantian equilibrium, which is an allocation feasible in the game.

Indeed, the argument is more general. Let an allocation rule be specified by $\mathbf{X} = (X^1,...,X^n)$ where $X^i : \mathfrak{R}^n_+ \to \mathfrak{R}_+$ with the identity $\sum_i X^i(E^1,...,E^n) = G(E^S)$ for all effort vectors $(E^1,...,E^n)$. Suppose that the rule has a common diagonal, meaning that:

$$(\forall E \geq 0)(\forall i)(X^i(E,E,...,E) = \frac{G(nE)}{n}) . \tag{2.6}$$

Of course, the proportional rule X^{Pr} has a common diagonal in this sense. Then:

PROPOSITION 2.4 *The SKE for any concave production economy and any symmetric allocation rule is Pareto efficient in the economic environment.*

PROOF. The typical producer maximizes $u(\frac{1}{n}G(nE),E)$, using the definition at (2.6), and the characterizing first-order condition is (2.5). ∎

Another historically important allocation rule for hunter-gatherer societies was the *equal-division rule*, defined by:

$$X^{ED,i}(E^1,...,E^n) = \frac{G(E^S)}{n} . \tag{2.7}$$

Because the equal-division rule is symmetric, it follows from Proposition 2.4 that the simple Kantian equilibrium for hunting societies—which often used this rule—is Pareto efficient in the economy. Again, the Nash equilibrium of the game defined by X^{ED} is Pareto inefficient. But the tragedy is of a different sort from that in the fisher economy: this time, hunters hunt *too little* at the Nash equilibrium. The characterizing condition for an interior Nash equilibrium is:

$$-\frac{u_2[i]}{u_1[i]} = \frac{1}{n}G'(E^S) . \tag{2.8}$$

As long as $n > 1$, the MRS for each player is less than the MRT. Note that this is also the case when G is linear, and in this sense the tragedy is deeper than in the fishing economy.

In sum, Kantian optimization can resolve inefficiencies that plague autarkic optimization in simple fishing and hunting economies. Did the producers in some such economies, in ancient times, learn to optimize in the Kantian manner, leading to the greater success of their communities? Is it possible that Kantian thinking became a meme, passed down through the generations, so that the individual fitness of the members of these groups was greater than of those in groups using the Nash optimization protocol? Can we see today, in hunting and fishing economies that remain, indications of Kantian reasoning?

2.6 Four Models

I propose a 2 × 2 typology of modeling, shown in table 2.6.

Table 2.6 **A typology of models**

preferences → optimization ↓	Self-Interested	Altruistic / Complex
Nash	classical	behavioral economics
Kant	this book, most chapters	this book, chapter 5

The northwest cell in the matrix is the classical model. Behavioral economists alter the column of the matrix by proposing nonclassical preferences but retaining Nash optimization; my proposal is to change the row of the matrix but retain classical preferences. (The southeast cell of the matrix studies Kantian equilibrium with altruistic preferences, considered in chapter 5.) To entertain this proposal one must of course relax one's belief that autarkic optimization is the *only rational* way of thinking in a game. Although this may be a correct statement for a decision problem, it is not obviously so for a game: recall Methods One and Two at this chapter's beginning. Those of us who have been schooled in Nash equilibrium tend to view many examples of successful cooperation as irrational. Would it not perhaps be more modest to think that we have not properly characterized rationality in games? In some social situations, at least, people may adopt the Kantian protocol; they may reason cooperatively, as it were, resolving free-rider problems.

At the danger of belaboring the point, I repeat: the main idea of this book is that we understand cooperation, not by altering preferences from classical self-regarding ones, but by altering the manner in which players optimize. The curious reader may ask: Is this a distinction without a difference—that is, could we always represent a simple Kantian equilibrium as a Nash equilibrium where players have altered preferences of some kind? I will argue, below in chapter 6, that the answer is no.

2.7 Literature Notes

Jean-Jacques Laffont (1975) wrote: "To give substance to the concept of a new ethics, we postulate that a typical agent assumes (according to Kant's moral) that the other agents will act as he does, and he maximizes his utility function under this new constraint. . . . Our proposition is then equivalent to a special assumption of others' behavior. It is clear that the meaning of 'the same action' will depend on the model and will usually mean 'the same *kind* of action'" (430). Not only does Laffont deserve credit for suggesting what is argued here, but his recognition that a Kantian must generally think in terms of the same *kind* of action will become clear in chapter 3.

Ted Bergstrom (1995), in a discussion of selective adaptation, defines the "Kantian golden rule for asexual siblings" as "Act toward your siblings as would be in your own best interest if your siblings' action would mimic your own" (61).

Robert Sugden (1982) discusses philanthropy and argues, with empirical evidence, that the Nash assumption (that donors take the contributions of others as given) is not empirically verified. He writes: "Or suppose that each person, instead of having Nash conjectures, believes that if he gives a certain minimum sum of money, everyone else will do the same, but he gives less, everyone else will give nothing" (342). This is his Kantian premise.

Tim Feddersen (2004) offers a "group-based ethical model" to explain the voting paradox. He writes, "First, ethical agents evaluate alternative behavioral rules in a Kantian manner by comparing the outcomes that would occur if everyone who shares their preferences were to act according to the same rule" (107).

Kjell Arne Brekke, Snorre Kverndokk, and Karine Nyborg (2003) propose that in a symmetric contribution game with a public good, agents define the moral action as the simple Kantian equilibrium (not those words). But they then introduce a penalty term in utility, which decreases utility to the extent that the player deviates from the Kantian action, so that it becomes a Nash equilibrium to play the simple Kantian equilibrium. From my viewpoint, this a gratuitous move: Why say that players pay a "cost" for deviating from the Kantian action, rather than just saying that they play the action they think is the right thing to do? Is not the latter simpler, although heretical from the classical viewpoint?

Heterogeneous Preferences

Multiplicative and Additive Kantian Optimization

3.1 Monotonicity and Pareto Efficiency

We now consider games $\mathbf{V} = \{V^i \mid i = 1, \ldots, n\}$ where the strategies (efforts) are chosen from the set $S = [0, \infty)$, but the payoff functions are in general different. The concept of simple Kantian equilibrium is no longer useful: generally, a simple Kantian equilibrium will not exist.[1]

Suppose that the game models the problem of fishers on a lake, where the labor expended by each fisher reduces the marginal productivity of the lake, because of congestion effects. The payoff function for a fisher is his utility, which is a function of fish caught and effort expended. The payoff functions of the game are given in equation (2.1).

Suppose, at an effort allocation $(E^1, \ldots, E^n)$ a fisher thinks: "I'd like to increase my fishing time by 10 percent. But I should do this only if I would be happy if all were to increase their fishing time by 10 percent." Do not at this point ask where this thought comes from, but let's define an equilibrium with respect to such thinking.

DEFINITION 3.1 A *multiplicative Kantian equilibrium* in a game $\{V^i\}$ is an effort vector $(E^1, \ldots, E^n)$ such that *nobody* would prefer to rescale *everybody's* effort by *any* nonnegative factor. Formally:

$$(\forall i)(\forall r \geq 0)(V^i(E^1, \ldots, E^n) \geq V^i(rE^1, \ldots, rE^n)) . \tag{3.1}$$

We denote such an allocation a $K^\times$ *equilibrium*.

Note that multiplicative Kantian equilibrium assumes a game in which the strategy spaces of players are intervals of real numbers. Thus, games with discrete strategy spaces consisting of two alternatives, such as the prisoner's dilemma, must be formulated as mixed-strategy games, so that the strategy space is the interval $[0,1]$. In this chapter, the focus will be on games induced by production economies, where we take the strategy space (effort choice) to be $\mathfrak{R}_+$.

The reader should note the formal similarity between multiplicative Kantian and Nash equilibrium. Both use ordinal preferences only. Each considers a counterfactual: with Nash reasoning, the counterfactual is that I alone change my strategy, whereas in Kantian reasoning, I imagine that all players change their strategies in a prescribed way. An equilibrium, in either case, is a strategy profile that dominates all admissible counterfactual profiles. An optimizing agent in both cases evaluates the counterfactual profile using his own preferences only. Other similarities will appear in the discussion of existence and dynamics (chapter 7).

The fishing game is a strictly monotone decreasing game: if anyone else increases his effort, my catch decreases, because the productivity of the lake decreases. We generalize Proposition 2.1:

PROPOSITION 3.1 *Let* $\mathbf{E} = (E^1,...,E^n)$ *be a strictly positive* $K^\times$ *equilibrium in a strictly monotone (increasing or decreasing) game. Then it is Pareto efficient in the game.*

PROOF.

1. Let the game be strictly monotone decreasing. Suppose that $\mathbf{E}$ were Pareto dominated by an effort vector $\mathbf{E}_* = (E_*^1,...,E_*^n)$. Let k be an index such that $\dfrac{E_*^i}{E^i}$ is minimized. Define $r = \dfrac{E_*^k}{E^k}$. Note that $rE^k = E_*^k$ and for $j \neq k$, $rE^j \leq E_*^j$, by definition of r. Furthermore, for at least one j, $rE^j < E_*^j$. For otherwise, $\mathbf{E}_* = r\mathbf{E}$, and since $\mathbf{E}_*$ Pareto dominates $\mathbf{E}$, at least one agent would prefer $r\mathbf{E}$ to $\mathbf{E}$, which contradicts the fact that $\mathbf{E}$ is a $K^\times$ equilibrium. It follows that:

$$V^k(r\mathbf{E}) > V^k(\mathbf{E}_*) \geq V^k(\mathbf{E}), \qquad (3.2)$$

where the first inequality follows because the game is strictly monotone decreasing, and the second follows because $\mathbf{E}_*$ Pareto dominates $\mathbf{E}$. But (3.2) contradicts the fact that $\mathbf{E}$ is a $K^\times$ equilibrium—agent k would advocate changing the scale of $\mathbf{E}$ by a factor of r. This contradicts the supposition that $\mathbf{E}$ is not Pareto efficient in the game.

2. If the game is strictly monotone increasing, then we define k to be an index that *maximizes* $\frac{E_*^i}{E^i}$. The positivity of the vector $\mathbf{E}$ guarantees that this number is not infinite. The proof proceeds as above. ■

Strictly monotone decreasing games are ones in which congestion effects abound, and strictly monotone increasing games are ones possessing positive externalities, such as when the efforts of players are directed at producing a public good from which everyone benefits.

The counterfactual in Definition 3.1 to which players compare the present allocation is one in which the entire strategy profile is rescaled by a nonnegative constant. Alternatively, we might consider *translating* the strategy profile by a constant. This leads to another Kantian equilibrium concept:

DEFINITION 3.2 An *additive Kantian equilibrium* (K^+) is an allocation such that nobody would prefer to translate all efforts by a (positive or negative) constant. That is:

$$(\forall i)(\forall r \geq -E^i)(V^i(E^1,...,E^n) \geq V^i(E^1 + r,...,E^n + r)), \tag{3.3}$$

where it is understood that we replace $E^i + r$ with zero if $E^i + r < 0$.

Note that the permissible values of the constant, r, by which agent i contemplates translating the effort vector are those that are feasible for him — that is, will not render his effort negative. The analog of Proposition 3.2 continues to hold — except this time, we need not require that the equilibrium allocation be positive.

PROPOSITION 3.2 *Let* $\mathbf{E} = (E^1,...,E^n)$ *be a K^+ equilibrium in a strictly monotone (increasing or decreasing) game. Then it is Pareto efficient in the game.*

PROOF. Suppose that the game is strictly monotone increasing but $\mathbf{E}$ is Pareto dominated by $\mathbf{E}_. = (E_*^1,...,E_*^n)$. Write $r^i = E_*^i - E^i$, and let $r^* = \max r^i$, which is achieved for some agent i^*. Define $\hat{\mathbf{E}} = \mathbf{E} + (r^*,...,r^*)$. Now:

$$V^{i^*}(\hat{\mathbf{E}}) > V^{i^*}(\mathbf{E}_.) \geq V^{i^*}(\mathbf{E}), \tag{3.4}$$

where the first inequality follows by strict monotonicity and the second by Pareto domination. This contradicts the fact that $\mathbf{E}$ is a K^+ equilibrium, because agent i^* would have preferred translating the effort vector $\mathbf{E}$ by r^*. The contradiction proves the proposition. An analogous proof works if $\mathbf{V}$ is strictly monotone decreasing. ■

For the next proposition, we require a restriction on the class of abstract games that models the interpretation of the strategy space as a space of *efforts*—that is, actions that have a cost to the individual.

DEFINITION 3.3 A game $\mathbf{V} = \{V^i\}$, where each player's strategy space is $\mathfrak{R}_+$, is *quasi-economic* if for all i and any vector $\mathbf{E}^{-i} = (E^1,...,E^{i-1},E^{i+1},...,E^n)$, $V^i(E^i,\mathbf{E}^{-i})$ is quasi-concave in E^i and becomes unboundedly negative as $E^i \to \infty$.

A quasi-economic game is one in which, fixing the efforts of all players but i, the payoff to player i has a unique local maximum on his strategy space $\mathfrak{R}_+$, and effort becomes unboundedly costly to the player as it becomes large. Thus, fixing the contributions of others, player i's payoff may initially increase with his effort, but eventually the cost of effort overwhelms the benefit he accrues from it. I call such a game *quasi-economic* because it restricts the meaning of "effort" to having a property that we attribute to effort in economic contexts.

Let us now contrast Kantian equilibrium with Nash equilibrium, with regard to Pareto efficiency. We know that the tragedy of the commons (implying Pareto inefficiency) is a property of Nash equilibrium in some games with negative externalities and that the free-rider problem (Pareto inefficiency) afflicts Nash equilibrium in some games with positive externalities. The next proposition shows that tragedies of the commons and free-rider problems are universal ones for Nash equilibrium in quasi-economic monotone games.

PROPOSITION 3.3 *Let* $\mathbf{V} = \{V^i\}$ *be a strictly monotone, continuously differentiable, quasi-economic game. Let* $\mathbf{E} = (E^1,...,E^n)$ *be an interior NE of the game. Then* $\mathbf{E}$ *is Pareto inefficient in the game.*

PROOF.

1. We assume $n = 3$ for notational simplicity. Let the game be strictly monotone increasing. Define the function $f^1(y,z)$ for nonzero vectors $(y,z) \in \mathfrak{R}_+^2$ by:

$$f^1(y,z) = \mathrm{lub}\{x \mid 0 \le x' < x \Rightarrow V^1(\mathbf{E}+(x',y,z)) > V^1(\mathbf{E})\}. \qquad (3.5)$$

Note that:

(*a*) $f^1(0,0) = 0$, because $\mathbf{E}$ is an NE;

(b) $f^1(y,z) > 0$ if $(y,z) \neq (0,0)$, because **V** is strictly monotone increasing and continuous;

(c) $f^1(y,z) < \infty$ because **V** is quasi-economic; and

(d) $V^1(\mathbf{E} + (f^1(y,z),y,z)) = V^1(\mathbf{E})$ by the least-upper-bound property.

Property (b) holds because, by strict monotonicity, $V^i(\mathbf{E} + (0,y,z)) > V^i(\mathbf{E})$; property (c) holds because V^i eventually becomes arbitrarily small as x increases.

2. In like manner define:

$$f^2(x,z) = \text{lub}\{y \mid 0 \leq y' < y \Rightarrow V^2(\mathbf{E} + (x,y',z)) > V^2(\mathbf{E})\} \tag{3.6}$$

$$f^3(x,y) = \text{lub}\{z \mid 0 \leq z' < z \Rightarrow V^3(\mathbf{E} + (x,y,z')) > V^3(\mathbf{E})\}. \tag{3.7}$$

Clearly functions f^2 and f^3 satisfy the analogs to (a), (b), and (c) in step 1.

3. Suppose that we can find a vector $(x,y,z) \in \mathfrak{R}^3_+$ such that:

$$x \leq f^1(y,z), \quad y \leq f^2(x,z), \text{ and } z \leq f^3(x,y), \tag{3.8}$$

with at least one of the three inequalities strict. Then it follows that:

$$(\forall i) \ V^i(\mathbf{E} + (x,y,z)) \geq V^i(\mathbf{E}),$$

with at least one inequality strict, and so **E** is not Pareto efficient. This is our task.

4. Choose (y,z) small and positive, and define $x = f^1(y,z)$. Then we have:

$$\begin{aligned} V^1(\mathbf{E} + (f^1(y,z),y,z)) &= V^1(\mathbf{E}) \\ V^2(\mathbf{E} + (x,f^2(x,z),z)) &= V^2(\mathbf{E}) \\ V^3(\mathbf{E} + (x,y,f^3(x,y))) &= V^3(\mathbf{E}). \end{aligned} \tag{3.9}$$

We know that:

$$\frac{\partial V^1}{\partial E^1}(\mathbf{E} + (f^1(y,z),y,z)) < 0 \tag{3.10}$$

by the quasi-concavity of V^1 in E^1. Now differentiate the first equation in (3.9) with respect to y:

$$\frac{\partial V^1}{\partial E^1}(\mathbf{E} + (f^1(y,z),y,z))f^1_1(y,z) + \frac{\partial V^1}{\partial E^2}(\mathbf{E} + (f^1(y,z),y,z)) = 0. \tag{3.11}$$

By strict monotonicity of **V**, the second term in (3.11) is positive, and by (3.10), the $\dfrac{\partial V^1}{\partial E^1}$ factor in the first term is negative for small (y,z) not equal to $(0,0)$. However, when $(x,y,z) = (0,0,0)$, $\dfrac{\partial V^1}{\partial E^1} = 0$, a necessary condition of NE. It follows from (3.11) and the implicit function theorem that the function f^1 is indeed differentiable when $(y,z) > (0,0)$, and its derivatives are given by:

$$(f_1^1(y,z), f_2^1(y,z)) = (-\frac{\partial V^1}{\partial E^2} / \frac{\partial V^1}{\partial E^1}, -\frac{\partial V^1}{\partial E^3} / \frac{\partial V^1}{\partial E^1}). \tag{3.12}$$

Furthermore, it follows that:

$$\lim_{y,z \to 0} f_1^1(y,z) = \infty = f_2^1(y,z), \tag{3.13}$$

by (3.11) and its analog, produced by differentiating the first equation in (3.9) with respect to z.

5. In like manner, by differentiating the second and third equations in (3.9), we deduce:

$$\lim_{x,y \to 0} f_1^3(x,y) = \infty = \lim_{x,y \to 0} f_2^3(x,y) = \lim_{x,z \to 0} f_1^2(x,z) = \lim_{x,z \to 0} f_2^2(x,z). \tag{3.14}$$

6. We finally prove what is required from step 3 above, that for sufficiently small (y,z):

$$y \leq f^2(x,z) \text{ and } z \leq f^3(x,y).$$

By the definition of x (step 4), we must show:

$$y \leq f^2(f^1(y,z),z) \text{ and } z \leq f^3(f^1(y,z),y), \tag{3.15}$$

with at least one inequality strict. Note that, since y and z are small, we have:

$$(y',z') \in [0,y] \times [0,z] \Rightarrow 1 < f_1^2(f^1(y,z),z)f_1^1(y,z)$$
$$(y',z') \in [0,y] \times [0,z] \Rightarrow 1 < f_1^3(f^1(y,z),y)f_2^1(y,z) \tag{3.16}$$

because all the partial derivatives of the functions f^i become arbitrarily large as $(y,z) \to (0,0)$, by (3.13) and (3.14). But the inequalities in (3.16) integrate to give (3.15), and both inequalities are strict.

Hence, the NE **E** is inefficient.

7. If **V** is a strictly monotone decreasing game, an analogous argument works. The proof obviously generalizes to $n > 3$, and the proof for $n = 2$ is simpler. ∎

This proposition enables us to draw a sharp distinction between Nash and Kantian equilibrium: Nash equilibria are universally inefficient in monotone, quasi-economic games, and Kantian equilibria are almost always efficient.

3.2 Fishing and Hunting Economies

We return to the study of production economies of chapter 2, but we now suppose that the fishers/hunters have arbitrary concave preferences over consumption and effort represented by (distinct) utility functions $\{u^i \mid i = 1,...,n\}$. In the fishing economy, X^{Pr} continues to be the allocation rule "each fisher keeps her catch." A simple Kantian equilibrium will (generally) not exist: that is, each fisher would (generally) choose a different effort vector on the diagonal of $\Re_+^n$ as the common level of effort. Even if we relax the definition and define E^{*i} as the effort that fisher i would like all to expend, the vector $(E^{*1},...,E^{*n})$ will not be Pareto efficient.

Now let the game $\{V^i\}$ be the fishing game derived from the production economy; that is:

$$V^i(E^1,...,E^n) = u^i(\frac{E^i}{E^S}G(E^S), E^i) .$$

The fact that any positive multiplicative Kantian equilibrium is Pareto efficient *in the game* $\{V^i\}$ does not imply that it is Pareto efficient in the *economic environment* $e = (u^1,...u^n,G)$, where feasible allocations are not restricted to be proportional allocations. As I pointed out in chapter 2, the *game* requires allocations to be proportional, but there may be some *nonproportional* allocation in the economy (requiring transfers among fishers) that Pareto dominates the multiplicative Kantian equilibrium. The next proposition shows that this is not the case.

DEFINITION 3.4 A proportional allocation that is Pareto efficient in the economic environment $(u^1,...u^n,G)$ is a *proportional solution*. (This definition was introduced in Roemer and Silvestre 1993.)

PROPOSITION 3.4 *Any strictly positive $K^\times$ equilibrium in the fishing economy, which employs the proportional allocation rule, is Pareto efficient (in the economic environment). Conversely, any proportional solution is a $K^\times$ equilibrium.*

PROOF. By concavity, the first-order condition is sufficient to establish $K^\times$ equilibrium:

$$(\forall i)(\frac{d}{dr}\bigg|_{r=1} u^i(\frac{rE^i}{rE^S}G(rE^S), rE^i) = 0. \tag{3.17}$$

Compute that (3.17) reduces to:

$$u^i_1 \cdot (\frac{E^i}{E^S}G'(E^S)E^S) + u^i_2 E^i = 0; \tag{3.18}$$

dividing through by the *positive* number E^i, and rearranging, we have:

$$(\forall i) \quad -\frac{u^i_2[i]}{u^i_1[i]} = G'(E^S). \tag{3.19}$$

But this is the statement that, for every fisher, the marginal rate of substitution between fish and effort equals the marginal rate of transformation of effort into fish, which is the characterizing condition for Pareto efficiency of an interior solution because the economy is convex.

To prove the converse, let $\{(x^i, E^i) \mid i = 1, \ldots, n\}$ be a proportional solution. We must show that:

$$(\forall i) \, (u^i(\frac{E^i}{E^S}G(rE^S), rE^i) \text{ is maximized at } r = 1). \tag{3.20}$$

Suppose that $E^i > 0$ but (3.20) is false for some i. Then by concavity:

$$\frac{d}{dr}\bigg|_{r=1} u^i(\frac{E^i}{E^S}G(rE^S), rE^i) \neq 0,$$

which reduces to $-\dfrac{u^i_2(x^i, E^i)}{u^i_1(x^i, E^i)} \neq G'(E^S),$

contradicting the fact that the allocation is Pareto efficient. On the other hand, if $E^i = 0$, then (3.20) is trivially true. ∎

Recall Laffont's comment: "It is clear that the meaning of 'the same action' will depend on the model and will usually mean 'the same *kind* of action.'" In the fishing game, the same *kind* of action means "changing all efforts by a scale factor." This is, admittedly, more complex than "taking the action I'd like all to take," the thought process defining simple Kantian equilibrium. The efficiency result suggests that successful fishing communities may have discovered multiplicative Kantian equilibrium reasoning through cultural evolution (see Boyd and Richerson 1985).

Now let us consider hunting economies, which use the allocation rule X^{ED}. Hunters fan out into the bush searching for game, and after several days they return to camp, dividing the capture equally. The relevant game is given by:

$$V^i(E^1,...,E^n) = u^i(\frac{G(E^S)}{n}, E^i).$$

At an effort allocation $(E^1,...,E^n)$, suppose that a hunter thinks, "I'd like to take a two-hour nap under that tree. But I should do this only if I would be happy if all hunters took a two-hour nap." This time, the *kind* of action that the Kantian contemplates is additive rather than multiplicative.

PROPOSITION 3.5 *Any K^+ equilibrium in the hunting economy, which employs the equal-division allocation rule, is Pareto efficient (in the economic environment). Conversely, any Pareto-efficient equal-division allocation is a K^+ equilibrium.*

PROOF. The first-order condition generated by Definition 3.4 that characterizes a K^+ equilibrium is:

$$\begin{cases} \frac{d}{dr}\bigg|_{r=0} u^i(\frac{G(E^S+nr)}{n}, E^i+r) = 0, \text{ if } E^i > 0 \\ \frac{d}{dr_+}\bigg|_{r=0} u^i(\frac{G(E^S+nr)}{n}, r) \leq 0, \text{ if } E^i = 0 \end{cases}, \qquad (3.21)$$

where $\frac{d}{dr_+}$ denotes the right-hand derivative. This expands to:

$$\begin{cases} u_1^i \cdot \frac{G'(E^S)}{n} n + u_2^i = 0, \text{ if } E^i > 0 \\ u_1^i \cdot \frac{G'(E^S)}{n} n + u_2^i \leq 0, \text{ if } E^i = 0 \end{cases}, \qquad (3.22)$$

which immediately reduces to $MRS^i \geq MRT$, with equality when $E^i > 0$. This is precisely the condition for Pareto efficiency.

The proof of the converse mimics the proof in Proposition 3.4. ∎

So Kantian reasoning resolves the tragedy of the commons in fishing games and the free-rider problem in hunting games with heterogeneous preferences—but the *kind* of action that a producer must contemplate universalizing changes with the allocation rule. My conjecture is that there are good reasons that fishing economies adopt the proportional allocation rule and hunting economies the equal-division rule. (For instance, "each keeps his catch," giving the proportional rule, economizes on monitoring and avoids the necessity of an institution that redistributes the communal catch. The justification of the equal-division rule is more complex; perhaps it evolved as a kind of insurance system to ensure that nobody went hungry.) Having done so, societies of these types that discover the correct Kantian optimization protocol will do better than ones that do not discover it, by these efficiency arguments. I can think of no reason that fishers might be led to think multiplicatively and hunters additively; if these communities discover the right kind of Kantian counterfactual, that engenders Pareto efficiency, this would be due to chance—selective adaptation of random cultural mutations.

What is the relation between multiplicative, additive, and simple Kantian equilibrium? We have:

PROPOSITION 3.6 *In a production game where all players have the same preferences u and the allocation rule X is symmetric, any positive SKE is both a $K^\times$ and a K^+ equilibrium.*

PROOF. Let the SKE be E^*. Define the share functions θ^i by:

$$\theta^i(E^1,...,E^n)G(E^S) = X^i(E^1,...,E^n).$$

To show that E^* is a $K^\times$ equilibrium, we need to show that:

$$\left.\frac{d}{dr}\right|_{r=1} u(\theta^i(rE^*,...,rE^*)G(rE^S), rE^*) = 0, \tag{3.23}$$

which reduces to:

$$u_1 \cdot (\theta^i(E^*,...,E^*)G'(nE^*)nE^* + \nabla\theta^i \cdot E^*) + u_2 E^* = 0, \tag{3.24}$$

where $\nabla\theta^i$ is the gradient vector of θ^i at $\mathbf{E}^* = (E^*,...,E^*)$. Because $E^* > 0$, we may rewrite (3.24) as:

$$-\frac{u_2[i]}{u_1[i]} = \frac{\theta^i G'(nE^*)nE^* + \nabla\theta^i \cdot E^*}{E^*}; \tag{3.25}$$

the right-hand side of (3.25) reduces to the MRT $G'(nE^*)$ if:

$$\frac{\theta^i(\mathbf{E}^*)nE^*}{E^*} = 1 \text{ and } \nabla\theta^i(\mathbf{E}^*) \cdot \mathbf{E}^* = 0.$$

The first condition is true, because, by symmetry, $\theta^i(\mathbf{E}^*) = 1/n$, and the second condition is likewise true by symmetry, for it says that the directional derivative of θ^i at $\mathbf{E}^*$ in the direction $\mathbf{E}^*$ is zero—and this is true, because θ^i is constant at $1/n$ along that path. Therefore, a positive SKE is a $K^\times$ equilibrium.

The demonstration that an SKE is a K^+ equilibrium is similar. ∎

Thus, multiplicative and additive Kantian equilibria are true generalizations of the natural concept of simple Kantian equilibrium to the case of heterogeneous preferences for the two simplest, ubiquitous allocation rules in common-pool resource problems: division of the product in proportion to effort and equal division of the product.

3.3 Incentive Compatibility

Let us look more carefully at the Kantian equilibria in the fishing and hunting economies for the special case, canonical in optimal taxation theory, in which workers have the same preferences over consumption and labor time (L), but their skills are different. Suppose that everyone has preferences over consumption and labor represented by a concave utility function $u(x,L)$, but productivities, w, are distributed according to some distribution function F, so that utility functions expressed as functions of consumption and efficiency units of labor are given by:

$$u^w(x,E) = u(x,\frac{E}{w}) . \tag{3.26}$$

So, although workers share the common preferences u, the differential skills they possess make this a case of heterogeneous preferences when we express labor in efficiency units.

We can ask whether the fishing and hunting equilibria are incentive compatible in the sense that, at the equilibrium, utility increases with skill. In the production economies studied above, the condition for Pareto efficiency is that $u_1^i G'(E^S) + u_2^i = 0$ for all i. For the special case of (3.26), this becomes:

$$(\forall w) \quad u_1 w G'(E^S) + u_2 = 0 , \tag{3.27}$$

where u is evaluated at the argument $(x,E/w)$.

Example: Kantian equilibrium in a quasi-linearity continuum economy

Assume $u(x,L) = x - \frac{1}{2}L^2$, and let skill levels w be distributed according to a continuous distribution function F. Let $G(E) = 2\sqrt{E}$. In the continuum economy, we replace E^S with $\bar{E} = \int E(w)\,dF(w)$, and E^i with $E(w)$. Thus, (3.27) becomes:

$$\bar{E}^{-1/2}w = \frac{E(w)}{w} \text{ or } \bar{E}^{-1/2}w^2 = E(w). \qquad (3.28)$$

Integrating this equation gives:

$$\bar{E}^{-1/2}\mu_2 = \bar{E} \text{ and so } \bar{E} = (\mu_2)^{2/3}, \qquad (3.29)$$

where $\mu_2 \equiv \int w^2\,dF(w)$ is the second moment of the real wage distribution. It now follows from (3.28) that $E(w) = \dfrac{w^2}{(\mu_2)^{1/3}}$. By recalling that the consumption of individual w is $\dfrac{E(w)}{\bar{E}}G(\bar{E})$ in the multiplicative Kantian equilibrium, we can compute that w's utility at the solution is given by:

$$u^{K^\times}[w] = u(\frac{E(w)}{\bar{E}}G(\bar{E}), \frac{E(w)}{w}) = \frac{3}{2}\frac{w^2}{(\mu_2)^{2/3}}. \qquad (3.30)$$

Hence utility[2] is indeed increasing in w.

Let us compute the Nash equilibrium of this fishing game. The first-order condition for Nash equilibrium is $\dfrac{d}{dE}u(E\dfrac{G(\bar{E}^N)}{\bar{E}^N}, \dfrac{E}{w}) = 0$, or:

$$\frac{2(\bar{E}^N)^{1/2}}{\bar{E}^N} = \frac{E^N(w)}{w^2}, \qquad (3.31)$$

or $E^N(w) = \dfrac{2w^2}{\sqrt{\bar{E}^N}}$, which integrates to give:

$$(\bar{E}^N)^{3/2} = 2\mu_2 \text{ or } \bar{E}^N = (2\mu_2)^{2/3}, \qquad (3.32)$$

and it follows that $E^N(w) = \dfrac{2w^2}{(2\mu_2)^{1/3}}$. Compute that utilities at the Nash equilibrium are given by:

$$u^N[w] = \frac{w^2}{\mu_2}2(2\mu_2)^{1/3} - \frac{1}{2}(\frac{2w}{(2\mu_2)^{1/3}})^2 = 2^{1/3}\frac{w^2}{(\mu_2)^{2/3}}. \qquad (3.33)$$

Comparing (3.33) with (3.30), we see that all players are strictly better off in the Kantian equilibrium, because $\dfrac{3}{2} > \sqrt[3]{2}$.

Let us now compute the utilities at the additive Kantian equilibrium for this example at the equal-division solution. Because of the quasi-linear structure, the values of $E(w)$ are the same for all Pareto-efficient allocations. We therefore know that $E(w) = \dfrac{w^2}{(\mu_2)^{1/3}}$ in the hunting economy. The only change from the multiplicative Kantian equilibrium is that consumption for all agents is $G(\bar{E}) = 2(\mu_2)^{1/3}$. It follows that utilities in the additive Kantian equilibrium of the X^{ED} economy are given by:

$$u^{K^*}[w] = 2(\mu_2)^{1/3} - \frac{w^2}{2(\mu_2)^{2/3}}. \tag{3.34}$$

The first-order condition for Nash equilibrium in the equal-division economy is $\frac{d}{dE}u(G(\hat{E}^N), \frac{E}{w}) = 0$, where $\hat{E}^N$ is the average efficiency units of effort expended in this Nash equilibrium. This first-order condition reduces to $\frac{u_2}{w} = 0$, so all efforts are zero in the Nash equilibrium of the equal-division economy. From (3.34), it follows that the additive Kantian equilibrium is not incentive compatible because utility is decreasing in w.

How disturbing or relevant is this? In ancient hunting economies, young men, who were the hunters, acquired their skills during youth and adolescence, when praise and respect were showered by their elders on those who developed high skill. Hunters in the bush had their reputations to maintain, so utility is incompletely represented by functions like u. In modern times, we think of the more radical kibbutzim in Israel, which used, more or less, an equal-division allocation rule. Some members with high earning power and who worked outside the kibbutz contributed more than others to the common pool of consumption goods. In the presence of a cooperative ethos, incentive incompatibility is not a death sentence, although we can expect that the cooperative ethos is more difficult to maintain if the variance in skills is high. Moreover, the incentive incompatible nature of the equal-division solution suggests that the additive Kantian equilibrium will be harder to maintain than the proportional multiplicative Kantian equilibrium.[3]

In the rest of this chapter, I apply the concept of Kantian equilibrium to a sequence of examples.

3.4 Oligopolistic Collusion[4]

Consider n producers in an oligopolistic market, who face a demand curve $D(p)$, where we assume that D^{-1} is a concave function, and where producer i has a convex cost function $c^i(y)$. The oligopolist game, where firms choose quantities, is given by the payoff functions:

$$V^i(y^1,...,y^n) = D^{-1}(y^S)y^i - c^i(y^i) .\tag{3.35}$$

Because D^{-1} is a decreasing function, the game so defined is strictly monotone decreasing, and hence by Proposition 2.1, the multiplicative Kantian equilibrium is Pareto efficient (for the community of producers).

3.5 Strikes

A group of N workers is contemplating a strike. Each worker's strategy is the probability that she will join the strike, π^i. If she does not join the strike, she scabs. Workers are of types i, with n^i workers of type i, and I types of worker. The probability that the strike wins is $p(m)$ where $m = \sum \pi^i n^i / N$, the fraction of workers who strike, and $p(\cdot)$ is monotone increasing. A strategy profile is a vector $(\pi^1,...\pi^I)$,

The utilities of a striker of type i are:

A^i if the strike wins, B^i if it loses, where $A^i > B^i$,

and strike-breakers earn, in addition, $d(m)$. We assume that $d(\cdot)$ is increasing, because the firm puts more value on having a worker cross the picket line, the more effective the strike is likely to be (large participation), and also because greater inducements are needed to attract scabs, the more solid the strike is.

The expected utility of a worker (striker or scab) at a profile $\pi = (\pi^1,... \pi^n)$ is:

$$EU^i = p(m)A^i + (1 - p(m))B^i + (1 - \pi^i)d(m).\tag{3.36}$$

Note that scabs enjoy the outcome of the strike, whatever it is. Because d is an increasing function of m, the game is monotone increasing, since $A^i - B^i > 0$, and hence a strictly positive multiplicative Kantian equilibrium, if it exists, is Pareto efficient. (Any additive Kantian equilibrium is efficient.)

We compute the condition for an interior multiplicative Kantian equilibrium, which requires solving for the strategy vector $(\pi^1,...\pi^I)$ that no worker-type would like to rescale. This requires solving:

$$\frac{d}{dr}\bigg|_{r=1} p(rm)(A^i - B^i) + B^i + (1 - r\pi^i)d(rm) = 0,$$

which reduces to:

$$p'(m)m(A^i - B^i) + (1 - \pi^i)d'(m)m - \pi^i d(m) = 0 \text{ or}$$

$$\forall i \quad p'(m)(A^i - B^i) = -(1 - \pi^i)d'(m) + \pi^i \frac{d(m)}{m}. \tag{3.37}$$

At the Kantian equilibrium, the right-hand side of (3.39) must be positive. The right-hand side of (3.37) is increasing in π^i, holding m fixed. It follows that lower equilibrium values of π^i are associated with lower strike gains, $A^i - B^i$. In other words, those who will gain less from the strike are the most likely to scab.

Let us now suppose that the number of workers is large and ask what the Nash equilibrium of the game is. If an individual worker can have only a very small impact on the size of m, then each worker should choose $\pi^i = 0$ (refer to the payoff functions at equation (3.38)): there is no other Nash equilibrium.

Here is a numerical example. Let:

$$p(m) = \begin{cases} am^2, \text{ if } m^2 < \dfrac{1}{a} \text{ and } d(m) = bm; \\ 1 \text{ otherwise} \end{cases} \tag{3.38}$$

define $\Delta^i = A^i - B^i$, $\overline{\Delta} = \sum n^i \Delta^i / N$, and suppose that:

$$a < 1 \text{ and } \Delta^i < \frac{b}{a} - \overline{\Delta}, \text{ all } i. \tag{3.39}$$

Note that, from (3.39), $b > 2a\overline{\Delta}$. (Multiply the ith inequality in (3.39) by n^i and add them up.) The first-order condition (3.37) for multiplicative Kantian equilibrium is $2am\Delta^i = 2b\pi^i - b$, if $p(m) < 1$; averaging this condition over all i allows us to solve:

$$m = \frac{b}{2(b - a\overline{\Delta})}.$$

m is positive and less than unity because $b > 2a\overline{\Delta}$. Now the first-order condition gives us $\pi^i = \dfrac{\dfrac{a\Delta^i}{b - a\overline{\Delta}} + 1}{2}$, which is less than one for all i by (3.39). Finally, we must check that $am^2 < 1$; this reduces to the inequality $a < 1$, which is true. We have found the unique positive multiplicative Kantian equilibrium for this example.

It may be possible to explain participation in strikes by positing that striking workers will impose severe costs on scabs, thus altering payoff functions to render it individually optimal to participate. Certainly, such penalties and ostracism occur in reality. The important question is whether it is the fear of punishment or Kantian morality that motivates participation for most strikers. The language of solidarity that is ubiquitous in the labor movement, especially concerning participation in militant and potentially costly actions, certainly suggests that workers attempt to support one another in their choice of the Kantian protocol. Is this a diversion, with the real work being done by fear of punishment? This seems most unlikely to me.

Contrast this Kantian analysis of strike behavior with a recent proposal by Salvador Barberà and Matthew O. Jackson (2016), who present a model of protests and revolutions. The problem is to derive a Nash equilibrium with positive participation, when the conventional analysis will produce a unique Nash equilibrium with zero participation. The authors achieve this by proposing the payoff matrix for an individual i as shown in table 3.1.

Table 3.1 **Payoff matrix in Barberà and Jackson (2016)**

	Success	Failure
Participate	θ^i	$-C$
Not Participate	0	0

θ^i is positive and is i's "unhappiness with the government." What's important here is that the utility achieved if the revolution succeeds depends on whether one participated in the protests. This is an example of the "warm glow" approach to explaining collective action (due to Andreoni 1990); the authors evidently assume that, the unhappier one is with the regime, the greater satisfaction one achieves from participating than not participating. Alternatively, one might think of the utility from participation as "expressive," as has been proposed in the theory of expressive voting (Brennan and Lomasky 1993). Having posited the warm glow/expressive feature, the authors derive Nash equilibria with positive participation.

But I question the warm glow approach to explaining protests. I offer the counter suggestion that many who participate do so because they are reasoning in the Kantian manner—as in the model of strikes above. Note that, in the strike model, the payoff to a participating agent if the strike succeeds is A^i, which is *less* than the payoff to the agent who does not participate (if the strike succeeds), which is $A^i + d(m)$. *Despite* this fact, there is positive participation in the strike when individuals maximize in the Kantian manner. (The payoff to both kinds of agent, should the strike fail, is also greater for the nonparticipator.) Do participators get a warm glow from participating? Surely this is often the case. But I conjecture that the warm glow is the *consequence* of having "done the right thing," not the *cause* of participation.

The "expressive" explanation is somewhat different, especially in one-off events, such as mass demonstrations. Expressing one's opposition to the regime can be a motivation for action. It is harder to believe that this is the case for participation in a protracted protest, such as a long strike, or an ongoing movement (such as the civil rights movement), or a lifetime of dissidence. In these cases, I think the Kantian explanation is superior.

3.6 Lindahl Equilibrium for a Public-Good Economy

Individuals in a society have utility functions u^i defined over arguments (y, E^i) where y is the value of a public good, E^i is i's contribution to the public good, and the cost function is $C(y) = E$. The production function G is the inverse of the cost function.

The payoff function of individual i is $u^i(G(E^S), E^i)$. The multiplicative Kantian equilibrium (if it exists) is characterized by:

$$\frac{d}{dr}\Big|_{r=1} u^i(G(rE^S), rE^i) = 0 \text{ or } u_1^i G'(E^S)E^S + u_2^i E^i = 0,$$

which can be written:

$$\frac{-u_1^i}{u_2^i} = \frac{E^i}{E^S} \frac{1}{G'(E^S)}. \tag{3.40}$$

Now $\dfrac{1}{G'(E^S)} = C'(y)$, and so adding (3.40) over all i gives:

$$\sum \frac{1}{MRS^i} = C'(y), \tag{3.41}$$

which is the Samuelson condition for efficiency in the public good economy.

DEFINITION 3.5 A *linear cost-share equilibrium* is a vector of shares $(b^1,...,b^n) \in [0,1]^n$ such that $\sum b^i = 1$, a contribution vector $(E^1,...,E^n)$ and a public good level y, which is feasible, such that:

$$(\forall i)(E^i = b^i C(y) \text{ and } y \text{ maximizes } u^i(y, b^i C(y))).$$

(See Mas-Colell and Silvestre 1989.)

A linear-cost-share equilibrium is a special case of a Lindahl equilibrium. Suppose that the $K^\times$ equilibrium characterized by (3.40) exists. Define $b^i = \dfrac{E^i}{E^S}$. Then the linear-cost-share equilibrium for the vector b solves:

$$\text{for all } i, y \text{ maximizes } u^i(y, b^i C(y)).$$

The first-order conditions for this problem are:

$$\text{for all } i, \quad u_1^i + u_2^i b^i C'(y) = 0. \tag{3.42}$$

But these equations are identical to (3.40), and so Kantian optimization decentralizes the Lindahl equilibrium. Andreu Mas-Colell and Joaquim Silvestre (1989) prove that such an equilibrium exists, and therefore the multiplicative Kantian equilibrium exists as well.

3.7 Affine Taxation in a Semi-Walrasian Economy

Consider an economy that produces a private good according to a concave production function G. The firm chooses its labor demand to maximize profits, observing the wage w per unit of efficiency labor and the price of output, which is unity. Individuals receive Arrow-Debreu profit shares according to a specified vector $\theta = (\theta^1,...,\theta^n)$. There is affine taxation of all income, at a rate t. The proceeds from taxation are distributed as a demogrant to the population. Utilities are $u^i(y^i, E^i)$ defined on income and labor. Define a *quasi-Walrasian additive Kantian equilibrium* to be a vector of efficiency labors $\mathbf{E} = (E^1,...,E^n)$ and a wage w such that:

(1) the firm maximizes profits given w at labor demand $E^S = \sum E^i$; and

(2) given w, no worker would prefer to *translate* the vector $\mathbf{E}$ by any constant.

What does (2) mean? Changing the vector $\mathbf{E}$, workers suppose, will change their individual wage income wE^i and also the demogrant, which they understand to be $\dfrac{tG(E^S)}{n}$; it will also change total profits. The myopia involved is that the wage is assumed to be fixed—and it would not be fixed if the labor supply were changed, assuming that the firm equalizes the value marginal product to the wage (the price of output is the numéraire).

Thus, the first-order conditions for a quasi-Walrasian additive Kantian equilibrium are:

(1) $w = G'(E^S)$ (from profit maximization); and

$$(2) \quad \left.\frac{d}{dr}\right|_{r=0} u^i((1-t)w(E^i + r) + (1-t)\theta^i(G(E^S + nr) - w(E^S + nr)) +$$
$$\frac{tG(E^S + nr)}{n}, E^i + r) = 0$$

Calculate that the second condition reduces to:

$$u_1^i \cdot \left((1-t)w + tG'(E^S) + (1-t)\theta^i(G'(E^S)n - wn)\right) + u_2^i = 0;$$

however, using $w = G'$, this reduces to $u_1^i G' + u_2^i = 0$, and so the allocation is Pareto efficient.

Thus, additive Kantian optimization, in the sense defined here, allows the polity to choose its tax rate, and then implement it efficiently in a decentralized way. In other words, this equilibrium *solves the equity-efficiency trade-off*, in the sense of completely separating the distributional question (the value of t) from efficiency.

If production is linear, then we need not inject the myopic behavior with respect to the wage, because the marginal rate of transformation is a constant independent of the labor employed.

This example is generalized in chapter 13.

3.8 A Firm with Stochastic Output[5]

Suppose the world has s states. In state σ, the production function of the firm is a concave function G^σ. The probability of state σ is p^σ. Player i will receive a share of output equal to $\theta^i(\mathbf{E})$, independent of the state. Players' utility functions over consumption and effort are as usual concave$\{u^i\}$, but now we assume that these are von Neumann–Morgenstern utility functions, so each player is concerned with expected utility $\sum\limits_{\sigma} p^{\sigma} u^{i}[\sigma]$, where $u^{i}[\sigma]$ is the utility at the allocation to receive in state σ.

For specificity, suppose that $\theta^{i}(\mathbf{E}) = \dfrac{E^{i}}{E^{S}}$. A multiplicative Kantian equilibrium is defined in the usual way. Is such an equilibrium Pareto efficient? The condition for Pareto efficiency of an interior vector of efforts $\mathbf{E}$ is:

$$(\forall i)(\sum_{\sigma} p^{\sigma} \left(u_1^i[\sigma](G^{\sigma})'(E^{S}) + u_2^i[\sigma]\right) = 0. \tag{3.43}$$

The necessary and sufficient condition for $\mathbf{E}$'s being a multiplicative Kantian equilibrium is:

$$(\forall i) \quad \frac{d}{dr}\bigg|_{r=1} \sum_{\sigma=1}^{s} p^{\sigma} u^{i}(\frac{E^{i}}{E^{S}} G^{\sigma}(rE^{S}), rE^{i}) = 0, \tag{3.44}$$

which, when expanded, becomes exactly (3.43). So interior multiplicative Kantian equilibria are Pareto efficient in the stochastic economy.

The same result holds if we use the equal-division shares, and additive Kantian equilibrium.

What happens if the share functions depend upon the state? If the problem is symmetric, then the simple Kantian equilibrium is Pareto efficient. But if it is not symmetric, there is no generalization.

3.9 Gift Exchange

In a well-known paper, George Akerlof (1982) explains that in some firms, workers work more than a stipulated, required minimum, and firms pay more than the market wage, as a gift exchange.

Here is a model of Akerlof's observation. The firm's profit function is $P(w,e)$, a concave function, increasing in the effort of workers e and also increasing in w, the wage, for sufficiently small w, but decreasing in w thereafter. We interpret the wage as the weekly income of the worker, independent of her effort e. The existence of a region in which $P_1 > 0$ is explained by the fact that increasing the wage induces low turnover of workers by increasing the opportunity cost of quitting, which is of greater value to the firm than the increased cost of labor, as long as the wage is not too high. The worker's utility function is $u(w,e)$, concave, increasing in w and decreasing in e.

Normal firms specify a minimal acceptable effort level e_m, and the equilibrium in a normal labor-firm relationship is a Nash equilibrium in which w is the firm's strategy and e is the worker's. The unique Nash equilibrium in the firm-worker game is given by:

$$e^N = e_m, \quad P_1(w^N, e_m) = 0. \tag{3.45}$$

However, Akerlof observes that there are other firms where workers offer more effort than e_m, employers pay a wage greater than w^N, and presumably both workers' utility and firm profits are greater than in the normal firm. Akerlof explains this as a gift relationship: the workers provide a gift to the employer by working harder than necessary, and in return the employer offers a gift to the workers of a higher than normal wage.

I will propose an alternative explanation to Akerlof's, which is that the players in the game are playing a multiplicative Kantian equilibrium. A multiplicative Kantian equilibrium is a pair (w,e) such that:

$$1 = \arg\max_r P(rw, re) \text{ and } 1 = \arg\max_r u(rw, re) \tag{3.46}$$

Notice that this is a strictly increasing monotone game: each player's payoff is strictly increasing in the other player's strategy. It follows by Proposition 3.1 that the solution, if it exists, is Pareto efficient. Typically, the Nash equilibrium in the game will not be Pareto efficient: so it is certainly possible that the Kantian equilibrium Pareto dominates the Nash equilibrium, and the other observations made above hold—that $e^K > e_m$ and $w^K > w^N$. We cannot, however, deduce these inequalities without more structure.

Consider this example:

$$u(w,e) = w - \alpha e, \quad P(w,e) = w - \frac{\beta}{2}w^2 + \gamma e,$$

where (α, β, γ) are positive numbers. Kantian equilibrium, the solution of (3.46), is given by:

$$w = \alpha e, \quad (1 - \beta w)w + \gamma e = 0,$$

which solves to:

$$w^K = \frac{1}{\beta}(1 + \frac{\gamma}{\alpha}), \quad e^K = w^K / \alpha,$$

$$u(w^K, e^K) = 0, \quad P(w^K, e^K) = \frac{1}{2\beta}(1 + \frac{\gamma}{\alpha})^2. \tag{3.47}$$

On the other hand, the Nash equilibrium is given by:

$$w^N = \frac{1}{\beta}, \quad e^N = e_m, \quad u(w^N, e^N) = \frac{1}{\beta} - \alpha e_m, \quad P(w^N, e^N) = \frac{1}{2\beta} + \gamma e_m.$$

One can compute that both players do better in the Kantian equilibrium than in the Nash equilibrium if and only if:

$$\frac{1}{2\beta\alpha} < e_m < \frac{1}{2\beta}\frac{1}{\alpha}(2 + \frac{\gamma}{\alpha}). \tag{3.48}$$

The wage is always greater in the Kantian equilibrium, and effort is greater if and only if:

$$\frac{1}{\alpha\beta}(1 + \frac{\gamma}{\alpha}) > e_m. \tag{3.49}$$

Check that (3.49) is implied by (3.48). It follows that all the features of the observed characteristics of the normal and "gifting" firms hold precisely when (3.48) is true.

So there are certainly environments in which the phenomenon Akerlof observes is explained by Kantian optimization. Many firms are caught in a noncooperative Nash equilibrium, and some have achieved cooperation, in the sense that the worker and employer are optimizing in the Kantian manner. Both gift and Kantian explanations are based upon trust: for Akerlof, each side trusts that the other side will make a gift if it does, and in my explanation, each side trusts that the other will optimize in the Kantian manner if it does. It may be very difficult to decide if one explanation is better than the other. Indeed, the "gift" explanation may just be another way—but an imprecise one—of stating Kantian optimization.

The advantage of the Kantian approach is that it gives an exact solution to the game. Akerlof's explanation is incomplete, for it does not determine how large the gifts will be. To do that, the utility functions of the players would have to be altered to include an exotic argument.

3.10 Sustainability in a Dynamic Setting

The fishing game is a very simple example of the tragedy of the commons. More realistically, one should examine the nature of stationary states where a common-pool renewable resource is exploited by a community. Here we modify slightly a model proposed by Andries Richter and Johan Grasman in 2013.

Consider a community that exploits a renewable resource, such as a fishery. At any point in time, the harvest will be proportional to the total extraction effort of the community, where the factor of proportionality is itself proportional to the total amount of the resource—that is:

$$H(t) = qX(t)E^S(t), \tag{3.50}$$

where X and E^S are total supply of the resource (the fish population in the lake) and total effort of extraction and H is the harvest at time t. Think of (3.50) as follows: in unit time, an amount proportional to the total fish population can be extracted, $qX(t)$—we view qX as a measure of the density of the fish in the lake. We now assume that there are constant returns in effort, at least for efforts that are not too large relative to X. Formulation (3.50) is standard in resource economics.

The law of motion of the renewable resource is given by:

$$X(t+1) = X(t) + rX(t)(1 - \frac{X(t)}{K}) - H(t), \tag{3.51}$$

where K is the maximum possible population of fish, or the capacity constraint of the lake. In other words, the fish population renews itself at a rate that is decreasing as the resource approaches the maximum capacity. It follows that the *stationary states*, where X is constant over time, are given by:

$$H = rX(1 - \frac{X}{K}) \tag{3.52}$$

or, using (3.50):

$$qE^S = r(1 - \frac{X}{K}). \tag{3.53}$$

Suppose that the utility function of producer i is given by:

$$u^i(x, E) = x - v^i E^2, \tag{3.54}$$

where x is consumption of the resource and E is extraction effort. The community wishes to choose among possible *sustainable extraction rules*: that is, it wishes to choose a stationary state (X, E^S) as defined by (3.53). As well as choosing the stationary state, it must choose the individual efforts E^i so that $E^S = \sum E^i$. Either because they have sufficiently low discount rates or because they care about future generations of producers, the community limits its search to sustainable states.

Production is carried out by individuals: thus, each keeps the resource he harvests. Since each producer is equally likely to extract a unit of the resource with the application of a unit of labor (in efficiency units), the total harvested resource is allocated in proportion to the efforts expended.

We examine a *multiplicative Kantian equilibrium* for such a problem. Imagine that the community is considering a particular stationary state (X, E^S). Suppose that everyone were to multiply his effort by a positive number ρ: then a new stationary fish population X^ρ would ensue, where this quantity is defined by:

$$q\rho E^S = r(1 - \frac{X^\rho}{K}), \text{ or } X^\rho = K(1 - \frac{q\rho E^S}{r}). \tag{3.55}$$

It is assumed for simplicity that producers will exert the same effort at every date, forever. Thus, they will quickly converge to a stationary state once the total effort is fixed. (This follows from an examination of (3.51).) Implicitly, producers are maximizing a discounted sum of their period utilities, and we ignore the issue of transition to a stationary state. Since maximizing the present value of a constant stream of utilities is equivalent to maximizing the single-period utility, we need not further consider the discounted sum, although it is their looking into the future that motivates the fishers to study the stationary (sustainable) states.

Now a Kantian equilibrium in such a situation is a vector of effort levels $\mathbf{E} = (E^1, \dots, E^n)$, inducing a total effort E^S, and a stationary state via (3.53), such that no producer would advocate changing *all* effort levels by *any* constant factor, passing to the associated new stationary state. In other words, $\mathbf{E}$ has the following property:

$$(\forall i)(1 = \arg\max_\rho [\frac{E^i}{E^S} q X^\rho \rho E^S - v^i (\rho E^i)^2]). \tag{3.56}$$

To understand (3.56), note that at (X, E^S), the amount of the resource (fish) that agent i gets is equal to his fraction of the total extraction time multiplied by the total harvest, which is qXE^S. So if i were to advocate multiplying all efforts by ρ, her new resource harvest would be $\frac{E^i}{E^S} q X^\rho \rho E$, and her new utility would be the expression in square brackets in (3.56). Thus, (3.56) is the condition for the effort vector's being a multiplicative Kantian equilibrium.

Substituting for X^ρ from (3.55), the above maximization is:

$$\max_{\rho} E^i q\rho K(1-\frac{q\rho E^S}{r})-\rho^2 v^i (E^i)^2, \tag{3.57}$$

which is concave in ρ, and hence we examine the first-order condition for the solution to (3.57) at $\rho = 1$, which reduces to:

$$E^i = \frac{qK(1-\frac{qE^S}{r})-\frac{q^2 KE^S}{r}}{2v^i}. \tag{3.58}$$

Adding (3.58) over all i gives us an equation in E^S, which solves to give:

$$E^S = \frac{\Omega}{2}qK(1-\frac{2qE^S}{r}), \tag{3.59}$$

where $\Omega \equiv \sum \frac{1}{v^i}$, which in turn gives:

$$E^S = \frac{\Omega qKr}{2(r+\Omega q^2 K)}. \tag{3.60}$$

Now the value of X follows from (3.53), and the individual effort levels are given by substituting E^S into (3.58); they turn out to be:

$$E^i = \frac{qK}{2v^i}\frac{r}{r+\Omega q^2 K}. \tag{3.61}$$

Unsurprisingly, the individual efforts are inversely proportional to the *disutilities* of effort (v^i). They are also increasing in r, the regeneration rate of the resource.

We next ask about the welfare properties of this solution to the commons problem. If the society limits itself to sustainable stationary states, what are the Pareto-efficient allocations of the resource and effort? To solve this problem, we maximize the utility of an arbitrary agent i subject to placing lower bounds on the utilities of all other agents and restricting ourselves to sustainable solutions. The problem is:

$$\max x^i - v^i (E^i)^2$$

subj. to

$$(\forall j \neq i)\ x^j - v^j(E^j)^2 \geq k_j \qquad (\lambda_j)$$

$$\sum_{\text{all } j} E^j = E^S \qquad (b) \qquad (3.62)$$

$$qXE^S \geq \sum_j x^j \qquad (a)$$

$$qE^S = r(1-\frac{X}{K}) \qquad (c),$$

where I have listed Lagrangian multipliers to the right of the constraints. Constraints (b) and (a) are feasibility constraints, and (c) is the sustainability constraint. The variables that must be chosen are $\{x^j, E^j, E^S, X\}$. The Kuhn-Tucker conditions for a solution to this problem are:

$$(\partial x^i)\, a = 1$$

$$(\partial x^i, j \neq i)\quad \lambda_j = a$$

$$(\partial E^i)\, E^i = \frac{b}{2v^i}$$

$$(\partial E^j, j \neq i)\, E^j = \frac{b}{2\lambda_j v^j} = \frac{b}{2v^j}\,. \qquad (3.63)$$

$$(\partial X)\, qE^S = \frac{cr}{K}$$

$$(\partial E^S)\, qX = b + cq$$

It immediately follows that $a = 1 = \lambda_j$ and $E^S = \frac{b\Omega}{2}$. From the last condition, $b = q(X - c) = (X - q\frac{E^S K}{r})$, and so $E^S = \frac{\Omega}{2} q(X - q\frac{E^S K}{r})$, which solves to give:

$$E^S = \frac{\Omega q X r}{2r + \Omega q^2 K}\,. \qquad (3.64)$$

Now, substituting into (3.64) from the last constraint in (3.62), we compute:

$$E^S = \frac{\Omega q r K}{2(r + \Omega q^2 K)}\,. \qquad (3.65)$$

But this is identical to the total effort in the Kantian equilibrium; see (3.60). Moreover, the individual efforts E^i are also identical to those of the Kantian equilibrium: this is obvious, since we note from (3.63) that the individual efforts are also inversely proportional to the v^i and must add up to the same total effort. *Any* allocation of the harvested resource among the producers generates a Pareto-efficient solution—the Kantian equilibrium picks out the allocation where "each keeps his catch."

To complete the Kuhn-Tucker analysis, we must check the sign of the shadow prices. $c = \frac{qKE^S}{r} > 0$ from the (∂X) condition. It remains only to check that $b \geq 0$. Now $b = q(X - c)$, so we need check that $X \geq c$, that is, $rX \geq qKE^S$. Using constraint (c) in (3.62), this becomes $E \leq^? \dfrac{r}{2q}$, or $\dfrac{\Omega qrK}{2(r + \Omega q^2 K)} \leq \dfrac{r}{2q}$ or $\dfrac{\Omega q^2 K}{(r + \Omega q^2 K)} \leq 1$, which is true. This completes the argument.

Thus, multiplicative Kantian optimization is a protocol for solving the problem of efficient, sustainable exploitation of a renewable resource.

3.11 Efficient Provision of the Quality of Work

The neoclassical convention is to model a worker's well-being as an increasing function of consumption and a decreasing function of work time. In fact, this surely undervalues the importance of meaningful work in peoples' lives. Let us suppose that a worker's utility function is $u(x,E,\omega)$, where x and E are consumption and efficiency units of labor expended, and ω is the quality of the work environment. (This might represent the speed of the assembly line or the degree of worker autonomy in the labor process.) Utility is increasing in its first and third arguments and decreasing in the second. Production is a function $G(E^S,\omega)$, a concave function of two variables that is decreasing in ω. Thus, there is a trade-off between output and the quality of working conditions. (Even if there is a range in which G is increasing in ω, we can ignore this part, because the only salient part of G's domain is the part where there is a trade-off between output and working conditions.)

We suppose that an economic environment consists of workers with utility functions of this kind, u^i, and a production function G. A feasible allocation is a vector of consumptions $\mathbf{x}$, of efforts $\mathbf{E}$, and of a value ω such that:

$$x^S \leq G(E^S, \omega). \tag{3.66}$$

The quality of working conditions is a public good, which is costly to produce (because G is decreasing in ω). Because of this, it is not surprising that an interior allocation is Pareto efficient exactly when:

$$(i')\,(\forall i)\; G_1(E^S,\omega) = -\frac{u_2^i(x^i,E^i,\omega)}{u_1^i(x^i,E^i,\omega)} \text{ and } (ii')\; G_2(E^S,\omega) = -\sum\left(\frac{u_3^i(x^i,E^i,\omega)}{u_1^i(x^i,E^i,\omega)}\right). \tag{3.67}$$

The first condition is the familiar equality of the marginal rates of substitution between labor and output and the marginal rate of transformation, and the second condition is the Samuelson condition for efficiency in the presence of a public good.[6]

Now suppose that we allocate output according to an allocation rule:

$$x^i = X^i(E^1,...,E^2),$$
(3.68)

for any fixed value ω. We now define:

DEFINITION 3.6 A $K^\times$ *equilibrium with work quality* is a feasible allocation $\{(x, E), \omega\}$ such that:

   (*i*) given ω, E is a $K^\times$ equilibrium for the economy (u^i, G)

   (*ii*) given E, no agent would prefer a different value of ω.   (3.69)

We now stipulate that the allocation rule X is the proportional rule:

$$X^i(\mathbf{E}) = \frac{E^i}{E^S} G(E^S, \omega).$$

We have:

PROPOSITION 3.7 A *strictly positive* $K^\times$ *equilibrium with work quality, where output is distributed in proportion to effort expended, is Pareto efficient.*

PROOF. Given concavity of the utility functions and the production function, an interior $K^\times$ equilibrium with a public good is characterized by two first-order conditions:

$$\begin{aligned}
&(i) \quad (\forall i)(\frac{d}{dr}\bigg|_{r=1} u^i(\frac{E^i}{E^S}G(rE^S, \omega), rE^i, \omega) = 0) \\
&(ii) \quad (\forall i)(\frac{d}{d\omega} u^i(\frac{E^i}{E^S}G(E^S, \omega), E^i, \omega) = 0)
\end{aligned}$$
(3.70)

Check that condition (*i*) of (3.70) implies condition (*i'*) of (3.67). Condition (*ii*) of (3.70) says that:

$$(\forall i)(u_1^i \cdot \frac{E^i}{E^S}G_2(E^S, \omega) + u_3^i = 0) \text{ or } (\forall i)(\frac{E^i}{E^S}G(E^S, \omega) = -\frac{u_3^i}{u_1^i}).$$

Adding up the last set of equations over i gives condition (*ii'*) of (3.67). ∎

Of course, the Walrasian equilibrium of an economy where the quality of working conditions is a public good will not be Pareto efficient.

Clearly, there is an analog to Proposition 3.7 where we use the equal-division rule to allocate the private good and additive Kantian equilibrium.

3.12 Summary Thoughts

Kantian optimization provides microfoundations for the efficient solution of many phenomena involving public goods and bads: in common-pool resource problems, collusion among oligopolists, by decentralizing Lindahl equilibrium, resolving the voting paradox, Akerlovian gift exchange, participation in strikes, and the provision of an efficient level of work-place quality. The virtue of the approach is that it gives a precise solution to many games (modulo the existence question), a solution that does not depend upon parameterizing the role of "exotic" arguments that behavioral economists typically insert into preferences. Preferences in all the examples I have given are classical (self-regarding and nonexotic). With heterogeneous preferences, we have introduced Kantian protocols that, mathematically, sound a lot like Nash optimization: we have chosen the counterfactual to which the agent compares the present strategy profile in a different manner from Nash.

As we now see that there are different varieties of Kantian optimization in economies with heterogeneous agents, how might we theorize which kind of Kantian optimization cooperators choose? Is there a reason that fishers should choose multiplicative variation and hunters additive variation? I am not particularly interested, however, in this question: as I will argue below (see chapter 11), these kinds of Kantian equilibrium should mainly be viewed, not as descriptive (positive economics), but rather as prescriptive. They provide instructions for how a group whose members wish to cooperate can find a normatively attractive solution to its design problem.

Perhaps this is an appropriate place to expand on the morality of Kantian optimization of the additive or multiplicative variety. After all, the justification given for Method Two in section 2.1 no longer applies, because symmetry no longer exists. When a fisher believes she must justify an expansion in her own labor supply by 10 percent by asking how *she would feel* if others similarly expanded their labor supplies, she is internalizing the negative externality that her labor expansion imposes on others (via reducing the lake's productivity). As I noted earlier, she does not internalize this by contemplating how the reduction in the lake's productivity will hurt others (that would be altruism): rather, she asks how *similar* behavior by others would affect *her*. This approach to moral thinking has several advantages: first, it does not require that the optimizer know the preferences of others, and second, it does not require her to care about others. (Indeed, the same trick to engender moral behavior is embedded in "Do unto others as you would have them do unto you.") We often invoke the same mechanism in teaching our children not to litter: we ask the child how *he* would feel if *others* were to litter the way he is doing, rather than relying on his altruism to desist from throwing his candy wrapper on the sidewalk. Our practice with littering children suggests to me that appealing to the categorical imperative is more persuasive than appealing to altruism.

I have cited the work of Michael Tomasello (2016) and Philip Kitcher (2011), who propose theories for how cooperation and the morality that supports it evolved among humans over the past 400,000 years, and, in particular, among *Homo sapiens* in the 140,000 or so years of its existence before the advent of agriculture 10,000 years ago. My own feeling is that concepts of fairness (and hence morality) have very much to do with symmetry. Our brains have evolved to focus on symmetry, to search for symmetry in situations, and it is not a stretch to believe that our concepts of fairness, likewise, depend upon symmetry. The proportional and additive deviations that characterize the multiplicative and additive versions of Kantian equilibrium involve what are probably the two simplest mathematical conceptions of symmetric deviation from a given vector of efforts. It does not seem to me far-fetched to suppose that these forms of symmetric deviation are associated with moral alternatives by human minds. But why assume that others in the game are engaging in the same kind of thinking? This must still be induced by the common knowledge assumption (Tomasello's joint intentionality) that all participants are thinking in the same way, as in Method Two of section 2.1.

If, after all, we accept Nash equilibrium, which models an individual as examining a counterfactual strategy profile where only she deviates, why not consider it credible that an individual consider a *morally salient* counterfactual profile with a symmetric deviation?

Thus, when the game is no longer symmetric, symmetric *deviations* from an existing strategy vector may continue to appear to humans as reasonable alternatives in a situation in which they desire to act cooperatively.

The cooperative flavor of Kantian optimization is that when each of us considers counterfactual strategy vectors, we consider them in a *common set* (namely, the line generated by rescaling the current strategy vector in $\mathfrak{R}_+^n$), as opposed to Nash optimization, in which each individual has his own, idiosyncratic set of counterfactual strategy vectors in $\mathfrak{R}_+^n$. This is illustrated in fig. 3.1.

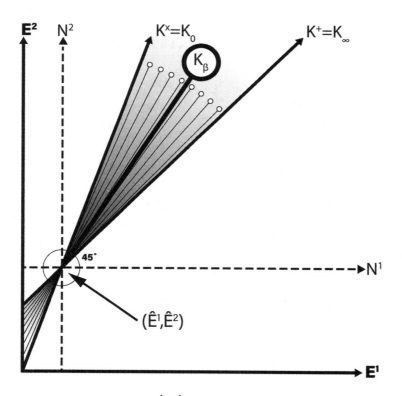

Figure 3.1 At a strategy pair $(\hat{E}^1, \hat{E}^2)$ a Nash player 1 will contemplate the set of counterfactual strategy profiles given by the horizontal line N^1, and a Nash player 2 will contemplate the set of counterfactual strategy profiles given by the vertical line N^2. But if the players are using multiplicative Kantian optimization, they will *each* contemplate strategy profiles in the ray $K^\times$, and if they are using additive Kantian optimization, they will each contemplate counterfactual strategy profiles in the 45° line K^+. The use of a common set of counterfactual profiles models joint intentionality.

3.13 Literature Notes

In Roemer and Silvestre (1993), we proved that, in economies more general than the ones defined here, allocations exist in which consumption is proportional to labor expended *and* which are Pareto efficient. We viewed this is a canonical "socialist allocation": it adjoins to the socialist principle of proportionality of consumption to labor, Pareto efficiency, mostly ignored in the socialist tradition. We dubbed this allocation a proportional solution (Definition 3.4). In Roemer (1996), I noted that the proportional solution possesses the multiplicative Kantian property, and so named it a "Kantian equilibrium."

Joaquim Silvestre suggested varying the Kantian protocol to "additive." He noted that one advantage of additive Kantian equilibrium is that it eliminates a nonefficient (multiplicative) Kantian equilibrium in the fishing game, where all efforts are zero. In general, one need not specify positivity in additive Kantian equilibrium to guarantee Pareto efficiency, whereas one does, for multiplicative Kantian equilibrium.

The proof presented here that positive multiplicative Kantian equilibria in a strictly monotone game with heterogeneous preferences is Pareto efficient (in the game) is due to Colin Stewart, who was then a Yale graduate student.

The presentation in this book is nonchronological. I first discovered multiplicative Kantian equilibrium and its relation to Pareto efficiency for the proportional allocation rule and only much later saw the simpler idea of simple Kantian equilibrium in symmetric games, to which I credit Brekke, Kverndokk, and Nyborg (2003).

FOUR

Other Forms of Kantian Optimization

4.1 A Continuum of Kantian Equilibria

Multiplicative and additive Kantian optimization each employ a method of universalizing one's action, and as we have seen, these ways of optimizing implement efficient allocations for the two classical rules for allocating a joint product: proportionally to effort, and equally. Can other allocation rules be efficiently implemented in production economies with some kind of Kantian optimization?

We can generalize the multiplicative and additive Kantian optimization protocols as follows. Consider the function:

$$\varphi^{\times}(E, r) = rE \tag{4.1}$$

defined on the domain $\mathfrak{R}_{+}^{2}$. Let a game be defined by payoff functions $\{V^{i}\}$ on strategy profiles $(E^{1},\ldots,E^{n})$. We can define a multiplicative Kantian equilibrium as a profile $(E^{1},\ldots,E^{n})$ such that:

$$(\forall i) \quad V^{i}(\varphi^{\times}(E^{1},r),\ldots,\varphi^{\times}(E^{n},r)) \text{ is maximized at } r = 1. \tag{4.2}$$

Similarly, define:

$$\varphi^{+}(E, r) = E + r - 1. \tag{4.3}$$

Then an additive Kantian equilibrium is a profile $(E^{1},\ldots,E^{n})$ such that:

$$(\forall i) \quad V^{i}(\varphi^{+}(E^{1},r),\ldots,\varphi^{+}(E^{n},r)) \text{ is maximized at } r = 1. \tag{4.4}$$

(In this case, r can take on negative values.)

More generally:

DEFINITION 4.1 A function $\varphi(E,r): \mathfrak{R}_{+} \times \mathfrak{R} \to \mathfrak{R}_{+}$ such that $\varphi(E,1) = E$ and φ is increasing and concave in r is a *Kantian variation*.

Consider the convex economic environments with production $e = (u^1, \ldots u^n, G)$ that we have been studying: denote the domain of such economic environments by $\mathfrak{E}$. The environment e becomes an *economy* if we append to it an allocation rule, which is a set of functions $\{X^i : \mathfrak{R}^n_+ \to \mathfrak{R}_+, i = 1, \ldots, n\}$ such that:

$$\forall (E^1, \ldots, E^n) \quad \sum_{i=1}^n X^i(E^1, \ldots, E^n) = G(E^S).$$

Alternatively, we may define an allocation rule as a set of output-share functions θ^i, where $X^i(E^1, \ldots, E^n) = \theta^i(E^1, \ldots, E^n)G(E^S)$. We have studied two allocation rules, X^{Pr} and X^{ED}. Given a pair (e,X), we have an economy with respect to which we can define a game whose strategies are the effort levels of its members. What we have shown is that the positive Kantian equilibria of economies (e,X^{Pr}) with respect to the Kantian variation $\varphi^\times$ are Pareto efficient for all $e \in \mathfrak{E}$ and that the Kantian equilibria of economies (e,X^{ED}) with respect to the Kantian variation φ^+ are Pareto efficient for all $e \in \mathfrak{E}$. This motivates the definition:

DEFINITION 4.2 An ordered pair (X,φ) consisting of an allocation rule and a Kantian variation is an *efficient Kantian pair* if the Kantian equilibria with respect to the variation φ of economies (e,X) for all $e \in \mathfrak{E}$ are Pareto efficient in the economic environment e.

The question naturally arises: Are there any efficient Kantian pairs other than the ones generating additive and multiplicative Kantian equilibrium? Indeed, we will show there is a whole continuum of such pairs that span a set of which the two polar members are $(X^{Pr}, \varphi^\times)$ and (X^{ED}, φ^+).

Define the allocation rule X_β for any $\beta \in [0, \infty)$:

$$X_\beta^i(E^1, \ldots, E^n) = \frac{E^i + \beta}{E^S + n\beta} G(E^S) \tag{4.5}$$

and the Kantian variation:

$$\varphi_\beta(E,r) = rE + (r-1)\beta. \tag{4.6}$$

Notice that as $\beta \to \infty$, $X^\beta(E^1, \ldots, E^n) \to \dfrac{G(E^S)}{n}$. Let us therefore define $\varphi_\infty(E,r) = \varphi^+(E,r)$.[1] Notice that for $\beta = 0$, we have the proportional allocation rule and the multiplicative Kantian variation. We have:

PROPOSITION 4.1 *For all* $0 < \beta \le \infty$, (X_β, φ_β) *is an efficient Kantian pair.*

Proof.

1. An effort vector $\mathbf{E} = (E^1, \ldots, E^n)$ is a Kantian equilibrium in the economy $(u^1, \ldots, u^n, G, X_\beta)$ with respect to the Kantian variation φ_β if and only if:

$$(\forall i = 1, \ldots, n)(\frac{d}{dr}\Big|_{r=1} u^i(\frac{E^i + \beta}{E^S + n\beta} G(rE^S + n(r-1)\beta), rE^i + (r-1)\beta) = 0). \quad (4.7)$$

To verify that (4.7) is correct, compute that the fraction $\dfrac{E^i + \beta}{E^S + n\beta}$ is invariant with respect to application of the function φ_β to all the effort levels. Now (4.7) expands to:

$$u_1^i \cdot \frac{E^i + \beta}{E^S + n\beta} G'(E^S)(E^S + n\beta) + u_2^i \cdot (E^i + \beta) = 0, \quad (4.8)$$

which reduces to:

$$u_1^i G'(E^S) + u_2^i = 0, \quad (4.9)$$

which uses the fact that $E^i + \beta > 0$ because $\beta > 0$. This proves the claim for $\beta \in (0, \infty)$.

2. The case $\beta = \infty$—which is K^+ equilibrium—has been shown in Proposition 3.6. ∎

We see from the last part of step 1 of the proof why we do not require the restriction to *positive* Kantian equilibria, for $\beta > 0$, that is required in Proposition 3.5.

Proposition 4.1 demonstrates the existence of a continuum of efficient Kantian pairs spanning economies from fishing ($\beta = 0$) to hunting ($\beta = \infty$).[2] What do these allocation rules X_β look like? Let's write:

$$\frac{E^i + \beta}{E^S + n\beta} = \lambda \frac{E^i}{E^S} + \frac{(1-\lambda)}{n}, \quad (4.10)$$

and compute that its solution λ is:

$$\lambda^* = \frac{E^S}{E^S + n\beta}. \quad (4.11)$$

λ^* is independent of i, so (4.11) implies that:

$$(\forall i = 1, \ldots, n) \quad X_\beta^i(E^1, \ldots, E^n) = \lambda^* \frac{E^i}{E^S} G(E^S) + (1 - \lambda^*) \frac{G(E^S)}{n}. \quad (4.12)$$

We can describe these equilibrium allocations as follows. They are Pareto efficient: a fraction λ^* of the product is divided in proportion to effort, while

75

the rest is equally divided among the participants. The value of λ^* is endogenous—it depends upon the vector E. We do know that as β travels from zero to infinity, λ^* travels from one to zero. But we cannot specify a priori a particular convex combination λ we wish to implement and immediately choose the right β. That is to say, the mapping from λ to β is complicated, depending on the equilibrium value of E^S (that is, $\beta = \dfrac{E^S(1-\lambda)}{\lambda}$). Indeed, these rules have appeared quite often in axiomatic resource-allocation analysis (see Moulin 1987, Ju, Miyagama, and Sakai 2007, Chambers and Moreno-Ternero 2017, and Thomson 2015).

Indeed, we can extend Proposition 4.1 to the case of negative values of β:

PROPOSITION 4.2 *For any* $\beta \leq 0$, *let* $(E^1,\ldots,E^n)$ *be a Kantian equilibrium of a production economy using the allocation rule* X_β, *with respect to the Kantian variation* φ_β, *such that for all i,* $E^i + \beta \neq 0$. *Then the allocation is Pareto efficient.*

I have separated this case out rather than including it in Proposition 4.1 because, as we will show in chapter 7, β–Kantian (that is, K_β) equilibria for the production economies indeed exist for all $\beta \geq 0$, but this is not true for all $\beta < 0$. The proof of Proposition 4.2 is identical to the proof of Proposition 4.1.

An example will be useful to illustrate. Let

$$n = 2, \, G(E) = aE - \frac{b}{2}E^2, \quad u^1(x,E) = x - \frac{\alpha_1}{2}E^2, \quad u^2(x,E) = x - \frac{\alpha_2}{2}E^2,$$
$$\alpha_1 > \alpha_2 > 0.$$

The equations for a K_β equilibrium are:

$$\alpha_1 E_1 = a - bE^S$$
$$\alpha_2 E_2 = a - bE^S$$
$$x_1 = \frac{E_1 + \beta}{E^S + 2\beta} G(E^S), \, x_2 = \frac{E_2 + \beta}{E^S + 2\beta} G(E^S). \tag{4.13}$$

In addition, it is necessary that either $E^i + \beta > 0$ for both i or $E^i + \beta < 0$ for both i—otherwise, one output share would be negative. One can solve the two linear equations in (4.13) for the $\{E^i\}$:

$$E^i = \frac{a\alpha_j}{\alpha_1\alpha_2 + b(\alpha_1 + \alpha_2)}, \quad i \neq j.$$

We have two cases where K_β equilibria exist:

CASE 1. $E^i + \beta > 0$ or $\beta > \max(-E^i)$.

In this case, $\beta > -\dfrac{a\alpha_2}{\alpha_1\alpha_2 + b(\alpha_1 + \alpha_2)} = v_2$.

CASE 2. $E^i + \beta < 0$ or $\beta < \min(-E^i)$.

In this case, $\beta < -\dfrac{a\alpha_1}{\alpha_1\alpha_2 + b(\alpha_1 + \alpha_2)} = v_1$.

Note $v_1 < v_2$. Thus, K_β equilibria for this quasi-linear economy exist for $\beta \in (-\infty, v_1) \cup (v_2, \infty)$. For $\beta \in (v_1, v_2)$ there are no K_β equilibria.

There is a geometric representation of the family of Kantian variations φ_β: return to fig. 3.1. The common set of counterfactual strategy profiles that players consider if they are using the optimization protocol φ_β, for some $0 < \beta < \infty$, is a straight line through the point $(\hat{E}^1, \hat{E}^2)$ lying in the cone generated by the lines K^+ and $K^\times$.

I do not think there is any practical application of Kantian optimization for the rules given by $0 < \beta < \infty$ or for the rules with negative β. The ways of thinking required by the variations φ_β in these cases are too complicated. These results are of theoretical interest, however, because of Proposition 4.3 and Corollary 4.4 below.

We now show that the only allocation rules that can be efficiently implemented on the domain $\mathfrak{E}$ by any Kantian variation are the rules X_β. Let φ be *any* differentiable Kantian variation. Define the two first partial derivatives of φ:

$$\varphi'(E,r) \equiv \frac{d\varphi(E,r)}{dr}, \quad \varphi_1(E,r) \equiv \frac{d\varphi(E,r)}{dE}.$$

We have:

PROPOSITION 4.3 *Let φ be any differentiable Kantian variation that is strictly increasing in r, let θ be any differentiable share rule depending only on the effort vector E, and suppose that (θ,φ) is an efficient Kantian pair for positive vectors E.*

Then:

$$(\forall i, E)(\theta^i(E) = \frac{E^i + \beta}{E^S + n\beta}) \tag{4.14}$$

for some $\beta \in \Re$.

PROOF.

1. $E > 0$ is a K^φ equilibrium for the economy $(\mathbf{u}, G, \theta, n)$ if and only if:

$$(\forall i)\, u_1^i \cdot \left(\theta^i(\mathbf{E}) G'(E^S) \sum \varphi'(E^j 1) + (\nabla \theta^i \bullet \varphi'(\mathbf{E}, 1)) G(E^S) \right) + \tag{4.15}$$
$$u_2^i \varphi'(E^i, 1) = 0,$$

where $\varphi'(\mathbf{E}, 1)$ is the n-vector whose jth component is $\varphi'(E^j, 1)$.

2. Therefore, if (θ, φ) is an efficient Kantian pair, it must be the case that (4.15) reduces to:

$$(\forall i)(u_1^i G'(E^S) + u_2^i) = 0, \tag{4.16}$$

which implies that:

$$(a)\ \ \theta^i(\mathbf{E}) \sum \varphi'(E^j, 1) = \varphi'(E^i, 1), \text{ and } (b)\ \ (\nabla \theta^i \cdot \varphi'(\mathbf{E}, 1)) = 0, \tag{4.17}$$

two equations that are identities on $\Re_{++}$. Why must (4.17) be true for any $\mathbf{E} \in \Re_{++}^n$? Because for any positive effort vector, one can produce an environment $(u^1, ..., u^n, G) \in \mathfrak{E}$ such that (4.15) holds at $\mathbf{E}$. To do this, pick any concave production function G; then pick u^i such that its marginal rate of substitution at $(\theta^i(\mathbf{E}) G(E^S), E^i)$ is given by the ratio of the coefficients of u_1^i and u_2^i in (4.15). Then $\mathbf{E}$ will be a K^φ equilibrium for that environment.

3. Since φ is strictly increasing in r, $\varphi'(E^i, 1) > 0$, for all i, and it immediately follows from (4.17) part (a) that:

$$\theta^i(\mathbf{E}) = \frac{\varphi'(E^i, 1)}{\sum \varphi'(E^j, 1)}. \tag{4.18}$$

4. From (4.18), compute that:

$$\text{for } j \neq i, \quad \frac{\partial \theta^i}{\partial E^j} = -\frac{\varphi'(E^i, 1) \varphi_1'(E^j, 1)}{(\varphi'(\mathbf{E}, 1) \bullet \mathbf{1})^2},$$

$$\frac{\partial \theta^i}{\partial E^i} = \frac{-\varphi'(E^i, 1) \varphi_1'(E^i, 1) + (\varphi'(\mathbf{E}, 1) \bullet \mathbf{1}) \varphi_1'(E^i, 1)}{(\varphi'(\mathbf{E}, 1) \bullet \mathbf{1})^2},$$

giving us the gradient vector $\nabla \theta^i(\mathbf{E})$. Using the fact that $\varphi'(E^j, 1) > 0$ for all j, calculate that:

$$(\nabla \theta^i \cdot \varphi'(\mathbf{E}, 1)) = 0 \Leftrightarrow$$
$$\sum_j \varphi_1'(E^j, 1) \varphi'(E^j, 1) = \varphi_1'(E^i, 1)(\varphi'(\mathbf{E}, 1) \cdot \mathbf{1}) \tag{4.19}$$

From (4.17) part (*b*), it therefore follows that the statement to the right of the equivalence sign in (4.19) is true, and this implies that $\varphi_1'(E^i,1)$ is a positive constant k, independent of i. But since $\mathbf{E}$ can be any interior vector in $\mathfrak{R}_{++}^n$, it follows that $\varphi_1'(E,1)$ is equal to k for all $E \in \mathfrak{R}_{++}$, because we can vary the vector $\mathbf{E}$ in a single component, always maintaining the validity of (4.19). Integrating with respect to E, we have $\varphi'(E,1) = kE + b$.

5. Therefore, again invoking (4.18), we have $\theta^i(\mathbf{E}) = \dfrac{kE^i + b}{kE^S + nb}$. Therefore, θ is the X_β allocation rule with $\beta = \dfrac{b}{k}$, as was to be proved. If $k = 0$, we have the equal-division rule, or θ_∞. ∎

Consider the Kantian variations studied in section 4.1: $\varphi_\beta(E,r) = rE + \beta(r-1)$. We have $\varphi_\beta'(E,r) = E + \beta$, and so it follows immediately that the allocation rule X_β is in fact the rule given by (4.18). We summarize Propositions 4.1, 4.2, and 4.3 with:

COROLLARY 4.4 *Let* $\{\theta^i\}$ *be a differentiable allocation rule where the shares* θ^i *depend only on the effort vector* $\mathbf{E}$. *Then there is a Kantian variation* φ *that implements* $\{\theta^i\}$ *efficiently on* $\mathbf{E}$ *if and only if* $\theta^i(\mathbf{E}) = \dfrac{E^i + \beta}{E^S + n\beta}$, *some* $\beta \in \mathfrak{R}$.

Thus, the allocation rules that can be implemented on our domain of economic environments are exactly the mixtures of equal division and proportional division, which are the two classical rules of cooperative societies.

4.2 Kantian Variations in Abstract Games

If we look at abstract monotone games, the relation between Kantian equilibria and Pareto efficiency holds for any Kantian variation:

PROPOSITION 4.5 *Let* $\mathbf{V} = \{V^i\}$ *be a strictly monotone game. Let* φ *be any Kantian variation and let* $\mathbf{E}^* = (E^{*1},...,E^{*n})$ *be a Kantian equilibrium with respect to the Kantian variation* φ *such that* $\varphi(E^{*i},\cdot)$ *is strictly increasing and maps onto* $\mathfrak{R}_+$ *for all i. Then* $\mathbf{E}^*$ *is Pareto efficient in the game.*

PROOF. The proof applies the same technique as the proof of Proposition 3.1. We assume that the game is monotone increasing.

Let the game $\mathbf{V}$ be strictly increasing. Suppose that the claim were false; let $\mathbf{E} = (E^1,...,E^n)$ Pareto dominate $\mathbf{E}^*$. Because $\varphi(E^{*i},\cdot)$ maps onto $\mathfrak{R}_+$ for each i, there is a value r^i such that $E^i = \varphi(E^{*i},r^i)$. Let $\hat{r} = \max_i r^i$. It cannot be that $\hat{r} = r^i$ for all i, for if that were so, then some i would surely prefer to rescale $\mathbf{E}^*$ to $\varphi(\mathbf{E}^*, \hat{r})$, contradicting the assumption that $\mathbf{E}^*$ is a $\varphi-$ Kantian equilibrium. Let j be a player such that $\hat{r} = r^j$. Then $V^j(\varphi(\mathbf{E}^*, \hat{r})) > V^j(\mathbf{E})$ because V^j is strictly increasing in the components $i \neq j$, and $\varphi(\mathbf{E}^*, \hat{r}) \geq \mathbf{E}$. This uses the fact that $\varphi(E^{*i}, \cdot)$ is strictly increasing for all i. But $V^j(\mathbf{E}) \geq V^j(\mathbf{E}^*)$, because $\mathbf{E} = (E^1, \ldots, E^n)$ Pareto dominates $\mathbf{E}^*$, and so $V^j(\varphi(\mathbf{E}^*, \hat{r})) > V^j(\mathbf{E}^*)$, which contradicts the fact that $\mathbf{E}^*$ is a $\varphi-$ Kantian equilibrium. ∎

In particular, K_β equilibria in monotone games are Pareto efficient (in the game) for all positive β.

4.3 Final Comment

I stress that I see no application for the Kantian optimization protocols K_β for $0 < \beta < \infty$ or for $\beta < 0$; it stretches the imagination to think of people optimizing in these complicated ways. What's interesting is that an allocation rule can be implemented efficiently by *some* kind of Kantian optimization if and only if it is a mixture of equal division and proportional division.[3] Because the equal-division and proportional share rules are the oldest conceptions of cooperative distribution of a joint product, this fact should reinforce my claim that Kantian optimization is a cooperative optimization protocol. And to reiterate one of my themes, no altruism is necessary to implement these share rules in a decentralized way: cooperation in the Kantian sense suffices.

FIVE

Altruism

In this chapter, we study the nature of Kantian equilibria when individuals are altruistic. We will restrict ourselves to examining multiplicative Kantian equilibria in economies (e,X^{Pr}) where e is an environment in the convex domain $\mathfrak{E}$. The results, however, generalize to the kinds of Kantian equilibria we have discussed in chapter 4: that is, K_β equilibria economies (e,K_β) where the Kantian variation is φ_β, $\beta \in [0,\infty]$.

5.1 Altruistic Preferences and Pareto Efficiency

We will now assume, for the first time, that individuals have altruistic preferences of the form:

$$U^i(\mathbf{x},\mathbf{E}) = u^i(x^i,E^i) + \alpha^i S(u^1(x^1,E^1),...,u^n(x^n,E^n)), \tag{5.1}$$

where $(\mathbf{x},\mathbf{E})$ is the entire allocation of consumptions and efforts, S is a Bergson-Samuelson social welfare function (which is concave, differentiable, and increasing in its arguments), and $\alpha^i \geq 0$. If $\alpha^i = 0$, the individual is self-interested, and if $\alpha^i = \infty$, she is a pure altruist, caring only about social welfare.

We begin by characterizing what the Pareto-efficient allocations will be in economies with the "all-encompassing preferences U^i" and a concave production function G.

PROPOSITION 5.1 *Suppose that $\alpha^i = \alpha$ for all i. An interior allocation $(\mathbf{x},\mathbf{E})$ is Pareto efficient in the economy $(\{U^i\},G)$ if and only if:*

$$(\forall i) \quad -\frac{u_2^i(x^i,E^i)}{u_1^i(x^i,E^i)} = G'(E^S), \text{ and} \tag{5.2}$$

$$\alpha \le \left(\max_i (u_1^i \cdot S_i \sum_k (u_1^k)^{-1} - \sum_k S_k \right)^{-1}, \tag{5.3}$$

where S_k is the kth partial derivative of S. All functions are evaluated at the allocation $(\mathbf{x}, \mathbf{E})$.[1]

The first condition (5.2) simply says that the allocation is Pareto efficient in the economy with self-interested preferences, when $\alpha = 0$. Clearly, this is a necessary condition for efficiency in the economy with $\alpha > 0$. For suppose that the allocation were not efficient in the self-interested economy. Then find a Pareto-dominating allocation. Notice that S must increase, because it is an increasing function of the utilities of all members of the society. Therefore, U^i will increase for everyone—strictly, if S is strictly increasing in its arguments. Therefore, the allocation was not Pareto efficient in the altruistic economy, a contradiction.

Because of altruism, if an allocation gives individuals very unequal utilities and S is strictly concave, then even if it is efficient in the self-interested economy (that is, if (5.2) holds), it will fail to be efficient in the $\alpha-$ economy, if α is sufficiently large, because everyone would prefer a redistribution that increases social welfare, even at the cost of a reduction in one's own personal utility. This is the consideration that condition (5.3) formalizes.

PROOF. To characterize Pareto efficiency in the economic environment $(\mathbf{u}, G, n, \alpha)$, we solve the program:

$$\max u^1(x^1, E^1) + \alpha S(u^1(x^1, E^1), ..., u^n(x^n, E^n))$$
subject to

$$\sum x^j \le G(E^S) \qquad (\rho)$$

$$j \ge 2 : u^j(x^j, E^j) + \alpha S(u^1(x^1, E^1), ..., u^n(x^n, E^n)) \ge k^j \qquad (\lambda^j).$$

The Kuhn-Tucker conditions are, letting $\lambda^1 = 1$:

$$(\forall j)(\lambda^j u_1^j + \alpha S_j u_1^j \Lambda = \rho)$$
$$(\forall j)(\lambda^j u_2^j + \alpha S_j u_2^j \Lambda = -G'(E^S)\rho)' \tag{5.4}$$

where $\Lambda = \sum \lambda^j$. Substituting the first of these equations into the second gives:

for all j $(G'u_1^j + u_2^j)(\lambda^j + \alpha S_j \Lambda) = 0$,

and so:

$$G'u_1^j + u_2^j = 0 \text{ for all } j, \tag{5.5}$$

since the second term is positive. (Recall that $S_j > 0$.) Equation (5.5) says that $MRS^i = MRT$ for all agents j.

Now (5.4) implies that $\lambda^j + \alpha S_j \Lambda = \dfrac{\rho}{u_1^j}$. Adding up these equations over j and solving for Λ gives:

$$\Lambda = \rho A \text{ where } A \equiv \frac{\sum_j \dfrac{1}{u_1^j}}{1 + \alpha \sum_j S_j}.$$

It follows that $u_1^1(1 + \alpha S_1 \Lambda) = \Lambda / A$, and so we solve:

$$\Lambda = \frac{u_1^1}{1/A - \alpha u_1^1 S_1}.$$

By substituting this value into the other equations, we compute that:

$$\frac{\lambda^j}{\Lambda} = \frac{1}{Au_1^j} - \alpha S_j.$$

Consequently, our KT nonnegativity condition is that:

$$\text{for all } j: \frac{1}{Au_1^j S_j} \geq \alpha.$$

Now substitute the expression for A and solve for α, giving:

$$\text{for all } j: 1 \geq \alpha \left(u_1^j S_j \sum_k \frac{1}{u_1^k} - \sum_k S_k \right).$$

If at least one of the terms in parentheses is positive, then this condition is equivalent to:

$$\alpha \leq \frac{1}{\max\limits_j \left(u_1^j S_j \sum_k \dfrac{1}{u_1^k} - \sum_k S_k \right)}. \tag{5.6}$$

Suppose to the contrary that the parenthetical terms are all nonpositive. This means that:

$$\text{for all } j: \frac{S_j}{\sum S_k} \leq \frac{1/u_1^j}{\sum 1/u_1^k}.$$

This inequality is of the form $\dfrac{a_j}{\sum a_k} \leq \dfrac{b_j}{\sum b_k}$ where all a's and b's are positive. It follows that all the inequalities are *equalities*; for if one is strict, both sums cannot add to one. Therefore, in this case we have $\left(u_1^j S_j \sum_k \dfrac{1}{u_1^k} - \sum_k S_k \right) = 0$ for all j, and hence (5.6) is true since the right-hand side is infinite.

Therefore, an interior allocation is Pareto efficient if and only if conditions (5.5) and (5.6) hold. ∎

Define $PE(\alpha;\mathbf{u},G,S)$ as the set of Pareto-efficient allocations when the economic environment is $(\mathbf{u},G,S)$ and α is the common altruistic parameter, which we will abbreviate as $PE(\alpha)$ when there is no possibility of confusion. Notice that as α increases, condition (5.3) becomes increasingly restrictive. It follows that the sets $PE(\alpha)$ are nested; that is:

$$\alpha < \alpha' \Rightarrow PE(\alpha') \subseteq PE(\alpha). \tag{5.7}$$

It therefore follows that $PE(\infty) = \bigcap_{\alpha \geq 0} PE(\alpha)$. Typically, in the purely altruistic economy, where $\alpha = \infty$, there will be a unique allocation maximizing social welfare—indeed, this must be the case if S is strictly concave. Therefore, the set of Pareto-efficient points shrinks to a single point as α increases when S is strictly concave. The intuition is clear. If everyone cares only about social welfare, then any allocation that does not maximize social welfare can be improved upon, from the viewpoint of each individual, by moving to the allocation that does maximize social welfare.

To get more intuition about condition (5.3), consider the case of a quasi-linear economy, where $u^i(x,E) = x - h^i(E)$. Then $u_1^i \equiv 1$. Let $\alpha \to \infty$. Then condition (5.3) becomes:

$$(\forall i) \quad n S_i \leq \sum_k S_k \text{ or } S_i \leq \frac{1}{n} \sum_k S_k. \tag{5.8}$$

Summing the last set of inequalities over i gives $\sum_i S_i \leq \sum_k S_k$. But this last expression must be an *equality*. It therefore follows that $S_i = \dfrac{1}{n} \sum_k S_k$ for all i, which is to say that for all (i,j), $S_i = S_j$. If S is an anonymous strictly concave social welfare function,[2] this implies that:

$$(\forall i,j) \quad u^i(x^i,E^i) = u^j(x^j,E^j). \qquad (5.9)$$

We have proved:

PROPOSITION 5.2 *If S is an anonymous strictly concave social welfare function and the individual utility functions are quasi-linear, then the only Pareto-efficient point in the purely altruistic economy equalizes all individual utilities.*

5.2 Kantian Equilibrium and Efficiency with Altruism

We fix the allocation rule X^{Pr}. The first remark is: *There may be no Pareto-efficient allocations in* $(\mathbf{u},G,\alpha,X^{Pr})$ *that can be implemented with the rule* X^{Pr}. Suppose that α is very large —say, infinity. Then the unique Pareto-efficient allocation in the economic environment $(\mathbf{u},G,\infty)$ is the one that maximizes social welfare. But this allocation may not (in general, it *will* not) be a proportional allocation. Consider the quasi-linear example of Proposition 5.2. If S is strictly concave and anonymous, the unique maximizer of the social welfare function (and therefore the unique Pareto-efficient point in this economy) is the one which maximizes the surplus (this determines the effort vector) *and* distributes output to equalize utilities. This allocation will only, by coincidence, be a proportional allocation. It therefore follows that we cannot expect the Kantian equilibrium of economies $(\mathbf{u},G, \alpha,X^{Pr})$ to be Pareto efficient (always, with respect to the all-encompassing preferences U^i).

Denote the set of $K^\times$ equilibria for the economy $(\mathbf{u},G,\alpha,X^{Pr})$ by $K^\times(\alpha,X^{Pr})$. We have:

PROPOSITION 5.3[3] *For all* $\alpha \geq 0$, $K^\times(\alpha,X^{Pr}) = K^\times(0,X^{Pr})$.

Proposition 5.3 says that *the Kantian equilibria for an economy with a positive degree of altruism, with respect to an allocation rule, are identical to the Kantian equilibria for the associated economy with purely self-regarding preferences.* Indeed, the proposition is more general than stated: it is easy to check that different agents can have different values of the altruistic parameter α^i, and the proof goes through.

PROOF. An allocation $(\mathbf{x},\mathbf{E})$ is a $K^\times$ equilibrium for the economy $(\mathbf{u},G,\alpha,X^{\text{Pr}})$ if and only if:

$$(\forall i) \quad \frac{d}{dr}\bigg|_{r=1} \begin{pmatrix} u^i(\dfrac{E^i}{E^S}G(rE^S),rE^i)+ \\[2mm] \alpha S(u^1(\dfrac{E^1}{E^S}G(rE^S),rE^1),..., \\[2mm] u^n(\dfrac{E^n}{E^S}G(rE^S),rE^n)) \end{pmatrix} = 0. \tag{5.10}$$

Denote $\dfrac{d}{dr}\bigg|_{r=1} u^i(\dfrac{E^i}{E^S}G(rE^S),rE^i) \equiv D_r u^i$. Then (5.10) can be written:

$$(\forall i) \quad D_r u^i + \alpha\sum_k S_k \cdot D_r u^k = 0, \tag{5.11}$$

from which it follows that for all i, $D_r u^i = c$, a constant over i. Substituting this constant into (5.11), we have:

$$c + \alpha c\sum_k S_k = 0.$$

Since $\sum_k S_j > 0$, it immediately follows that $c = 0$. But this says that $D_r u^i = 0$ for all i, which is exactly the condition that the allocation is a $K^\times$ equilibrium in the economy $(\mathbf{u},G,\alpha,X^{\text{Pr}})$, proving the claim. ∎

The important consequence of Proposition 5.3 is that Kantian equilibria of economies with and without altruism are *observationally equivalent*. If a community has learned to cooperate in the sense of employing Kantian optimization, we cannot tell by observing the equilibrium whether its members hold altruistic preferences or not—at least, with altruism modeled in this way. Their altruism has no impact on what happens in the economy at equilibrium. Although Kantian reasoning can deal quite effectively with many kinds of externality (such as the tragedy of the commons, and so on), it has no bite in addressing altruism. This result does not depend upon the number of individuals being large: indeed, it holds for economies with two people.

5.3 Review

If members of a community are altruistic toward one another, and if each is applying the Kantian protocol, the observed outcome is observationally equivalent to what it would be if each had self-regarding preferences. In this sense, altruism is a gratuitous assumption, which does not appear to have much impact if cooperation is already present. Of course, we cannot expect this result to generalize to other ways of modeling altruism: here, we have taken the traditional approach of appending a social welfare function to each individual's self-interested utility function.

Because of this result, it follows that Kantian equilibria in the presence of altruism will not in general be Pareto efficient (with respect to the altruistic preferences)—Kantian optimization will not take into account the consumption externalities in agents' preferences.

One should not read too much into Proposition 5.3. The relation between altruism and cooperation in the evolution of our species is another question. Tomasello (2016) argues that cooperation with nonkin may have been induced by altruism in the family. Bowles and Gintis (2011) argue that altruism explains the participation, in hunter-gatherer societies, of young men in battles against competing groups. Perhaps the above proposition has some bearing on these issues, as it shows that cooperation (viewed as Kantian optimization) cannot address the externality due to altruism. One cannot infer from this, however, that altruism is inactive in reality, or that altruism and cooperation are unrelated. The essential point here is that Kantian optimization is a way that efficiency can be achieved in cooperative settings; it does not, however, appear to solve the inefficiencies due to the consumption externalities typical of altruism.

SIX

Is Kantian Optimization Really Nash Optimization under Another Guise?

6.1 Maximizing Total Payoff versus Kantian Optimization

Is it the case that the Kantian equilibrium of a production game where players have traditional self-interested preferences is indeed the Nash equilibrium of a game whose players have extended preferences defined on the entire alloca-tion? For most of this chapter, I will work with the economic environments with production $\mathfrak{E}$ studied in chapter 3. Indeed, I will assume that the al-location rule X^{Pr} is in place and that the Kantian protocol that players use is $K^{\times}$. Thus, any positive Kantian equilibrium of such an economy is Pareto efficient.

One who is skeptical about the novelty of Kantian optimization may pose the italicized question above. For if the answer to the question were affirma-tive, then one could say that players in the game were in fact optimizing in the Nash manner, but using preferences with (what I've called) exotic arguments. In fact, were the answer to the question affirmative, and the extended preferences had a "nice" interpretation, this would provide a jus-tification of what I've characterized as the approach of behavioral econom-ics—namely, to deduce cooperation as following from Nash optimization with extended preferences.

There is an almost trivial response to the posed question. Suppose that we have a convex economy $(u^1,u^2,G,X^{\mathrm{Pr}})$ in $\mathfrak{E}$ and its Pareto-efficient mul-tiplicative Kantian equilibrium, $(\bar{E}^1,\bar{E}^2)$. Because the utility possibilities set is convex, the utilities at the Kantian allocation, $(\bar{u}^1,\bar{u}^2)$, lie on the boundary of that set and can be supported by a tangent line of the form $au^1+(1-a)u^2=k$, some $a \in (0,1)$. Define

$$U\left(E^1, E^2\right) = au^1(\frac{E^1}{E^s}G(E^S), E^1) + (1-a)u^2(\frac{E^2}{E^S}G(E^S), E^2)$$
,

and consider the game where each player maximizes the function U with respect to his or her strategy. Then $\left(\bar{E}^1, \bar{E}^2\right)$ is a *Nash* equilibrium of this game. The proof is immediate. Given that the first player plays $\bar{E}^1$, the second player maximizes U by playing $\bar{E}^2$, for by definition of the supporting tangent, there is no effort level for the second player that can achieve a higher value of U. This concludes the proof.

Another way of phrasing this result is that, in the modified production economy, each player is maximizing the *social welfare function* $V^a\left(u^1, u^2\right) = au^1 + (1-a)u^2$.

This example, however, shows that the question in the first paragraph above is not sufficiently nuanced. To rephrase that question: The challenge is whether Kantian equilibrium can be viewed as a Nash equilibrium of a game with extended preferences, *which, it could be credibly argued, the players are in fact playing.* This cannot be the case just described—for how would the players come to coordinate on just that value of a defining the function V that works? I assert that there is no way. In the words I used in the second paragraph of this chapter, the function V^a is not "nice."

What we must ask is whether there is a *natural transformation* of preferences (u^1, u^2) into preferences (V^1, V^2), where each V^i is defined on the entire allocation, such that the Kantian equilibrium of (u^1, u^2, G, X^{Pr}) is a Nash equilibrium of (V^1, V^2, G, X^{Pr}). Let us, therefore, rephrase the "Nash challenge" as follows:

> Is it the case that the Kantian equilibrium of a production game (u^1, u^2, G, X^{Pr}), where players have traditional self-interested preferences, is indeed the Nash equilibrium of a production game (V^1, V^2, G, X^{Pr}) where the preferences V^1, V^2 are defined over the entire allocation, and are derived from u^1, u^2 in a *natural way*?

It is only if the answer to this question is affirmative that the "Nash challenge" is powerful.

I begin by examining two cases in which the answer to the question posed is easily seen to be affirmative. The first case is when players have quasi-linear preferences; thus $u^i(x^i, E^i) = x^i - h^i(E^i)$ where $\{h^i\}$ are convex functions. Let us suppose that $n = 2$ to keep things simple. We modify the players' utility functions as follows. Both players will have the *same* extended utility function V given by:

$$V(u^1, u^2) = u^1 + u^2. \tag{6.1}$$

It is important to realize that in (6.1), each player has preferences over the whole allocation (x^1, E^1, x^2, E^2). Thus, we should write out (6.1) in full:

$$V(u^1(x^1, E^1), u^2(x^2, E^2)) = u^1(x^1, E^1) + u^2(x^2, E^2). \tag{6.2}$$

Formally, the composition $V \circ u$ maps $\Re_+^4 \to \Re$.

Let us write the payoff functions of the game where both players have the utility function V, where the strategies are effort levels:

$$\hat{V}(E^1, E^2) = \frac{E^1}{E^S} G(E^S) - h^1(E^1) + \frac{E^2}{E^S} G(E^S) - h^2(E^2); \tag{6.3}$$

here, we have just used the proportional allocation rule and substituted into (6.3). Although the players have the same preferences $\hat{V}$, the game is not symmetric with respect to the strategies of the two players. As always, player one controls E^1 and player two controls E^2. Now we look at the *Nash* equilibrium of this new game. The necessary first-order conditions for Nash equilibrium are:

$$\frac{\partial \hat{V}}{\partial E^1} = 0 \text{ and } \frac{\partial \hat{V}}{\partial E^2} = 0. \tag{6.4}$$

Compute that these conditions are exactly:

$$G'(E^S) = (h^1)'(E^1) \text{ and } G'(E^S) = (h^2)'(E^2). \tag{6.5}$$

But these are precisely the conditions for Pareto efficiency! Therefore, the Nash equilibrium of the game is a proportional allocation that is Pareto efficient: this is precisely the multiplicative Kantian equilibrium of the game with players whose preferences are given by (u^1, u^2).

In other words, the Kantian equilibrium of the game with self-interested (quasi-linear) preferences is exactly the Nash equilibrium of the game with players each of whom is concerned with maximizing the *sum of utilities* of the players. The two games are, in a word, observationally equivalent. Indeed, the utility function V defined by (6.1) does qualify as natural. There is, however, one drawback to this example: it requires a cardinal representation of the utility functions. For instance, if we used the utility function $2u^1$ for the first player, and continue to use u^2 for the second player, and define the extended preferences as $V = 2u^1 + u^2$, it is no longer the case that the Nash equilibrium of the new game is Pareto efficient. Indeed, with this V, the first-order condition for Nash equilibrium for the first player is:

$$\frac{G(E^S)}{E^S}\left(\frac{E^2}{E^3}\right)+G'(E^S)\left(1+\frac{E^1}{E^S}\right)=(h^1)'(E^1). \qquad (6.6)$$

The second case I propose is when all players have the *same* utility function u. Again, we define the extended preferences as the "altruistic" ones:

$$V(u,u)=u[1]+u[2], \qquad (6.7)$$

where the notation $u[i]$ means the utility of player i at the allocation (x^i,E^i) that i receives. The players now have the symmetric payoff function:

$$\hat{V}(E^1,E^2)=u(\frac{E^1}{E^S}G(E^S),E^1)+u(\frac{E^2}{E^S}G(E^S),E^2). \qquad (6.8)$$

The condition for Nash equilibrium is again (6.4). These conditions compute to:

$$\begin{aligned}
&u_1[1]\left(\frac{E^1}{E^S}(G'(E^S)-\frac{G(E^S)}{E^S})+\frac{G(E^S)}{E^S}\right) \\
&+u_2[1]+u_1[2]\left(\frac{E^2}{E^S}(G'(E^S)-\frac{G(E^S)}{E^S})\right)=0 \\
&u_2[2]\left(\frac{E^2}{E^S}(G'(E^S)-\frac{G(E^S)}{E^S})+\frac{G(E^S)}{E^S}\right) \\
&+u_2[2]+u_1[1]\left(\frac{E^1}{E^S}(G'(E^S)-\frac{G(E^S)}{E^S})\right)=0
\end{aligned} \qquad (6.9)$$

Let us look for a symmetric solution to equation (6.9). At such an allocation, we have $u_1[1]=u_1[2]$ and $u_2[1]=u_2[2]$. Then the first equation becomes:

$$\begin{aligned}
&u_1[1]\left(\frac{E^S}{E^S}(G'(E^S)-\frac{G(E^S)}{E^S})\right)+u_1[1]\frac{G(E^S)}{E^S}+u_2[1]=0 \\
&\text{or } u_1[1]G'(E^S)+u_2[1]=0
\end{aligned} \qquad (6.10)$$

and the second equation similarly reduces to $u_1[2]G'(E^S) + u_2[2] = 0$. But these two equations simply say that the marginal rate of transformation is equal to the marginal rate of substitution for both players. In other words, the multiplicative Kantian equilibrium (which is a symmetric, proportional allocation that is Pareto efficient) solves (6.7) and is therefore a Nash equilibrium of the game played by players with extended preferences.

Again, the same drawback applies: we must use cardinal utility functions that are identical for the two players for this conclusion to hold. We have shown:

PROPOSITION 6.1

a. Suppose that players have quasi-linear utility functions of the form $u^i(x^i, L^i) = x^i - h^i(E^i)$, *or suppose that all players have the same concave utility function u. Consider the new game where each player maximizes the sum of all the (cardinal) utility functions of players in the original game. Then there is a Nash equilibrium of the game with extended preferences that is the $K^\times$ equilibrium of the original game (with self-interested preferences).*

b. If we substitute K^+ for $K^\times$ in statement a, the statement is still true.

Proof of part *b* replicates the proof given for part *a*.[1]

It turns out that the result with identical utility functions extends to many other games. In the next proposition, we consider games in which player *i*'s payoff function is $P(E^i, E^S)$ for some function P. This covers symmetric public-good games (so-called trust games in lab experiments) and all two-person symmetric games.

PROPOSITION 6.2 *Consider a symmetric n-player game where the payoff of player i is $P(E^i, E^S)$, where P is a concave function and the strategy space is convex (an interval). Define the extended preferences* $V(E^1, E^2, ..., E^n) = \sum_i P(E^i, E^S)$.

If $\mathbf{E}^* = (E^*, ..., E^*)$ *is an SKE of the game where players' payoff functions are* $P(E^i, E^S)$, *then:*

(i) $\mathbf{E}^*$ maximizes V over all strategy profiles, and

(ii) $\mathbf{E}^*$ is an NE of the game where each player's payoff function is V.

It should be noted that the assumption of Proposition 6.2 that the strategy space is convex (an interval) is key. One can construct games with discrete strategy spaces for which the total-payoff-maximizing strategy profile is not the simple Kantian equilibrium of the game.

PROOF. If $\mathbf{E}^* = (E^*,\dots,E^*)$ is the SKE of the first game, then:

$$E^* \text{ maximizes } P(E, nE). \tag{6.11}$$

Suppose that the vector $\mathbf{E}^* = (E^*,\dots,E^*)$ does not maximize V. Then there exists a vector $\mathbf{E} = (E^1,\dots,E^n)$ such that:

$$\sum_{i=1}^{n} P(E^i, E^S) > nP(E^*, nE^*) \text{ or } \sum_i \frac{1}{n} P(E^i, E^S) > P(E^*, nE^*). \tag{6.12}$$

By concavity of P:

$$P\left(\frac{E^S}{n}, E^S\right) \geq \sum_i \frac{1}{n} P(E^i, E^S) \tag{6.13}$$

Note that (6.13) uses the fact that the strategy space is an interval, so that the strategy $\dfrac{E^S}{n}$ is feasible. But (6.12) and (6.13) together imply that $P(\hat{E}, n\hat{E}) > P(E^*, nE^*)$, where $\hat{E} = \dfrac{E^S}{n}$, which contradicts the fact that E^* is the SKE. This proves claim (*i*). Claim (*ii*) is immediate. ∎

There is, I believe, an important implication of Proposition 6.2. A number of authors argue that the cooperation that we observe among humans, and to a limited degree among other primates, is due to the evolution of altruism in the species. Altruism began, it is argued, in the relationship of the mother to the infant and extended over time to include other kin and eventually even nonkin. An important statement of this view is Kitcher (2011), who distinguishes among three types of altruism—biological, psychological, and behavioral. Biological altruism occurs when an individual takes an action that increases the fitness of another individual at a fitness cost to himself: this can be due to instinct and hard-wired. Psychological altruism occurs when an individual is motivated by a desire to help others: *intent* is key here. Behavioral altruism occurs when an individual has self-interested preferences but helps another individual as part of a Nash equilibrium in a game with stages, or a repeated game, in an equilibrium with reciprocation. It is questionable whether this should be called altruism at all: nonmyopic self-interest would seem to be more appropriate.

Kitcher argues that the ability to cooperate was engendered by psychological altruism that developed in nonkin primates.[2] But Proposition 6.2 tells us that we cannot distinguish altruism, in the sense that each player is maximizing the total payoff to all players in the game, from cooperation, in the sense that each is playing the simple Kantian equilibrium, where Kantian play is not motivated by altruism but (for instance) has evolved due to the symmetry of the game, a recognition that if we do not hang together, we will each hang separately.

There is, it seems to me, a reason to be suspicious of the altruistic explanation of cooperation in symmetric games. The total-payoff-maximizing strategy profile is one in which each player gives *equal weight* to the payoff of all players—in other words, each player is a utilitarian. But it would be more natural to assume that altruism is limited, so that each player weights her own payoff more highly than the other players' payoffs, and the simple Kantian equilibrium has no relation to the (different) strategy profiles that maximize a nonutilitarian sum of the payoffs.

Proposition 6.2 also tells us that it will be difficult to design laboratory experiments that distinguish between the hypothesis that players who play the Kantian equilibrium are using the Kantian protocol or are maximizing total payoff. To distinguish between these two hypotheses, the game must violate one of the premises of the proposition. Perhaps choosing a game with a discrete strategy space, having the property that the total-payoff-maximizing profile differs from the simple Kantian equilibrium, is the simplest way to proceed.

6.2 Asymmetric Production Games

We now ask whether these examples—of quasi-linear utility functions, or identical utility functions—can be extended. Fix a pair of concave utility functions (u^1, u^2) for the production economies. Consider the domain of economies $\Omega^{(u^1, u^2)} = \{(u^1, u^2, G, X^{Pr}) | G \text{ is nonlinear, concave}\}$. Any $K^\times$ equilibrium for an economy in this domain generates a pair of utilities for the players, say (a, b). Let $D^{(u^1, u^2)} \subset \Re^2$ be the set of such utility pairs. The next two propositions show that, indeed, we can "rationalize" $K^\times$ equilibria on $\Omega^{(u^1, u^2)}$ as Nash equilibria on economies where both players have extended utility functions over the domain of allocations in $\Re^4_+$.

PROPOSITION 6.3 *Suppose that there are extended utility functions* $V^1(u^1, u^2)$ *and* $V^2(u^1, u^2)$ *such that a positive NE of the game* (V^1, V^2, G, X^{Pr})

is a $K^\times$ equilibrium of the game $e = \left(u^1, u^2, G, X^{\text{Pr}}\right)$ for any $e \in \mathfrak{E}$ where G is nonlinear. Then V^1 and V^2 represent the same ordinal preferences [that is, have the same indifference map] on the set $D^{\left(u^1, u^2\right)}$.

Let's explain what this says. V^1 and V^2 are defined on allocations in $\mathfrak{R}_+^4$. However, they can also be viewed as having indifference curves in $\mathfrak{R}_+^2$, since any allocation produces a pair of utility numbers. The proposition claims that if a Kantian equilibrium can be rationalized as a Nash equilibrium with extended preferences on the domain $\Omega^{\left(u^1, u^2\right)}$, those preferences must be the same for both players. So the constructions of Proposition 6.1—where both players had the same extended preference order over utility pairs—was not a coincidence.

PROOF.

1. We are given a pair of extended utility functions $V^1\left(u^1, u^2\right)$ and $V^2\left(u^1, u^2\right)$. As before, we define the associated payoff functions of game with the proportional allocation rule by:

$$\text{for } i = 1, 2 : \hat{V}^i\left(E^1, E^2\right) = V^i\left(u^1(\frac{E^1}{E^S}G(E^S), E^1), u^2(\frac{E^2}{E^S}G(E^S), E^2)\right). \quad (6.14)$$

The first-order conditions for an NE of the extended games are:

$$\frac{\partial \hat{V}^1(E^1, E^2)}{\partial E^1} = \frac{\partial \hat{V}^2(E^1, E^2)}{\partial E^2} = 0. \quad (6.15)$$

Writing out the derivative[3] for $\hat{V}^1$, using (6.14), we have:

$$\left(V_1^1 u_1^1 \frac{E^1}{E^S} + V_2^1 u_1^2 \frac{E^2}{E^S}\right) G'(E^S) + \frac{G(E^S)}{E^S} \frac{E^2}{E^S}(V_1^1 u_1^1 - V_2^1 u_1^2) + V_1^1 u_2^1 = 0. \quad (6.16)$$

Dividing by u_1^1 (which is positive) and using the fact that $-G'(E^S) = \frac{u_2^1}{u_1^1}$, since by hypothesis the NE is a positive $K^\times$ equilibrium and is hence Pareto efficient, we have:

$$\left(V_1^1 \frac{E^1}{E^S} + V_2^1 \frac{u_1^2}{u_1^1} \frac{E^2}{E^S}\right) G'(E^S) + \frac{G(E^S)}{E^S} \frac{E^2}{E^S}(V_1^1 - V_2^1 \frac{u_1^2}{u_1^1}) - V_1^1 G'(E^S) = 0$$

$$G'(E^S)\left(V_1^1(\frac{E^1}{E^S} - 1) + V_2^1 \frac{u_1^2}{u_1^1} \frac{E^2}{E^S}\right) + \frac{G(E^S)E^2}{(E^S)^2}\left(V_1^1 - \hat{V}_2^1 \frac{u_1^2}{u_1^1}\right) = 0 \quad , \quad (6.17)$$

$$G'(E^S)\frac{E^2}{E^S}(-V_1^1 + V_2^1 \frac{u_1^2}{u_1^1}) + \frac{G(E^S)E^2}{(E^S)^2}\left(V_1^1 - V_2^1 \frac{u_1^2}{u_1^1}\right) = 0$$

from which it follows that either $V_1^1 = V_2^1 \dfrac{u_1^2}{u_1^1}$ or $G' = \dfrac{G(E^s)}{E^s}$. But the second possibility is false because G is concave but nonlinear. Therefore, we must have:

$$V_1^1 = V_2^1 \frac{u_1^2}{u_1^1} \tag{6.18}$$

at the proportional solution on the whole domain of economic environments. In like manner, we can expand the second condition in (6.15) to give:

$$V_2^2 = V_1^2 \frac{u_1^1}{u_1^2} \tag{6.19}$$

on the whole domain. Therefore, $\dfrac{V_2^2}{V_1^2} = \dfrac{V_2^1}{V_1^1}$ at all proportional solutions on the domain $D^{(u^1, u^2)}$.

2. Therefore, $\dfrac{V_2^2}{V_1^2} = \dfrac{V_2^1}{V_1^1}$ is an identity on $D^{(u^1, u^2)}$. But this means that the *marginal rates of substitution* of V^1 and V^2, viewed now as functions on the utility space $\Re^2$, are identical on domain $D^{(u^1, u^2)}$, and hence, V^1 and V^2 have identical indifference maps in $\Re_+^2$. Hence, they represent the *same preferences* over pairs of utilities, proving the claim. ■

Because Kantian and Nash equilibrium are both concepts defined on *preferences*, this means that we can assume that if Kantian equilibrium can be everywhere rationalized as a Nash equilibrium with extended preferences, those extended preferences (over pairs of self-interested utilities) are the same for the two players. In other words, if such a representation exists, we may take $V^1 = V = V^2$, for some function $V(u^1, u^2)$.

6.3 A Cobb-Douglas Example

We now come to the central question. When is the premise of Proposition 6.3 true—that is, when can we rationalize a multiplicative Kantian equilibrium as a Nash equilibrium where players each have a social welfare function as their utility function? I will begin by trying to construct the extended utility function V for a general Cobb-Douglas economy. Let $u^1(x, E) = x(1 - E)^m, u^2(x, E) = x(1 - E)^n, 0 < m < n < \infty$. These are two different utility functions representing Cobb-Douglas preferences. On the domain $\Omega^{(u^1,u^2)}$ we know that (positive) multiplicative Kantian equilibrium is Pareto efficient. We know that Nash equilibrium is defined and is always Pareto inefficient. We study whether it is possible to construct extended preferences V for each player such that the Nash equilibrium on the extended economy is the Kantian equilibrium for (u^1,u^2,G,X^{Pr}).

Note that if G were linear, then the Nash equilibria on $\Omega^{(u^1,u^2)}$ are efficient and that they therefore coincide with the multiplicative Kantian equilibria. I have eliminated this case from the domain.

Equation (6.19) tells us how the slopes of the indifference curves of V^i are related to the Kantian equilibrium. Now (6.19) says that it must be the case that:

$$\frac{V_2(a,b)}{V_1(a,b)} = \frac{(1-E^1)^m}{(1-E^2)^n},$$
(6.20)

where $a = u^1(x^1,E^1), b = u^2(x^2 E^2)$ at the Nash allocation (which is also the Kantian allocation of the original economy). To prove the affirmative claim, we must show that there exists a function $\Phi : \mathfrak{R}_+^2 \to \mathfrak{R}$ such that, at any Kantian equilibrium on the domain $\Omega^{(u^1,u^2)}$, it is true that $\Phi(a,b) = -\dfrac{(1-E^1)^m}{(1-E^2)^n}$, where (E^1,E^2) is the Kantian effort vector which yields utilities (a,b). For if this is true, then we have characterized $-\dfrac{V_2}{V_1}$ on its domain (namely: $-\dfrac{V_2^1(a,b)}{V_1^1(a,b)} = \Phi(a,b)$) and so will have characterized the indifference map of V. The proof will establish the existence of such a function Φ and then of V, which will also be differentiable.

We next observe that an interior Kantian allocation on the domain $\Omega^{(u^1,u^2)}$ is characterized by the following two equations and inequality:

$$\frac{mx^1}{1-E^1} = \frac{nx^2}{1-E^2},$$
(6.21)

$$\frac{x^1}{E^1} = \frac{x^2}{E^2},$$
(6.22)

and

$$m\frac{E^1}{1-E^1} < 1.$$
(6.23)

Equation (6.21) says the MRSs of the two players are equal. Equation (6.22) says the allocation is proportional. Equation (6.23) is equivalent to $m\dfrac{x^1}{1-E^1} < \dfrac{x^1}{E^1} = \dfrac{x^1+x^2}{E^1+E^2}$. We can therefore find a strictly concave G whose slope at the point (E^1+E^2, x^1+x^2) equals the MRS, because the last inequality tells us the marginal product of this G is less than its average product at this point, which is the condition for finding a nonlinear concave G passing through the point. Indeed, note that (6.23) can be rewritten as:

$$E^1 < \frac{1}{m+1}. \tag{6.24}$$

We now rewrite the equations characterizing the interior Kantian equilibria on the domain $\Omega^{(u^1, u^2)}$ as follows:

$$\begin{aligned}
mE^1 - nE^2 + (n-m)E^1 E^2 &= 0 \\
x^1 E^2 - x^2 E^1 &= 0 \\
x^1 (1-E^1)^m &= a \\
x^2 (1-E^2)^n &= b \\
E^1 &< \frac{1}{m+1}
\end{aligned} \qquad , \tag{6.25}$$

where we have also included the utility values. We can view these equations as ones defining the entire class of interior Kantian allocations on $\Omega^{(u^1, u^2)}$, where E^1 is restricted to the interval $(0, \dfrac{1}{m+1})$, as a function of the two parameters (a,b).

Our procedure will be to show, using the implicit function theorem, that the four variables E^1, E^2, x^1, x^2 can be defined as (differentiable) functions of (a,b) on the solution space of (6.25). It will then immediately follow that we have constructed the function $\Phi(a,b) = -\dfrac{(1-E^1(a,b))^m}{(1-E^2(a,b))^n}$, which will complete the proof. (Note that the denominator in the definition of Φ is never zero, because $E^2 < \dfrac{1}{n+1}$.)

To show this, we will demonstrate that the Jacobian of the system (6.25) never vanishes on the domain $D^{(u^1, u^2)}$. Order the variables (x^1, E^1, x^2, E^2) and compute that the Jacobian of (6.25) is:

$$J = \begin{pmatrix} 0 & \dot{m}+(n-m)E^2 & 0 & -n+(n-m)E^1 \\ E^2 & -x^2 & -E^1 & x^1 \\ (1-E^1)^m & -mx^1(1-E^1)^{m-1} & 0 & 0 \\ 0 & 0 & (1-E^2)^n & -nx^2(1-E^2)^{n-1} \end{pmatrix}. \quad (6.26)$$

Expanding the determinant of J and dividing by the positive number $(1-E^1)^{m-1}(1-E^2)^{n-1}$ demonstrates that $|J| \neq 0$ if and only if:

$$\overbrace{((n-m)E^1-n)}(1-E^2)x^2(1-E^1)\overbrace{(\frac{mE^1}{1-E^1}-1)}^{neg}+ $$
$$(1-E^1)\overbrace{(m+(n-m)E^2)}^{pos}x^1(1-E^2)\overbrace{(\frac{nE^2}{1-E^2}-1)}^{neg} \neq 0 \quad (6.27)$$

Suppose $|J|=0$. By (6.21) and (6.22), $(\frac{mE^1}{1-E^1}-1)=(\frac{nE^2}{1-E^2}-1)$, and so we can rewrite the *negation* of (6.27) as:

$$\overbrace{((n-m)E^1-n)}^{neg}(1-E^2)E^2(1-E^1)+ $$
$$(1-E^1)\overbrace{(m+(n-m)E^2)}^{pos}E^1(1-E^2)=0$$

and further simplify to:

$$E^2E^1(n-m)-nE^2+E^2E^1(n-m)+mE=0,$$

which in turn simplifies to:

$$nE^2 = mE^1. \quad (6.28)$$

But this contradicts the fact that $\frac{mE^1}{1-E^1} = \frac{nE^2}{1-E^2}$, since $m \neq n$, which proves that $|J| \neq 0$.

It therefore follows by the implicit function theorem that there is a differentiable function Φ that can be defined locally around any point (a,b). What is the relevant global extension of this result? We have to consider the domain $D^{(u^1,u^2)} \in \Re^2$ for which there exists a nonlinear concave differentiable production function G at which the multiplicative Kantian equilibrium of the economy (u^1, u^2, G, X^{Pr}) is a point $(a,b) \in E^{(u^1,u^2)}$. Our existence results (proved in chapter 7 below) will show that this is a large domain. The global inverse theorem of Hadamard[4] allows us to extend the locally defined function Φ to any compact subset of D. (We will not check this here.) Except for checking the Hadamard extension, we have therefore proved that there exists a continuously differentiable function $\Phi(a,b)$ that specifies the marginal rate of substitution of the social welfare function $V(a,b)$, whose existence we wish to prove, at every point (a,b) for which the system (6.25) can be solved.

We must finally ask: Can we indeed "integrate" the function Φ to find the function V? The answer is yes. Consider the differential equation:

$$\frac{da}{db} = \Phi(a,b). \tag{6.29}$$

Because Φ is continuously differentiable, by the Picard-Lindelöf theorem, there is a unique solution to the differential equation (6.29) for any initial condition on the function a. Denote the solution by $Q(a,b,k) = 0$, where k is a constant associated with the initial condition. Now differentiating this equation with respect to b gives:

$$Q_1 \frac{da}{db} + Q_2 = 0 \text{ or } \frac{da}{db} = \Phi(a,b) = -\frac{Q_2}{Q_1}.$$

But this means that the $Q(a,b,k) = 0$ is the locus of the kth indifference curve of the function V. By varying k, we sweep out the entire indifference map of V. The uniqueness guaranteed by the Picard-Lindelöf theorem tells us that the function V is unique, up to ordinal transformation, which will preserve the indifference map.[5]

PROPOSITION 6.4 *Let* $u^1(x,E) = x(1-E)^m, u^2(x,E) = x(1-E)^n, 0 < m$ $< n < \infty$. *Then there exists a differentiable function* $V : \mathfrak{R}^4 \to \mathfrak{R}$, *more precisely of the form* $V : \left(u^1(\cdot, \cdot), u^2(\cdot, \cdot)\right)$, *such that in a game induced by the economy* (V,V,G,X^{Pr}), *where G is any nonlinear concave differentiable production function, and where the preferences of each player are given by V, the NE is the $K^\times$ equilibrium of the game induced by* (u^1, u^2, G, X^{Pr}). *Furthermore, if* (V^1, V^2, G, X^{Pr}) *is any game with extended preferences whose NE is the $K^\times$ equilibrium of* (u^1, u^2, G, X^{Pr}), *then V^i is ordinally equivalent to V for $i = 1,2$.*

It is interesting to note where strict concavity of G enters. If a Kantian equilibrium is associated with a linear G, then (6.23) becomes an *equality*. This in turn means that the expression in (6.27) becomes *zero*, because $(\frac{mE^1}{1-E^1}-1)=(\frac{nE^2}{1-E^2}-1)=0$. Therefore, $|J|=0$. Note also that in Proposition 6.3, I used the fact that $G'(E^S)\neq\frac{G(E^S)}{E^S}$ to deduce (6.19), with which the proof of that proposition begins.

Let us calculate the slope of the indifference curves of V for the Cobb-Douglas example of Proposition 6.4, when $m = 1$ and $n = 2$. The equation (6.25) can in this case can be solved for E^1 as a function of (a,b):

$$(2-E^1)^3 b - 4a(1-E^1) = 0. \tag{6.30}$$

This cubic equation has a unique real root[6] given by:

$$E^1 = 2 - (2^{(5/3)} a)/(3^{(1/3)}(-9ab^2 + \sqrt{3}\sqrt{-16a^3b^3 + 27a^2b^4})^{(1/3)}) - \\ 2^{(1/3)}\left(-9ab^2 + \sqrt{3}\sqrt{-16a^3b^3 + 27a^2b^4}\right)^{1/3}/(3^{(2/3)}b) \tag{6.31}$$

Furthermore, we can show for this example that $E^2 = \dfrac{E^1}{2-E^1}$, so the function $\Phi(a,b)=-\dfrac{(1-E^1(a,b))^m}{(1-E^2(a,b))^n}$ reduces to $\Phi(a,b)=-1+E^1(a,b)/2$, and may be written down explicitly using (6.31). Recall that $\Phi(a,b)$ is the slope of indifference curve of V at the utility pair (a,b). V is hardly a "nice" function; the transformation of (u^1,u^2) into V can hardly be considered natural.

Let us note why it is easy to construct the extended preferences in the quasi-linear case and in the case when the players have the same utility function. In these two cases, the fundamental equation (6.19) becomes $-\dfrac{V_2}{V_1}=-1$. This means $V(a,b) = a + b$, which gives another proof of Proposition 6.1.

It is indeed possible to extend Proposition 6.3 to any pair of fixed concave, differentiable utility functions (u^1,u^2). We begin by replacing the system (6.21)–(6.23) with the general system:

$$\frac{u_2^1(x^1,E^1)}{u_1^1(x^1,E^1)} = \frac{u_2^2(x^2,E^2)}{u_1^2(x^2,E^2)}$$

$$x^1E^2 - x^2E^1 = 0$$

$$u^1(x^1E^1) = a \qquad\qquad (6.32)$$

$$u^2(x^2,E^2) = b$$

$$-\frac{u_2^1(x^1,E^1)}{u_1^1(x^2,E^2)} < \frac{x^1}{E^1}$$

and then compute its Jacobian, and so on. In general, the extended function V will not be computable in closed form.

The next question I ask is what happens to the function V if we replace $\{u^i\}$ with ordinal transformations of them. Let $\hat{u}^1 = f \circ u^1$ and $\hat{u}^2 = g \circ u^1$ where f and g are strictly monotone increasing functions. Consider·the analogous system to (6.32):

$$\frac{f'(a)u_2^1(x^1,E^1)}{f'(a)u_1^1(x^1,E^1)} = \frac{g'(b)u_2^2(x^2,E^2)}{g'(b)u_1^2(x^2,E^2)}$$

$$x^1E^2 - x^2E^1 = 0$$

$$f(u^1(x^1,E^1)) = f(a) \qquad\qquad (6.33)$$

$$g(u^2(x^2,E^2)) = f(b)$$

$$-\frac{f'(a)u_2^1(x^1,E^1)}{f'(a)u_1^1(x^2,E^2)} < \frac{x^1}{E^1}$$

A quick comparison shows this is *identical* to the original system (6.32)—just apply f^{-1} and g^{-1} to the third and fourth equations. Let the extended utility function for the new system be denoted by $\hat{V}$ and the extended preferences for the system (6.32) be denoted by V. Then we have:

$$\hat{V}(f(a),g(b)) = V(a,b), \qquad\qquad (6.34)$$

or, writing this slightly differently:

$$\hat{V}(f(u^1),g(u^2)) = V(u^1,u^2). \qquad\qquad (6.35)$$

This means that $\hat{V}$ and V define the *same preferences* on arguments $(x^1,E^1,x^2,E^2) \in \Re_+^4$.

Let us now move from the language of utility functions to the language of preference orders. Denote the set of self-interested preference orders over consumption and effort by $\mathbf{R}$. Denote the set of preference orders over the whole allocation for two players (an element in $\mathfrak{R}_+^4$) by $\mathbf{Q}$. The correct way of stating the central question of this chapter is: Given concavifiable preference orders $R^1, R^2 \in \mathbf{R}$, is there a mapping $F : \mathbf{R}^2 \to \mathbf{Q}$ such that the multiplicative Kantian equilibrium of the economy $(R^1, R^2, G, X^{\mathrm{Pr}})$ is always a Nash equilibrium of the economy $(F(R^1, R^2), F(R^2, R^1), G, X^{\mathrm{Pr}})$? F, in this case, is a social choice rule: given any two preference orders, it aggregates them into a preference order for society. Because the utility function is a derived concept, we must state the query using the fundamental notion of preference orders. We have:

PROPOSITION 6.5 *There exists a social choice rule* $F : \mathbf{R}^2 \to \mathbf{Q}$ *such that for any pair of self-interested preferences* $R^1, R^2 \in \mathbf{R}$, *the* $K^\times$ *equilibria of the economy* $(R^1, R^2, G, X^{\mathrm{Pr}})$ *is an NE of the economy with extended preferences* $(F(R^1, R^2), F(R^2, R^1), G, X^{\mathrm{Pr}})$ *for all increasing, concave production functions G.*

The proof is, in fact, the equation (6.35). For this equation says that the induced preferences on $\mathfrak{R}_+^4$ (for which the Nash equilibrium is the Kantian equilibrium of the problem with preference orders on $\mathfrak{R}_+^2$) are independent of the utility functions that are chosen to represent the self-regarding preferences. In other words, the induced preferences on the whole allocation that both players have in the "extended" game depend only on their *preferences* in the original game.

At this point, our skeptic can say: "Well, you see, Kantian optimization really isn't any different from Nash optimization. One just has to realize that people have preferences over the whole allocation." Proposition 6.5 could be taken to vindicate the program of behavioral economics.

But I disagree. For the function V that must be constructed, which represents the preferences of the players on the whole allocation, is in general extremely complex, as I have shown above for the Cobb-Douglas example. If the transformation from (u^1, u^2) were natural, as it is in the case when the $\{u^i\}$ are either quasi-linear or identical, then it would be plausible to assert that Kantian equilibrium is an unnecessary diversion: we could instead entertain the view that when people don't play what appears to be the Nash equilibrium from self-regarding preferences, they are being altruistic, using a social welfare function as their preferences. But given the complexity of the function V, and given the fact that V changes with (u^1, u^2), this view is impossible to maintain.

Let's take a *simple* example to illustrate the point. Suppose that the two players in a production game have utility functions:

$$\hat{u}(x^1, E^1) = (x^1 - h^1(E^1))^{1/3}, \quad \hat{u}(x^2, E^2) = (x^2 - h^2(E^2))^{1/2}. \quad (6.36)$$

This is how they think of their payoffs from "fishing" in cardinally meaningful units. Or these are the payoff functions provided by the experimenter in a lab experiment. Of course, the multiplicative Kantian equilibrium of this game, in the economy $(\hat{u}^1, \hat{u}^2, G, X^{\mathrm{Pr}})$, is identical to the Kantian equilibrium with the utility representation $u^i(x^i, E^i) = x^i - h^i(E^i)$. Now the monotonic transformations that relate the second (obviously quasi-linear) representation to the representation of (6.36) are $f(u) = u^3$ and $g(u) = u^2$. By Proposition 6.5 (or equation (6.35)), the extended preferences that each must maximize in the game whose Nash equilibrium will be the Kantian equilibrium of the original game are $\hat{V}(\hat{u}^1, \hat{u}^2) = (\hat{u}^1)^3 + (\hat{u}^2)^2$. But this is not a natural construction. The "nice" formula $V(u^1, u^2) = u^1 + u^2$ applies only if the representation of the quasi-linear preferences is given by $u^i = x^i - h(E^i)$. So it is *false* to say that in a quasi-linear economy, it suffices to rationalize the Kantian equilibrium as a Nash equilibrium that each player *maximize total welfare*. This formulation works only for a *particular* representation of players' preference orders by utility functions.[7]

Even in the case of quasi-linear *preferences* (that is, preferences that admit a quasi-linear utility representation), the extended preferences that players would have to be using are complex. Let us state this in terms of laboratory experiments. Suppose that the experimenter poses a prisoner's dilemma game to the players, whose payoffs are given by the matrix in table 6.1.

Table 6.1 A prisoner's dilemma

	Cooperate	Defect
Cooperate	(2,2)	(0,3)
Defect	(3,0)	(1,1)

According to Proposition 6.2, the simple Kantian equilibrium of this game is the same as the Nash equilibrium of the game where each player maximizes the *sum* of the payoffs $P^1 + P^2$. But now suppose that the experimenter proposes the payoff matrix shown in table 6.2.

Table 6.2 The same prisoner's dilemma as in table 6.1

	Cooperate	Defect
Cooperate	(2,4)	(0,4.5)
Defect	(3,3)	(1,3.5)

Table 6.2 is, in fact, the same prisoner's dilemma game as table 6.1: I have simply transformed the von Neumann–Morgenstern utilities of the second player by the positive affine transformation $\frac{1}{2}u + 3$. The Kantian equilibria of the two games are identical. But in order to produce the Kantian equilibrium of the second game as a Nash equilibrium of a game with extended payoff functions, the players must both maximize $P^1 + 2(P^2 - 3)$. Although maximizing the sum of payoffs might be natural, maximizing the latter function is not.

6.4 Summary

To reiterate, I take the results of this chapter to support the case that Kantian optimization is a fundamentally different protocol from Nash optimization. Formally, we can explain cooperation as the result of Nash reasoning with preferences defined on the entire allocation. In some cases, the utility function that players must adopt on the entire allocation to rationalize Kantian equilibria in this way seems natural. But in general, the extended utility function is not natural. Even for the simple case of quasi-linear preferences, producing a simple extended utility function (which "maximizes total utility") is achieved only with a particular choice of the utility representation of the original self-regarding preferences. The same is true with regard to rationalizing the prisoner's dilemma.

Although Nash rationalization of cooperation is mathematically possible, to make the story credible, one would have to explain how players move from their self-regarding preferences to the extended preferences that are required. Behavioral economists have limited themselves to situations and experiments, almost ubiquitously, in which the identification of the fair allocation is obvious or in which players have identical cardinal utility functions. In the latter case, the strategy profile that maximizes total payoff will coincide with the Kantian equilibrium of the game with self-regarding preferences. But this simple "altruistic" preference order on the entire allocation works only for players with symmetric preferences represented by *particular* cardinal utility functions (or payoff functions) and does not work at all when players have different self-regarding preferences.

In contrast, the Kantian explanation seems much simpler. It enables cooperation where it is not obvious *what* cooperation entails (for example, in the production economies)—that is, what the Pareto-efficient solution is. Of course, to complete the story, one must explain how people learn to optimize in the Kantian manner. When players are identical, simple Kantian optimization will work—and in this case, it is not hard to imagine the symmetry of the situation suggesting the simple Kantian protocol. How people might learn to optimize in the multiplicative or additive way, for games with heterogeneous players, is harder to explain. Nevertheless, in real life, there is often a focal "right" and "wrong" choice, and so the problem reduces to a simple game with two strategies, and simple Kantian optimization will work, even if the game is not symmetric.

SEVEN

Existence and Dynamics of
Kantian Equilibrium

Almost all the results up until now are of the form "If a Kantian equilibrium exists, it has such and such properties." In this chapter, I establish the existence of Kantian equilibria in the production economies we have been studying.

7.1 Existence of Strictly Positive $K^\times$ Equilibria
for Production Economies

Consider the following condition on utility functions $u(x,E)$:

Condition A. A utility function u satisfies Condition A if and only if

$$\lim_{\varepsilon \to 0} \lim_{x \to 0} -\frac{u_2(x,\varepsilon)}{u_1(x,\varepsilon)} = 0.$$

Examples: Let $u(x,E) = x^a(1-E)^{1-a}$. Then $-\dfrac{u_2(x,\varepsilon)}{u_1(x,\varepsilon)} = \dfrac{1-a}{a}\dfrac{x}{1-\varepsilon}$, and Condition A holds. Let $u(x,e) = x - h(E)$, where $h'(0) = 0$. Then $-\dfrac{u_2(x,\varepsilon)}{u_1(x,\varepsilon)} = h'(\varepsilon)$, and Condition A holds. Let $u(x,E) = (ax^r + (1-a)(1-E)^r)^{1/r}$.

Now $-\dfrac{u_2(x,\varepsilon)}{u_1(x,\varepsilon)} = \dfrac{1-a}{a}(\dfrac{1-\varepsilon}{x})^{r-1}$, and Condition A holds for $-\infty < r \le 1$, which is to say, for all concave CES utility functions.

Define the domain of utility functions as:

$$\mathbf{U} = \left\{ \begin{array}{l} u : \Re_+ \times [0,M] \to \Re, \text{ some } M > 0, u \\ \text{differentiable \& concave, Condition A holds} \end{array} \right\}.$$

Define the domain of production functions as:

$$\mathbf{G} = \left\{ \begin{array}{l} G : \Re_+ \to \Re_+; G \text{ increasing,} \\ \text{differentiable, concave; } G' > 0 \end{array} \right\}.$$

Define the domain of economies as:

$$\mathbf{D} = \left\{ \left(u^1, \ldots, u^n, G \right) \middle| u^i \in \mathbf{U}, G \in \mathbf{G} \right\}.$$

PROPOSITION 7.1 *For all economies* $e \in D$, *a strictly positive* $K^\times$ *equilibrium exists.*

Recall that a *multiplicative Kantian equilibrium* is a feasible allocation $\left(x^i, E^i \right)_{i=1,\ldots,n}$ such that:

$$(\forall i) \quad x^i = \frac{E^i}{E^s} G(E^s),$$

and for all i, $1 \in \arg \max_{0 \le \rho \le \frac{M}{E^i}} u^i \left(\frac{E^i}{E^s} G(\rho E^s), \rho E^i \right)$. (If $E^i = 0$, the domain of the argmax function is $0 \le \rho < \infty$.)

Let $M > 0$ and define the rectangle $R^\varepsilon = [\varepsilon, M]^n \subset \mathfrak{R}^n_{++}$ for any $0 < \varepsilon < M$. First, we prove a lemma:

LEMMA 7.2 *Fix* M. *For any* $G \in \mathbf{G}$, $\lim_{\varepsilon \to 0} \max_{E \in R^\varepsilon} \frac{E^i}{E^s} G(\varepsilon \frac{E^s}{E^i}) = 0$.

PROOF.

1. For any $\varepsilon > 0$, we must evaluate the solution of:

$$\max_Q \frac{1}{Q} G(\varepsilon Q)$$

$$s.t. \quad \frac{(n-1)\varepsilon + M}{M} \le Q \le \frac{(n-1)M + \varepsilon}{\varepsilon} \tag{7.1}$$

where $Q = \frac{E^s}{E^i}$.

There are three possibilities for the solution: (*a*) $Q = 1 + \frac{(n-1)\varepsilon}{M}$; (*b*) $Q = 1 + \frac{(n-1)M}{\varepsilon}$; or (*c*) $Q \in (1 + \frac{(n-1)\varepsilon}{M}, 1 + \frac{(n-1)M}{\varepsilon})$.

2. Case (*a*). At $Q = 1 + \frac{(n-1)\varepsilon}{M}$, the maximand is: $\frac{M}{M + (n-1)\varepsilon} G(\varepsilon + \frac{(n-1)}{M} \varepsilon^2) \to G(0) = 0$.

3. Case (*b*). In this case, the maximand is: $\frac{\varepsilon}{\varepsilon + (n-1)M} G(\varepsilon + (n-1)M) \to 0$.

4. Case (*c*). In this case, we compute the first-order condition with respect to Q, for the maximization problem (7.1). This condition is:

$$\frac{G(\varepsilon Q^*)}{Q^*} = \varepsilon G'(\varepsilon Q^*) \qquad (7.2)$$

at the solution Q^*. If εQ^* does not approach zero with ε, then the right-hand side of (7.2) does approach zero, as we wish to show. If Q^* does approach zero, it cannot approach faster than $1 + \frac{(n-1)\varepsilon}{M}$, and so $\varepsilon G'(\varepsilon Q) \le \varepsilon G'(\varepsilon + \frac{(n-1)\varepsilon^2}{M}) \to \varepsilon G'(\varepsilon) \le G(\varepsilon) \to 0$. This proves the lemma. ∎

PROOF OF PROPOSITION 7.1.

1. Given $(\mathbf{u}, G) \in \mathbf{D}$, consider the n-rectangle $R^\varepsilon = [\varepsilon, M]^n$ for some $0 < \varepsilon < M$. Define the individual best-reply correspondences on a domain R^ε as follows:

$$B^i(E^1, \ldots, E^n) = \{rE^i \mid r \in \arg\max_{0 \le \rho \le \frac{M}{E^i}} u^i(\frac{E^i}{E^S} G(\rho E^S), \rho E^i)\}.^1 \qquad (7.3)$$

Define $\mathbf{B} = (B^1, \ldots, B^n)$, a mapping whose domain is R^ε and whose range is $\mathfrak{R}_+^n$. The mapping $\mathbf{B}$ is convex-valued because $u^i(\frac{E^i}{E^S} G(\rho E^S), \rho E^i)$ is a concave function of ρ. It is upper hemicontinuous by the Berge maximum theorem. We must show that $\mathbf{B}$ maps R^ε into itself, for some sufficiently small $\varepsilon > 0$. That is:

for some $\varepsilon > 0$ and any $\mathbf{E} = (E^1, \ldots, E^n) \in R^\varepsilon$, $B^i(\mathbf{E}) \ge \varepsilon$ for all i.

The condition that guarantees the required inequality is:

$$(\exists \varepsilon > 0)(\forall i)(\forall \mathbf{E} \in R^\varepsilon)(\frac{d}{dr}\Big|_{r = \frac{\varepsilon}{E^i}} u^i(\frac{E^i}{E^S} G(rE^S), rE^i) \ge 0, \qquad (7.4)$$

for (7.4) guarantees that that scale factor r that maximizes i's utility is at least $\frac{\varepsilon}{E^i}$, and hence $B^i(E^i, E^{N\setminus i}) \ge \frac{\varepsilon}{E^i} E^i = \varepsilon$. Condition (7.4) expands to:

$$(\exists \varepsilon > 0)(\forall i)(\forall \mathbf{E} \in R^\varepsilon)G'(\frac{\varepsilon}{E^i} E^S) \ge -\frac{u_2^i}{u_1^i}(\frac{E^i}{E^S} G(\frac{\varepsilon}{E^i} E^S), \varepsilon). \qquad (7.5)$$

The argument of G' is bounded above as ε approaches zero, so the left-hand side of this inequality is bounded away from zero, because $G \in \mathbf{G}$. It therefore suffices to show that the right-hand side approaches zero as ε becomes small.

Now Lemma 7.2 tells us that the argument $\frac{E^i}{E^S} G(\frac{\varepsilon}{E^i} E^S)$ of the marginal rate of substitution on the right-hand side of (7.5) approaches zero, and therefore, by Condition A, the marginal rate of substitution approaches zero.

This concludes the demonstration that for small enough ε, **B** maps R^ε into itself.

2. Therefore, all the assumptions of Kakutani's fixed point theorem hold, and so a fixed point of **B** exists on some domain R^ε. But a fixed point on this domain is a strictly positive $K^\times$ equilibrium, which concludes the proof. ∎

7.2 Existence of K^β Equilibria for $0 \le \beta \le \infty$

Recall (chapter 4) the infinite family of efficient Kantian pairs (X_β, φ_β), for $0 \le \beta \le \infty$. Proposition 7.1 proves the existence of positive Kantian equilibria for $\beta = 0$, which is to say, Pareto-efficient Kantian equilibria. The proof for $\beta > 0$ is simpler, because of Proposition 4.1: that is, any K^β Kantian equilibrium for $\beta > 0$ is Pareto efficient. We do not need an analog to Lemma 7.2.

Let $\tilde{U} = \{u : \Re \times [0, M] \to \Re$, some $M > 0$, u differentiable & concave$\}$; let $\tilde{G} = \{G : \Re_+ \to \Re_+, G$ concave & differentiable$\}$; let $\tilde{D} = \{e = (u^1, \ldots, u^n, G), u^i \in \tilde{U}, G \in \tilde{G}\}$.

PROPOSITION 7.3 *For any $\beta > 0$, on the domain $\tilde{D}$, a Kantian equilibrium with respect to the allocation rule and Kantian variation (X_β, φ_β) exists.*

PROOF.

1. Consider $0 < \beta < \infty$. The domain of effort vectors is the convex, compact set $R^0 = [0, M]^n$. For any vector in the domain, define the best-reply correspondences:

$$B^i(E^1, \ldots, E^n) = \{rE^i + (r-1)\beta \mid r \in \arg\max_{\rho \in \left(\frac{\beta}{E^i + \beta}, \frac{M+\beta}{E^i+\beta}\right)}$$

$$u^i(\frac{E^i + \beta}{E^S + n\beta} G(\rho E^S + n(\rho - 1)\beta), \rho E^i + (\rho - 1)\beta). \tag{7.6}$$

The domain restriction on ρ in the maximization guarantees that $B^i(E^1, \ldots, E^n) \subseteq R^0$.[2] Define the vector-valued best-reply correspondence by $\mathbf{B} = (B^1, \ldots, B^n)$. **B** is convex-valued, because the argument in the maximization in (7.6) is a concave function of ρ. It is upper hemicontinuous by the maximum theorem. Hence, all the assumptions of the Kakutani fixed point theorem hold, and so a fixed point of **B** exists. But such a fixed point is a K^β equilibrium.

2. For $\beta = \infty$ (that is, K^+ equilibrium), a separate argument is required. It is obvious how to define the best-reply correspondence, and the same approach works. ■

7.3 Is There an Allocation Rule That Nash Equilibrium Implements Efficiently on the Domain $\tilde{D}$?

What Propositions 7.1 and 7.3 show is that for every Kantian variation K^β, for $0 \le \beta \le \infty$, there is (at least) one allocation rule that optimization according to the K^β protocol implements efficiently on a large domain of production economies. We may ask: Is there *any* allocation rule that the Nash protocol implements efficiently on the domain $\tilde{D}$? The answer is negative.

PROPOSITION 7.4

a. There is no allocation rule that is efficiently implementable in NE on the domain $\tilde{D}$.

b. On continuum economies, Walrasian rules (with no taxation) are efficiently Nash implementable.

The Walrasian allocation rules are defined by the following way of sharing output. The share allocated to player i is equal to:

$$\text{for all } i, \ \theta^{i,Wa}(E^1,\dots,E^n,G) = \frac{G'(E^S)}{G(E^S)}E^i + \sigma^i(1 - \frac{G'(E^S)E^S}{G(E^S)}), \quad (7.7)$$

where the profit shares $(\sigma^1,\dots,\sigma^n)$ are fixed nonnegative numbers summing to one. Note that the share functions have the argument G as well as **E**. Equation (7.7) states that the output received by player i (that is, $\theta^{i,Wa}G(E^S)$) is equal to the sum of her labor income (her effort supply times the marginal productivity of effort) and her share of profits.

PROOF.

1. An interior allocation **E** is an NE on the domain of economies for the allocation rule θ if and only if:

$$\forall j \ u_1^j \cdot (\frac{\partial \theta^j(\mathbf{E})}{\partial E^j}G(E^S) + \theta^j(\mathbf{E})G'(E^S)) + u_2^j = 0. \quad (7.8)$$

Therefore, θ is efficiently Nash-implementable if and only if:

$$\forall j \; 1 = \theta^i(\mathbf{E}) + \frac{G(E^S)}{G'(E^S)} \frac{\partial \theta(\mathbf{E})}{\partial E^i}. \qquad (7.9)$$

2. Indeed, (7.9) must hold for the entire positive orthant $\mathfrak{R}^n_{++}$, for given any positive vector $\mathbf{E}$, we can construct n concave utility functions such that (7.8) holds at $\mathbf{E}$.

3. For fixed $\mathbf{E} = (E^1,\ldots,E^n)$, define $\psi^i(x) = \theta^i(E^1, E^2,\ldots,E^{i-1}, x, E^{i+1},\ldots E^n)$ and $\mu^i(x) = G(x + E^S - E^i)$. Then (7.9) gives us the differential equation:

$$1 = \psi^i(x) + \frac{\mu^i(x)}{(\mu^i)'(x)}(\psi^i)'(x), \qquad (7.10)$$

which must hold on $\mathfrak{R}_{++}$.

4. But (7.10) implies that:

$$\frac{(\psi^i)'(x)}{1 - \psi^i(x)} = \frac{(\mu^i)'(x)}{\mu^i(x)}, \qquad (7.11)$$

which implies that $\mu^i(x)(1 - \psi^i(x)) = k^i$, and therefore, $\psi^i(x) = 1 - \dfrac{k^i(\mathbf{E}^{-i})}{\mu^i(x)}$, where the constant k^i may depend on the ray $(E^1,\ldots,E^{i-1}, x, E^{i+1},\ldots E^n)$ on which ψ^i is defined — that is, upon $\mathbf{E}^{-i}$.

5. In turn, this last equation says that on the ray $(E^1,\ldots,E^{i-1}, x, E^{i+1},\ldots E^n)$ we have:

$$\begin{aligned} &\theta^i(E^1,\ldots,E^{i-1}, x, E^{i+1},\ldots E_n)G(x + E^S - E^i) \\ &= G(x + E^S - E^i) - k^i(\mathbf{E}^{-i}) \end{aligned} \qquad (7.12)$$

which says that "every agent receives his entire marginal product" on this space. To be precise:

$$\begin{aligned} &(\forall x, y > 0) \\ &(\theta^i(E^1,\ldots,E^{i-1}, x, E^{i+1},\ldots,E^n)G(x + E^S - E^i) - \\ &\theta^i(E^1,\ldots,E^{i-1}, y, E^{i+1},\ldots,E^n)G(y + E^S - E^i) = \\ &G(x + E^S - E^i) - G(y + E^S - E^i)). \end{aligned} \qquad (7.13)$$

6. Letting $n = 2$, for simplicity of exposition, we have, for any positive (interior) vector $\mathbf{E} = (E^1, E^2)$:

$$\begin{aligned} &(a)\, G(E^S) - G(E^2) = \theta^1(E^1, E^2)G(E^S) - \theta^1(0, E^2)G(E^2), \text{and} \\ &(b)\, G(E^S) - G(E^1) = \theta^2(E^1, E^2)G(E^S) - \theta^2(E^1, 0)G(E^1) \end{aligned} \qquad (7.14)$$

Adding (7.14a) and (7.14b) gives:

$$G(E^S) - G(E^1) - G(E^2) = -\theta^1(0, E^2)G(E^2) - \theta^2(E^1, 0)G(E^1). \qquad (7.15)$$

Since the allocation **E** is positive, we have, by strict concavity of G, that the left-hand side of equation (7.15) is negative. Therefore, either $\theta^1(0, E^2) > 0$ or $\theta^2(E^1, 0) > 0$—suppose the former. By (7.14) again:

$$G(E^2) = \theta^2(0, E^2)G(E^2), \qquad (7.16)$$

from which it follows that $\theta^2(0, E^2) = 1$ and hence $\theta^1(0, E^2) = 0$. This contradiction establishes part a.

7. The proof of part b is well known, for part b just says that Nash behavior, taking prices as given, at the Walrasian allocation rule, induces Pareto efficiency. ∎

The key point, in part a of Proposition 7.4, is that in a finite economy, an agent cannot ignore the effect of his labor supply on the marginal productivity of labor. It is only in an economy with an infinite number of agents that the wage is not affected by individual labor choices.

Proposition 7.4 is another way of stating the benefits of cooperation. Of course, cooperation works only on a "small" domain of allocation rules for production economies: the rules that allocate part of the product according to equal division and part according to proportional division.[3]

7.4 Dynamics

There is a convenient dynamic process that, for well-behaved games, will converge to a Nash equilibrium of the game from an arbitrary initial strategy vector. It is to iterate the Nash best-reply correspondence. If the payoff functions are sufficiently well behaved, "iterated best replies" converges to a Nash equilibrium of the game. We can use the same procedure for Kantian equilibrium: "iterated best replies" converges to a Kantian equilibrium, if the game is well behaved, using the Kantian best-reply correspondence defined in the proof of Proposition 7.1. The purpose of this section—to demonstrate this—is again to emphasize the formal similarity between Nash and Kantian equilibrium.

We will study a special case: there are two players, and they each have quasi-linear preferences $u^i(x,E) = x - c^i(E)$, for $i = 1,2$, where c^i are strictly convex, increasing, differentiable functions. We will work with the K^+ protocol and the equal-division rule. We are given an economy (u^1, u^2, G) with G concave. Define the best-reply function for effort vectors in $R^0 = [0, M]^2$:

$$\mathbf{B} = (B^1, B^2), \text{ where } B^i(E^1, E^2) = E^i + r^i(\mathbf{E}) \tag{7.17}$$

and $r^i(\mathbf{E}) = \underset{-E^i \le r \le M - E^i}{\arg\max} u^i(\dfrac{G(E^S + 2r)}{2}, E^i + r)$. For the utility functions specified, the argmax in (7.17) is unique, and so $\mathbf{B}$ is single-valued. Note that a fixed point of $\mathbf{B}$ is an additive Kantian equilibrium for the equal-division rule, since if $\mathbf{B}(E^1, E^2) = (E^1, E^2)$, then "$r = 0$" is the argmax for both players.

PROPOSITION 7.5 *The mapping* $\mathbf{B} : \mathfrak{R}_+^2 \to \mathfrak{R}_+^2$ *is a contraction mapping, and hence it possesses a unique fixed point.*[4]

It immediately follows that iterated application of $\mathbf{B}$ starting from any initial vector of efforts will converge to its fixed point, which is an additive Kantian equilibrium (indeed, the unique such equilibrium for the economy specified).

The proof of Proposition 7.5 uses the following mathematical fact:

LEMMA 7.6 (Courtesy of Roger Howe) *Let* $\| \ \|$ *be a norm on* $\mathfrak{R}^n$ *and let* $[\![A]\!]$ *be the associated sup norm on mappings* $A : X \to \mathfrak{R}^n$, *defined by* $[\![A]\!] = \underset{x \in X}{\sup} \dfrac{\|A(x)\|}{\|x\|}$, *where X is a closed, convex set in* $\mathfrak{R}^n$. *Let A be differentiable, and J be the* $n \times n$ *Jacobian matrix of A. If* $[\![J]\!] < 1$ *on X, then A is a contraction mapping.*

PROOF.

1. We must show that there is an $\varepsilon > 0$ such that:

$$\text{for all } x^0, x^1 \in X, \|A(x^1) - A(x^0)\| < (1 - \varepsilon)\|x^1 - x^0\|.$$

By convexity of X, $u(\lambda) := \lambda x^0 + (1 - \lambda)x^1 \in X$ for all $\lambda \in [0,1]$. By the fundamental theorem of calculus for mappings:

$$A(x^1) - A(x^0) = \int_\gamma J(u) \cdot du = \int_0^1 J(u(\lambda)) \cdot u'(\lambda) d\lambda$$
$$= \int_0^1 J(u(\lambda)) \cdot (x^1 - x^0) d\lambda, \tag{7.18}$$

where J is the Jacobian matrix of A and γ is the line segment connecting x^0 to x^1, defined above.

2. Define ε by $[\![J]\!] = 1 - \varepsilon$; since $[\![J]\!] < 1$, $\varepsilon > 0$. Hence, from (7.18) we compute:

$$\left\| A(x^1) - A(x^0) \right\| \leq \int_0^1 \left\| J(u(\lambda)) \cdot (x^1 - x^0) \right\| d\lambda \leq (1 - \varepsilon) \left\| x^1 - x^0 \right\|,$$

where the first inequality applies the triangle inequality to (7.18), and the second follows from the definition of $[\![J]\!]$. This establishes that A is a contraction mapping. ∎

PROOF OF PROPOSITION 7.5.

1. The Jacobian of the mapping $\mathbf{B}$ is $\begin{pmatrix} 1 + r_1^1 & r_2^1 \\ r_1^2 & 1 + r_2^2 \end{pmatrix}$, where $r_i^j(E^1, E^2) = \frac{\partial r^j}{\partial E^i}(E^1, E^2)$, assuming that these derivatives exist. Thus, Lemma 7.6 requires that we show that the norm of this matrix is less than unity. We take $\| \ \|$ to be the Euclidean norm on $\mathfrak{R}^2$. We must show that:

$$\| E \| = 1 \Rightarrow \left\| \begin{pmatrix} 1 + r_1^1(\mathbf{E}) & r_2^1(\mathbf{E}) \\ r_1^2(\mathbf{E}) & 1 + r_2^2(\mathbf{E}) \end{pmatrix} \begin{pmatrix} E^1 \\ E^2 \end{pmatrix} \right\| < 1. \qquad (7.19)$$

2. By differentiability of c^i, the function r^j is defined by the following first-order condition:

$$G'(E^S + 2r^j(\mathbf{E})) = (c^j)'(E^j + r^j(\mathbf{E})), \qquad (7.20)$$

which has a unique solution. By the implicit function theorem, the derivatives of $r^j(\cdot)$ are given by:

$$G''(y^j)(1 + 2r_i^j(\mathbf{E})) = (c^j)''(x^j)(\delta_i^j + r_i^j(\mathbf{E})),$$

where $y^j = G(E^S + 2r^j(\mathbf{E}))$, $x^j = E^j + r^j(\mathbf{E})$ and $\delta_i^j = \begin{cases} 1, & \text{if } i = j \\ 0, & \text{if } i \neq j \end{cases}$; or

$$r_i^j(\mathbf{E}) = \frac{\delta_i^j(c^j)''(x^j) - G''(y^j)}{2G''(y^j) - (c^j)''(x^j)}. \qquad (7.21)$$

3. It follows from (7.19) that the Jacobian of $\mathbf{B}$ is given by:

$$\begin{pmatrix} \dfrac{G''(y^1)}{2G''(y^1) - (c^1)''(x^1)} & \dfrac{-G''(y^1)}{2G''(y^1) - (c^1)''(x^1)} \\ \dfrac{-G''(y^2)}{2G''(y^2) - (c^2)''(x^2)} & \dfrac{G''(y^2)}{2G''(y^2) - (c^2)''(x^2)} \end{pmatrix},$$

and so, from step 1, we need only show that:

$$(Q^1(E^1 - E^2))^2 + (Q^2(E^1 - E^2))^2 < 1, \tag{7.22}$$

where $\|(E^1, E^2)\| = 1$ and $Q^j = \dfrac{G''(y^j)}{2G''(y^j) - (c^j)''(x^j)}$. Note that $|Q^j| < \dfrac{1}{2}$.

Inequality (7.22) reduces to showing that $\dfrac{1}{2}(1 - 2E^1 E^2) < 1$, which is obviously true, proving the proposition. ∎

7.5 Summary

The upshot of this chapter is that Pareto-efficient Kantian equilibria exist for the production games studied in chapter 3, under reasonable restrictions on the data of the economy. The allocation rules that can be so implemented are the mixtures of the equal-division and proportional rules. In contrast, there is no allocation rule that Nash equilibrium implements efficiently on our domain of economies. "Iterated best response" is a dynamic process that will converge to a Kantian equilibrium under some conditions, as is true for Nash equilibrium as well.

EIGHT

Evolutionary Considerations

Can Kantians Resist Invasion by Nashers?

In this chapter, we examine 2 × 2 symmetric games in which Kantian and Nash players meet each other repeatedly and play a game. The question is whether Kantian players can resist invasion by Nash players.

We assume there is a population, fraction v of whom are Kantian optimizers, and fraction $1 - v$ of whom are Nash optimizers (henceforth, Nashers). At each date, individuals from this population are randomly paired and play a game. The fitness of each group is equal to the average payoff of the members of that group. The population is stable when the fitness of both Kantian and Nash players is the same. If the fitness of Nashers is greater than the fitness of Kantians for all fractions v, then Nashers drive Kantians to extinction, and conversely.

8.1 2 × 2 Symmetric Games

We study games whose payoff matrices are given by table 8.1, where $(a,b) \in \Re^2$, a two-dimensional set of games.

Table 8.1 **The generic symmetric 2 × 2 game**

	X	Y
X	(1,1)	(a,b)
Y	(b,a)	(0,0)

I will call X the "cooperative strategy" and Y the "noncooperative strategy." We assume that the games are *generic*, which is here defined to mean that

$0 \neq a \neq 1, 0 \neq b \neq 1, 1 \neq a + b \neq 2$. Define the following subsets of the (a,b) plane:

$$N_1 = \{b < 1\}$$
$$N_2 = \{a < 0\}$$
$$N_3 = \{a > 0, b > 1, a + b > 1\}$$
$$N_4 = \{a < 0, b < 1\}$$
$$K_1 = \{a + b > 2\}$$
$$K_2 = \{a + b < 2\}$$

We assume that when a game is played, every Nasher plays the mixed strategy associated with the Nash equilibrium of the game, and every Kantian plays the mixed strategy associated with the simple Kantian equilibrium of the game. (If there are several Nash equilibria, a Nasher randomizes among them.) The strategy "play X with probability p and Y with probability $1 - p$" will be denoted "p."

Define the mixed strategies

$$p_1^* = \frac{a+b}{2(a+b-1)}, \qquad q_1^* = \frac{a}{a+b-1}, \tag{8.1}$$

in the case where the two probabilities so defined are in the interval $[0,1]$.

There is a frequency of Kantians v in the economy. At each date, agents are paired off and play the (a,b) game, for a given (a,b). Denote the simple Kantian equilibrium of the game in question by $p^*(a,b)$ and the (or one of the) Nash equilibrium(a) of the game by $q^*(a,b)$; we will abbreviate these strategies as p^* and q^* when there is no confusion. Kantians always play the strategy p^*, and Nashers always play the (or a) strategy q^*. When players are matched to play the game, neither can recognize the type of her opponent.

We first characterize the Nash and simple Kantian equilibria for these games.

LEMMA 8.1 *In the (a,b) game, the NEs are:*

$$(1,1) \Leftrightarrow (a,b) \in N_1,$$
$$(0,0) \Leftrightarrow (a,b) \in N_2$$
$$(q_1^*, q_1^*) \Leftrightarrow (a,b) \in N_3 \cup N_4.$$

In the nonempty intersections of these three regions (for example, $N_1 \cap N_2$), there are multiple NEs. The SKEs are:

$$(p_1^*, p_1^*) \Leftrightarrow (a,b) \in K_1$$
$$(1,1) \Leftrightarrow (a,b) \in K_2 \quad .$$

Since $K_1 \cap K_2 = \varnothing$, the SKE is always unique.

PROOF.

1. Let the row player play p and the column player play q. Then the payoff to the row player is:

$$V(p,q) = pq + p(1-q)a + (1-p)qb =$$
$$p(q + (1-q)a - qb) + qb \qquad , \qquad (8.2)$$

which is linear in p. Hence, the best (Nash) response of the row player, p, is given by:

$$p = 1 \text{ if } q + (1-q)a > qb$$
$$p = 0 \text{ if } q + (1-q)a < qb$$

It follows that $(1,1)$ is an NE if and only if $(a,b) \in N_1$ and $(0,0)$ is an NE if and only if $(a,b) \in N_2$.

If $q + (1-q)a = qb$—which is to say, $q = q_1^*$—then any p is a best response. Thus (q_1^*, q_1^*) is an NE exactly when $q_1^* \in [0,1]$, which means $(a,b) \in N_3 \cup N_4$.

2. To compute the SKE, we maximize the symmetric payoff:

$$V^K(p,p) = p^2 = p(1-p)a + (1-p)pb =$$
$$p^2(1-a-b) + p(1+b).$$

If $1 < a + b$, this is a concave function of p, and the first-order condition gives the maximum— $p = \dfrac{a+b}{2(a+b-1)}$. Thus, in this case, the solution is:

$$p = \begin{cases} p_1^*, & \text{if } K_1 \\ 1, & \text{if } 1 < a + b < 2 \end{cases}.$$

The second case is that $1 > a + b$. Then V^K is a convex function of p, and the solution is either $p = 0$ or $p = 1$. Check that $V^K(1,1) > (V^K)(0,0)$, so it is $p = 1$. It follows that $p = 1$ is the SKE when $1 < a + b < 2$ or $a + b < 1$, which is to say when K_2. This concludes the characterization. ∎

DEFINITION 8.1 A *pure coordination game* is one in which there are multiple pure-strategy NEs, which can be Pareto ranked.

LEMMA 8.2 *The pure coordination (a,b) games are precisely those in $N_1 \cap N_2$.*

PROOF. From Lemma 8.1, the games in $N_1 \cap N_2 = \{a < 0\} \cap \{b < 1\}$ are pure coordination games, because they possess two pure-strategy NEs, $(1,1)$ and $(0,0)$, which are Pareto ranked. Are there pure coordination games whose Pareto-ranked equilibria are not the symmetric equilibria $(1,1)$ and $(0,0)$? The answer is no. One easily verifies, using equation (8.2), that $(1,0)$ is an NE if and only if $a > 1$, and $(0,1)$ is an NE if and only if $b > 1$. Therefore, $(1,1)$ and $(1,0)$ are Nash equilibria if and only if $\{a > 1 \,\&\, b < 1\}$, but in this region these equilibria are not Pareto ranked since neither payoff vector $(1,1)$ nor vector (a,b) dominates the other. There is no region in which both $(1,0)$ and $(0,1)$ are both NEs. In other regions where multiple pure-strategy NEs exist, the equilbria are not Pareto ranked. ∎

DEFINITION 8.2 An (a,b) game is *supermodular* if $\dfrac{\partial^2 V(p,q)}{\partial p \partial q} > 0$: that is, if and only if $1 > a + b$.

The condition that defines supermodularity is often called strategic complementarity. One might say of these games that "increased cooperation begets increased cooperation."

We have:

LEMMA 8.3[1] *An (a,b) game is supermodular and possesses a mixed-strategy NE if and only if it is in $N_1 \cap N_2$.*

PROOF. From Lemma 8.1, a mixed-strategy NE exists if and only if $N_3 \cup N_4$. A game is supermodular if and only if $a + b < 1$. The intersection of these two conditions is $\{a > 0 \,\&\, b < 1\} = N_1 \cap N_2$. ∎

To study the behavior of Nash and Kantian players when they meet, we must examine each region $N_n \cap K_k$, for $1 \leq n \leq 4, 1 \leq k \leq 2$. The region $N_4 \cap K_1$ is empty. This leaves seven nonempty regions, which we name as in table 8.2, with their associated mixed- and pure-strategy (symmetric) equilibria for the two player types.

Some of these regions intersect (for example, $I \cap II \neq \varnothing$), and in these cases there are multiple possible outcomes.[2]

In a region, if Nashers play the strategy q^* and Kantians play the strategy p^*, the expected payoff to a Kantian player, who knows he will be matched with another Kantian with probability v and with a Nasher with probability $1 - v$, is:

$$\begin{aligned}
V^K(v) &= v(p^*)^2 + vp^*)(1 - p^*)(a + b) \\
&+ (1 + v)(p^* q^* + p^*(1 - q^*)a + (1 - p^*)q^* b)
\end{aligned}$$
(8.3)

Table 8.2 Characterization of symmetric NE strategies
and SKE strategies in 2 × 2 symmetric games

Region number	Region	NE	SKE
I	$N_1 \cap K_1$	1	p_1^*
II	$N_2 \cap K_1$	0	p_1^*
III	$N_3 \cap K_1$	q_1^*	p_1^*
IV	$N_1 \cap K_2$	1	1
V	$N_2 \cap K_2 \setminus N_1$	0	1
VI	$N_3 \cap K_2$	q_1^*	1
VII	$N_4 \cap K_2 = N_4$	q_1^*	1

In like manner, compute that the expected payoff to a Nasher is given by:

$$\mathbf{V}^N(v) = (1-v)\big((q^*)^2 + q^*(1-q^*)(a+b)\big) \\ + v\big(q^*p^* + q^*(1-p^*)a + (1-q^*)p^*b\big) \quad . \tag{8.4}$$

The average payoff (that is, fitness) of Kantians is greater than the average payoff of Nashers if and only if $\mathbf{V}^K(v) > \mathbf{V}^N(v)$, which occurs precisely when:

$$\begin{cases} Q(v) > 0, \text{ if } p^* > q^* \\ Q(v) < 0, \text{ if } p^* < q^* \end{cases}, \tag{8.5}$$

where $Q(v) = v(1-a-b)(p^* - q^*) + q^*(1-a-b) + a$.

PROPOSITION 8.4

a. For games in Region VII = $\{a < 0\} \cap \{b < 1\} = N_4$, *Kantians drive Nashers to extinction. This is true whether Nashers play either of their symmetric equilibrium strategies,* $q^* \in \{0, q_1^*\}$.[3] *These games are precisely stag hunts (chapter 2).*

b. In all other regions, either Kantians and Nashers play identically or Nashers drive Kantians to extinction.

c. Generically, there are no games in which Kantians and Nashers play different strategies and coexist at stable frequencies.

PROOF. We will first examine what happens for games in Regions I and VII.

Region I $(p^*, q^*) = (\dfrac{a+b}{2(a+b-1)}, 1)$.

In this case, $p^* < q^*$, so $\mathbf{V}^K > \mathbf{V}^N$ if and only if $Q(v) < 0$. Note that Q is linear in v; check that $Q(0) > 0$ and $Q(1) > 0$, and so it follows that Q is positive on the interval $[0,1]$ in this Region. Hence for games in this Region, Nashers drive Kantians to extinction.

Region VII $(p^*, q^*) = (1, \dfrac{a}{a+b-1})$

Since $p^* > q^*$, Kantians drive Nashers to extinction if and only if $Q > 0$ on $[0,1]$. Check that $Q(0)$ and $Q(1)$ are positive, and so Q is positive on the unit interval.

Regions II–VI

Similar analysis shows that Nashers drive Kantians to extinction in these regions regardless of the value of v.

This concludes the proof. ■

We now have:

COROLLARY 8.5 *For the class of (a,b) games, the following four conditions are equivalent:*

i. $a < 0$ and $b < 1$ (the stag hunt);

ii. Kantian players drive Nash players to extinction as long as the Nash and Kantian strategies are distinct;

iii. The game is one of pure coordination; and

iv. The game is supermodular and a mixed-strategy NE exists.

PROOF. *i* ⇔ *ii* by Proposition 8.4. *i* ⇔ *iii* by Lemma 8.2. *i* ⇔ *iv* by Lemma 8.3. ■

In words, Kantian optimizers possess an evolutionary advantage over Nashers precisely when the game is one of pure coordination. (If the Nashers were able to coordinate on the good equilibrium, then they and Kantians would appear, in these games, to be identical.) These games are all ones with strategic complementarity—the property that cooperation begets cooperation—but strategic complementarity alone is insufficient to guarantee that Kantians drive Nashers to extinction (*iv*).

The evolutionary importance of the Stag Hunt game has been emphasized by Brian Skyrms (2004). Skyrms's focus is on how Nash players can signal to each other that they will play the Cooperative (Share) equilibrium—that is, he focuses on the issue of *Nash equilibrium selection*. It is easy to see that if each of us believes that the other will play Share with sufficiently high probability, then we will each play Share (in fact, it suffices that this probability is at least $\dfrac{1-a}{2-(a+b)}$).

Note that the prisoner's dilemma games comprise the region $\{a < 0\} \cap \{b > 1\}$: Nashers drive Kantians to extinction in the prisoner's dilemma, whether it is a game where the simple Kantian equilibrium strategy is 1 or p_1^*. Because Skyrms stays within the confines of Nash equilibrium, he has no way of getting players to play Cooperate in the prisoner's dilemma, except to embed it in a repeated game.

8.2 Playing Several Games

According to Proposition 8.4, there are no (a,b) games where both Kantian and Nash players exist with positive frequencies in a stable equilibrium. In reality, we do see stable population fractions of the two types (so I claim). This could perhaps be achieved if Kantians punish Nashers. What other model will give this result? Suppose that at each date Nature flips a coin: with probability φ the population will face a pure coordination game, $(\hat{a}, \hat{b})$, and with probability $1 - \varphi$ it will face a prisoner's dilemma game (α, β).

We will study an example. Because $(\hat{a}, \hat{b})$ is a coordination game, we know from Corollary 8.4 that $\hat{a} < 0$ and $\hat{b} < 1$. Because (α, β) is a prisoner's dilemma game, we know that $\alpha < 0$ and $\beta > 1$. We further assume that $\alpha + \beta < 1$, so that the simple Kantian equilibrium of the prisoner's dilemma game is (X,X) or $p^{*,PD} = 1$. Of course, the Nash equilibrium of the prisoner's dilemma game is $q^{*,PD} = 0$. The simple Kantian equilibrium of the pure coordination game is $p^{*,coor} = 1$. There are three symmetric Nash equilibria of the coordination game, $q^{*,coor} \in \{0, 1, q_1^*\}$. We will assume that Nashers play $q^{*,coor} = 0$ in the coordination game.

We suppose, now, for simplicity, that time is continuous. Let the frequency of Nashers in the population at time t be $v(t)$. Denote by $\hat{V}^j(v; a, b)$ the average payoff to players of type j, for $j \in \{\text{Kantian, Nasher}\}$, if the game has parameters (a,b) and the frequency of Kantians is v. We suppose the following *replicator dynamics*:

$$v'(t) = \gamma(\hat{\mathbf{V}}^K(v(t), a, b,) - \hat{\mathbf{V}}^N(v(t), a, b,)), \tag{8.6}$$

where the game realized at date t is the (a,b) game, and $\hat{\mathbf{V}}^j(v, a, b)$ is the expected payoff of a type j player if the population frequency of Kantians is v and the game is (a,b). Under replicator dynamics, the frequency of Kantians in the population increases at a rate proportional to the difference in average payoffs of Kantians and Nashers.

It follows that the expected value of $v'(t)$ is zero precisely when:

$$\begin{aligned} &\varphi\gamma\left(\hat{\mathbf{V}}^K(v(t); \hat{a}, \hat{b}) - \hat{\mathbf{V}}^N(v(t); \hat{a}, \hat{b})\right) + \\ &(1-\varphi)\gamma\left(\hat{\mathbf{V}}^K(v(t); \alpha, \beta) - \hat{\mathbf{V}}^N(v(t); \alpha, \beta)\right) = 0 \end{aligned}, \text{ or:}$$

$$\begin{aligned} &\varphi\hat{\mathbf{V}}^N(v(t); \hat{a}, \hat{b}) + (1-\varphi)\hat{\mathbf{V}}^N(v(t); \alpha, \beta) \\ &= \varphi\hat{\mathbf{V}}^K(v(t); \hat{a}, \hat{b}) + (1-\varphi)\hat{\mathbf{V}}^K(v(t); \alpha, \beta) \end{aligned}. \tag{8.7}$$

We therefore seek a value of $v = v(t)$ such that (8.7) is true. That is, we assert that if the expected value of the rate of change of the population frequency of Kantians is zero, then the population is stable.

We compute, using (8.4), that:

$$\hat{\mathbf{V}}^N(v; \hat{a}, \hat{b}) = \mathbf{V}^N(v) = v\hat{b}. \tag{8.8}$$

(That is, we set $q^* = 0$.) In like manner, we have:

$$\hat{\mathbf{V}}^N(v; \alpha, \beta) = \mathbf{V}^N(v) = v\beta. \tag{8.9}$$

In like manner, using equation (8.3), we have:

$$\begin{aligned} \hat{\mathbf{V}}^K(v; \alpha, \beta) &= \mathbf{V}^K(v) = v + \hat{a}(1-v), \\ \text{and } \hat{\mathbf{V}}^K(v; \alpha, \beta) &= \mathbf{V}^K(v) = v + \alpha(1-v). \end{aligned} \tag{8.10}$$

Therefore, (8.7) can be written:

$$\varphi v\hat{b} + (1-\varphi)v\beta = \varphi(v + \hat{a}(1-v)) + (1-\varphi)(v + \alpha(1-v)), \tag{8.11}$$

which solves to give:

$$v = \frac{-\varphi\hat{a} - (1-\varphi)\alpha}{-\varphi\hat{a} - (1-\varphi)\alpha + 1 - \varphi\hat{b} - (1-\varphi)\beta}. \tag{8.12}$$

The numerator of this expression is positive, and so $v \in (0,1)$ if and only if:

$$1 > \varphi\hat{b} + (1-\varphi)\beta. \tag{8.13}$$

Since $\hat{b} < 1$ and $\beta > 1$, expression (8.13) is true if φ is sufficiently close to one.

Thus, there is a stationary state in which Nashers and Kantians coexist in the population, and play different strategies, if (8.13) holds, and the population frequency of Kantians at this state is given by (8.12). Is the stationary point stable? This will be the case if any small deviation from the stationary state is self-correcting; the condition for this is:

$$\frac{dv'(t)}{dv} < 0 \text{ at } v'(t) = 0. \tag{8.14}$$

To be precise, in the situation where either the prisoner's dilemma or pure coordination game may be played, we have:

$$v'(t) = \gamma\left(\varphi\hat{V}^K(v;\hat{a},\hat{b}) + (1-\varphi)\hat{V}^K(v;\alpha,\beta)\right)$$
$$-\gamma\left(\varphi\hat{V}^N(v;\hat{a},\hat{b}) + (1-\varphi)\hat{V}^N(v;\alpha,\beta)\right)$$

and so, substituting in the values for the $\hat{V}^J$, we compute that:

$$\frac{dv'(t)}{dv} = \gamma((\varphi(\hat{a}+\hat{b}-1) + (1-\varphi)(\alpha+\beta-1)) < 0, \tag{8.15}$$

where the inequality holds if φ is sufficiently close to one, or if $\alpha + \beta < 1$. Thus, the stationary state is stable with replicator dynamics, when the pure coordination game occurs sufficiently frequently.

To summarize:

PROPOSITION 8.6 *Suppose that the population play the pure coordination game* $(\hat{a},\hat{b})$ *with probability* φ *and the prisoner's dilemma game* (α,β) *with probability* $1 - \varphi$. *Suppose that the population frequency of Kantians is governed by replicator dynamics and that Nashers play their pure-strategy equilibrium Y in the pure coordination game. Then there is a stable population with both Nashers and Kantians if* φ *is sufficiently close to one.*

8.3 Conclusion

In games of pure coordination, Kantians drive Nashers to extinction. These are games with strategic complementarity, so cooperation begets cooperation. In such games, Kantians can survive without punishing those ex post who play the noncooperative strategy Y. Indeed, the advantage to cooperating in these games is sufficiently strong that Nashers do not survive, even though they are not punished for playing autarchically.

But if invasion by Nash players is a threat, and our result shows it will be if the game is not a pure coordination game, then Kantians, in order to survive, must learn either to recognize Nashers and to change their play accordingly or to punish them ex post. Punishment ex post is properly targeted when one knows that an opponent who plays Y must be a Nasher, and this is the case when the simple Kantian equilibrium is the pure strategy X. This is the case in a class of prisoner's dilemma games: see Proposition 2.2. If such games are prevalent, then we can expect that, if Kantians survive, they will have learned to punish Nashers. For otherwise, if that kind of prisoner's dilemma game is typical of real life, we would not observe Kantian behavior. In laboratory games, it is usually the case that it is impossible to identify the type of one's opponent, and one sees, ubiquitously, that noncooperators are punished by cooperators, in games where the Kantian equilibrium is to cooperate with probability one. Indeed, Robert Boyd and colleagues (2003) provide an argument based on group selection for how "altruistic" punishment can evolve.[4] They conclude that "group selection can maintain altruistic punishment and altruistic cooperation over a wider range of parameter values than group selection will sustain altruistic cooperation alone" (3533).

Corollary 8.5 suggests that we should see only Nashers or only Kantians, not the populations of mixed types that comprise reality. One explanation of the coexistence of both Nashers and Kantians is that the members of the population play several kinds of game. If the population plays both pure coordination games and prisoner's dilemma games—and if pure coordination games occur sufficiently often—then there are stable populations where both kinds of player coexist, even if Kantians do not punish Nashers who play noncooperatively. Hence, it is possible that there is an evolutionarily stable equilibrium where both types of player exist, even absent punishment (or, one might say, absent consistent punishment).

Samuel Bowles and Herbert Gintis (2004) give the following example of the failure of cooperation. Farmers in the Indian village of Palanpur can plant their seeds early or late. The farmers are caught in a bad Nash equilibrium, planting late. It's a bad equilibrium because the harvests are relatively small with late planting. However, if a (sole) farmer deviates from the late planting equilibrium and plants early, the birds will converge on his plot and eat his seed. It is also a symmetric Nash equilibrium to plant early: if all do this, the birds will take relatively few seeds from each plot, and the farmers enjoy a more abundant harvest than if all planted late. The early planting equilibrium Pareto dominates the late planting equilibrium. This is a pure coordination game, and the simple Kantian equilibrium is that all plant early. But lacking the Kantian optimization ethos—perhaps due to insufficient trust in others—Palanpur is stuck in the bad Nash equilibrium. Perhaps there are other communities facing a similar environment where farmers trust one another and all plant early.

In contrast, Christopher Boehm (2012) describes a band of !Kung bushmen who hunt for game by spreading their large nets at the edge of the forest. Women and children beat the bushes in the forest, scaring the game, which run into the nets. One day, Cephu secretly places his net closer to the forest than the nets of the other hunters and catches a large fraction of the game. Over the next few days, he is criticized by others, and ostracized. He is threatened with expulsion from the band. Soon, he takes the game he caught and shares it with the others. He cries and swears not to misbehave again. The question we must ask is whether Cephu is one of a small number of Nashers in a community that consists mainly of Kantians or whether everyone is a Nasher, kept in line by the threat of expulsion from the community as a punishment for noncooperative behavior. According to Boehm's account, the punishment does not occur immediately. It takes time for one hunter to raise his criticism of Cephu. It does not appear as if the first one to speak out against Cephu has a responsibility to do so and would have been punished by others had he failed to speak out. It does not appear from the account that his speaking out is part of a Nash equilibrium in a multistage game. But when he speaks out, others join the attack on Cephu.

Distinguishing the motives for cooperation between these two possibilities (that everyone is a Nasher but most are deterred from selfish behavior by the threat of punishment, versus the situation in which only a few Nashers exist but most are Kantians) is important but difficult. It seems to me natural to conjecture that the first hunter who criticized Cephu is a Kantian. He initiates costly punishment when others are holding back. Other hunters are conditional Kantians, who undertake punishing action once the ball gets rolling. Boehm describes how mild punishments usually succeed in controlling noncooperators. But sometimes they do not, and the noncooperators are either expelled from the band or, if their behavior is really costly to the group, executed. These responses to noncooperators in egalitarian bands of hunter-gatherers appear to be ubiquitous around the world.

Michael Tomasello (2016) discusses an example of competition for food between a male and female who are possible mates. Indeed, this game is a stag hunt. Each would like the food for him- or herself but also has an interest in keeping the other one well fed. This "interdependence," Tomasello writes, induces them to share food.

But Tomasello's argument is incomplete. We can represent the payoff matrix of this food competition (stag hunt) game as in table 8.3.

Table 8.3 **A stag hunt**

	Share	Grab
Share	(1,1)	(−1,0.5)
Grab	(0.5,−1)	(0,0)

As we discussed in chapter 2, this is a pure coordination game: both (Share, Share) and (Grab, Grab) are Nash equilibria. The fact that each individual values the other's welfare (that is, interdependence) is embodied in the payoff matrix—each player would rather share than take all the food—but this alone is insufficient to guarantee that mutual sharing will be the result. (Share, Share) is, indeed, a Nash equilibrium, but so is (Grab, Grab). However, the unique simple Kantian equilibrium is (Share, Share), and Corollary 8.5 tells us that there is an evolutionary advantage to being a Kantian in a world in which this kind of game is played. Interdependency alone is insufficient to explain why individuals in this situation may almost always play (Share, Share). It is not a mystery why Kantians may have survived, given their evolutionary advantage over Nashers in these pure coordination games.

We now observe that modifying the stag hunt game by injecting altruism explicitly in players' preferences does not assure that *Nash* players will play the simple Kantian equilibrium, (Share, Share). Suppose that altruism takes this form: each player maximizes his payoff in the original stag hunt matrix, plus a positive multiple λ of the other player's payoff. The payoff function for the row player, over a mixed-strategy profile (p,q), is:

$$V^R(p,q) = pq\{1+\lambda\} + p(1-q)(\frac{\lambda}{2}-1) + (1-p)q(\frac{1}{2}-\lambda)$$
$$= p\left(\frac{3q}{2}(1+\lambda)+\frac{\lambda}{2}-1\right) + q(\frac{1}{2}-\lambda)$$

Therefore, $p = 1$ is a best response to q if and only if $\left(\frac{3q}{2}(1+\lambda)+\frac{\lambda}{2}-1\right) \geq 0$. It follows by symmetry that $(1,1)$ is a Nash equilibrium if and only if $1 \geq \frac{2}{3}\left(\frac{1-(\lambda/2)}{1+\lambda}\right)$, which is true for all positive values of λ. However, $(0,0)$ is a Nash equilibrium if and only if $q = 0$ satisfies $\left(\frac{3q}{2}(1+\lambda)+\frac{\lambda}{2}-1\right) \leq 0$, that is, if and only if $\lambda \leq 2$. Thus, *even if each player weights the other player's payoff at twice the weight she puts on her own payoff*, Nash players can be trapped in a (Grab, Grab) equilibrium.

NINE

Alternative Approaches to Cooperation

9.1 The Traditional Approach

The traditional neoclassical approach to explain cooperation is to model it as a Nash equilibrium in a repeated game where players are self-interested but will be punished by others if they fail to play the "cooperative" strategy. Since punishment is postulated to be costly to the punisher, it must also be the case that those who fail to punish noncooperators are themselves punished by others in the next round of the game. Cooperation by all players comprises a Nash equilibrium only if the game has an infinite or unknown number of stages. For if there were a known last stage T, then at stage $T - 1$, players would fail to cooperate, because no rational self-interested player would punish those noncooperators at stage T. Hence cooperation unravels.

As I said earlier, I find this explanation of cooperation unconvincing as a general explanation of the many examples of cooperation that we observe. My objection is intuitive: I cannot believe that examples of human cooperation are maintained solely through the fear of punishment. It is much more reasonable, in my view, to think that many people have internalized the norm of cooperation, and they would cooperate, absent punishments. As I wrote in chapter 2, a given culture or society may possess a catalog instructing its members how to behave in many situations, and it is known that deviations from the instructions may incur punishment. Eventually, people learn to generalize rules from the catalog. Some may generalize and become Nash optimizers: play the cooperative solution only if there is a threat of punishment and otherwise maximize your own utility. But others will generalize to Kantian optimization: take the action I would like all to take.

Punishments are needed to keep the autarkic optimizers (the Nash players) in line. Indeed, the literature is full of examples of repeated games with a known number of stages (T) in which cooperation occurs at the early stages (at least), although the subgame perfect Nash equilibrium of the repeated game with self-regarding preferences is a complete failure of cooperation. Moreover, when punishment is possible, a large fraction of players cooperate for the whole game—and those who fail to cooperate at stage $T - 1$ are often punished by others at stage T, even though this is inconsistent with autarkic optimization (see, for example, Fehr and Gintis 2007).

Herbert Gintis (2000) denotes the cooperation that is enforced by punishment "weak reciprocity," and he contrasts this with his own theory of "strong reciprocity."

9.2 Strong Reciprocity

Gintis (2000) proposes that "a strong reciprocator is predisposed to cooperate with others and punish non-cooperators, even when this behavior cannot be justified in terms of self-interest, extended kinship, or reciprocal altruism" (169). More recently, he and Samuel Bowles write: "We commonly observe that people sacrifice their own payoffs in order to cooperate with others, to reward the cooperation of others, and to punish free-riding, even when they cannot expect to gain from acting in this way. We call the preferences motivating this behavior *strong reciprocity*" (2011, 20).

Gintis often speaks of the propensity to take actions that are not Nash-optimal responses in a game as *altruistic*. He is using the term in the sense that biologists use it: any action that an individual member of a species takes that helps others at a cost to itself is considered altruistic, regardless of the cause of the action. As I have noted, psychological altruism is what economists typically mean by the term—that an individual's preferences assign positive value to the welfare of others, and hence these costly actions that help others are motivated by an intent to help. Because Gintis uses the term in its biological sense, he denotes any action that objectively helps others at a cost to oneself as being the consequence of maximizing non-self-regarding preferences. But this does not follow. I may punish a noncooperator because I am offended that he has broken a norm—to behave cooperatively—not because I care about the welfare of others. Equating such motivations with having altruistic preferences in the psychological sense is, I believe, incorrect.

In contrast, the preferences of players in all chapters of this book except chapter 5 are self-regarding, yet nevertheless the Kantian equilibrium typically involves cooperation. I achieve this by asserting that players use an optimization protocol that is not Nash's, and that doing so is motivated *not* by psychological altruism but by understanding that, in a situation of solidarity, players must "hang together or hang separately." I do not object to calling this a moral code. Because Gintis does not consider the option of varying the optimization protocol, he must explain cooperation by saying that players have non-self-regarding preferences. There is a moral norm in my story, but it is not modeled as an argument of preferences but rather induces the choice of optimization protocol.

Is this a distinction without a difference? I believe not. The evidence for my claim is that the theory of strong reciprocity does not tell us how cooperation is achieved except in very simple cases, where the cooperative strategy profile is *obvious*. In contrast, the theory of Kantian optimization is *explicit* about the optimization program of each player and hence can define a concept of equilibrium even in "complex" games such as the production economies that we have employed to study common-pool resource and free-rider problems. In particular, players may possess different preferences. The cooperative equilibria, for example, in production economies that I called "fishing" economies, where the allocation rule is proportional, are far from being ex ante obvious. They are, however, multiplicative Kantian equilibria with standard, self-regarding preferences. In contrast, in chapter 6, I showed that to achieve these Pareto-efficient allocations as Nash equilibria of a game where players have extended preferences over the entire allocation is mathematically possible but unconvincing, since it would require a theory of how players adopt the "right" non-self-regarding preferences. For those extended preferences are *in general* not given by any simple social welfare function whose arguments are the players' utilities.

Ernst Fehr and Gintis (2007) advocate strong reciprocity to explain the results of experiments with a public-good game. The are N players. Each is endowed with an amount of resource Y. Each can contribute any amount $0 \leq y_i \leq Y$ to a common pot. The pot is multiplied by a number M by the experimenter, where $1 < M < N$. This expanded pot is then divided equally among all players. Thus, the payoff to a player i is:

$$Y - y_i + \frac{M}{N}\sum_i y_i. \tag{9.1}$$

The Nash equilibrium (where the strategies are $\{y_i\}$) in the one-shot game is that all players contribute zero. Since the game is symmetric, it is appropriate to look at the simple Kantian equilibrium. Each player, under the simple Kantian protocol, maximizes $Y - y + \frac{M}{N}Ny = Y + (M-1)y$ under the constraint $0 \leq y \leq Y$, and the solution is $y = Y$ because $M > 1$.

The one-shot game is, however, not the one that Fehr and Gintis (2007) describe but rather a repeated game with two treatments—either with or without the option to punish those who fail to cooperate. The experimental result is that, without the possibility of punishment, cooperation is quite high in the beginning stages but deteriorates by the last stage (10) to very little. With the possibility of punishing noncooperators, cooperation becomes virtually complete by the last stage, and some players in the last stage punish those who failed to cooperate in the penultimate stage.

How do I explain the tendency for "altruistic punishment" in one-shot games (such as the ultimatum game) or in the last stage of a repeated game? In chapter 8, I observed that in prisoner's dilemma games Kantian players would be driven to extinction if they did not learn to punish noncooperators who are present in their population. Thus, it's likely that the tendency to punish must have evolved if we are to observe cooperation in mixed populations.

Suppose that one wishes to rationalize cooperation in the one-shot public-good game of Fehr and Gintis (2007) by *psychological* altruism. Suppose that players append to the payoff function in (9.1) a utilitarian social welfare function, so that player i maximizes:

$$V^i(y_i; y_{-i}) = Y - y_i + \frac{M}{N}\sum_{j=1}^{N} y_j + \alpha^i \sum_{k \neq i} \left(Y - y_k + \frac{M}{N}\sum_{j=1}^{N} y_j \right). \tag{9.2}$$

We have $\frac{\partial V^i}{\partial y_i} = -1 + (1 + \alpha^i)\frac{M}{N}$. It therefore follows that the Nash equilibrium of this game is:

$$y_i = \begin{cases} Y, \text{if } (1+\alpha^i)\dfrac{M}{N} > 1 \text{ or } \alpha^i > \dfrac{N-M}{N} \\[2ex] [0,Y] \text{ if } (1+\alpha^i)\dfrac{M}{N} = 1 \\[2ex] 0, \text{if } (1+\alpha^i)\dfrac{M}{N} < 1 \end{cases}$$

The values for the Fehr-Gintis experiment are $M = 2$, $N = 10$. Thus, altruists would have to have $\alpha^i > 0.8$ in order to play fully "cooperatively." This strikes me as unreasonably high as a credible explanation of cooperation.

9.3 Conditional Cooperation

In reality, I think that there are very few individuals who always use the Nash protocol or who always use the Kantian protocol. Most people are *conditional Kantians*. As I've said, Jon Elster says that these people are behaving in a quasi-moral way. I propose that in many real cases, each person i has a threshold, q_i, and will optimize using the Kantian protocol if and only if she observes that fraction q_i of the relevant population (set of players) is cooperating. A typical cumulative distribution function of thresholds in a population is plotted in fig. 9.1.

In the case of fig. 9.1, the stable behavior is that fraction q^* of the population will play the cooperative strategy. For suppose that fraction $q < q^*$ were cooperating; then the fraction who desire to cooperate, given cooperation at level q, is greater than q, so q will increase. A similar argument shows that no value $q < q^*$ is stable.

In fig. 9.2, there are three equilibrium cooperation frequencies, q_1^*, q_2^*, and 1. Equilibrium q_1^* is stable—a slight displacement from it will induce a dynamic returning to q_1^*. But q_2^* is unstable. If a shock causes the number of cooperators to fall, the new equilibrium will be at q_1^*. If, perchance, a shock increases the frequency of cooperation, the new equilibrium will be at $q^* = 1$.

In many situations of solidarity, trust must be established to build cooperation. Often, there is a small core of individuals who are *saints*—their threshold is $q = 0$. In small communities, trust may be established via the

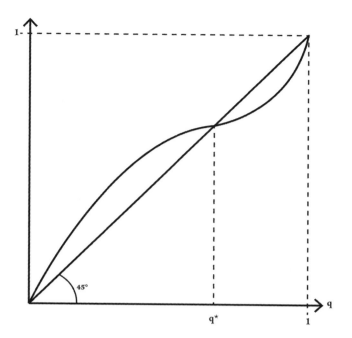

Figure 9.1

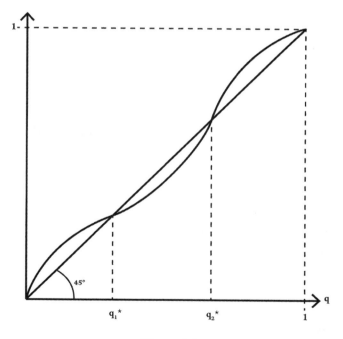

Figure 9.2

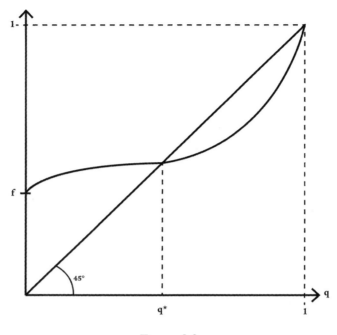

Figure 9.3

common knowledge assumption, as discussed in chapter 2. But what about large groups? In fig. 9.3, I have drawn a distribution function of thresholds where fraction f of the population are saints. Saints induce others, whose thresholds are strictly positive, to cooperate. Cooperation builds as those who are increasingly skeptical join — their trust of others increases as they see others joining the movement. Eventually, at q^*, the limit is reached. For the game of recycling, q^* is now quite high in many cities, even though there is scarcely any punishment or ostracism of those who fail to recycle. For the voting game, q^* varies across countries.

Of course, the dynamics described here can describe conditional strong reciprocators as well as conditional Kantians.

9.4 Rabin and the Kindness Function

Matthew Rabin has proposed an explanation of cooperation, which, I think, could provide microfoundations for Herbert Gintis's strong reciprocity. A relatively simple description of the approach is found in Rabin (2004). Strictly speaking, the approach is not a special case of Nash equilibrium, because players' actions depend not only on others' actions but on their beliefs about others' motives. Roughly speaking, players wish to be generous to other players who, they think, are motivated by being kind to them, and they wish to punish players who, they think, are motivated by being unkind to them. This produces extended utility functions, where arguments incorporating these behaviors are included. A *fairness equilibrium* is then defined as what Rabin (2004) describes as "the analog of Nash equilibrium for psychological games" (305).

I have three reservations about fairness equilibrium. My first reservation is that, when all is said and done, fairness equilibrium involves autarkic reasoning, as Rabin says when he writes that it is the analog of Nash equilibrium in psychological games. I return to my deepest motivation for the Kantian approach, which is that I think a fundamentally different kind of optimization protocol is needed to explain cooperation. Lest this reservation be viewed as too demanding or radical, let me remark that Kantian optimization *is* within the genre of what Jon Elster calls methodological individualism. That is, it provides an explanation of cooperation at the level of individual choice. A *truly* radical critique would argue that cooperation is an "emergent" phenomenon that cannot be explained at the individual level, a view to which I do not subscribe.

My second reservation is that fairness equilibrium assumes considerable sophistication on the part of players. It is required that higher-order beliefs match actual behavior. Thus, a player's payoff depends not only on the strategy profile but on his beliefs about the other player's strategy choice, and his beliefs about the other player's beliefs about his strategy choice. Now the complexity of reasoning required could be invoked to explain why cooperation is difficult to establish in reality; but I would rather say that cooperation is prevalent in reality, and a simpler explanation would be more convincing.

My third reservation is that it is unclear how the theory could be extended to more complex economic environments than 2×2 games. As with strong reciprocity, it appears to require an ex ante conception of what constitutes cooperative (or kind or fair) play. As I have been at pains to establish, it is often, in real life, not clear what the cooperative action is. In the fishing economy, how can I decide whether another fisher's labor supply is being kind or un-kind to me? Rabin's concept of reciprocating to the kindness of others may not be well defined in the production economies we have studied.

9.5 *Homo moralis* (Alger and Weibull 2013)

Ingela Alger and Jörgen W. Weibull (2013) propose a model in which agents are randomly matched in pairs, from an infinite population, and play one-shot games, where strategies are chosen from an abstract (compact, convex) strategy space X. The "material payoff" to a player is a function $\pi(x,y)$ of the strategy profile, where the function π varies across players. However, the *utility* function of the player is:

$$u_\kappa(x,y) = (1-\kappa)\pi(x,y) + \kappa\pi(x,x),\qquad(9.3)$$

for some $\kappa \in [0,1]$. Here is the authors' interpretation of (9.3):

> It is as if *homo moralis* is torn between selfishness and morality. On the one hand, she would like to maximize her own payoff. On the other hand, she would like to "do the right thing," that is, choose a strategy that, if used by all individuals, would lead to the highest possible payoff. This second goal can be viewed as an application of Kant's (1785) categorical imperative, to "act only on the maxim that you would at the same time will to be a universal law." Torn between these two goals, *homo moralis* chooses a strategy that maximizes a convex combination of them. If $\kappa = 0$, the definition of *homo moralis* coincides with that of "pure selfishness," or *homo oeconomicus*. At the opposite extreme, $\kappa = 1$, the definition of *homo moralis* coincides with that of "pure morality," or *homo kantiensis*; irrespective of what strategy the other party uses (or is expected to use), this extreme variety of *homo moralis* will use a strategy in $\arg\max_{x \in X} \pi(x,x)$. (2276)

The focus of their article is the study of when agents with preferences like *Homo moralis* can survive invasion by other agents. Under stipulated conditions, including assortative matching of players in the 2×2 games, they argue that such agents can successfully resist invasion. The equilibrium in the game played by two players (with preferences of this sort) is a Nash equilibrium (actually, Bayesian Nash). So the Kantian aspect of the model is embedded in the utility function of (9.3), not in the optimization protocol.

To compare this approach to mine, let's begin with the case when the two players are identical and when they are both type *Homo kantiensis*— that is, $\kappa = 1$. Then it is trivial to observe that (x^*,x^*) is a Nash equilibrium of the game where each maximizes $\pi(x,x)$, where x^* is the (unique) maximum of $\pi(x,x)$. (We have observed this earlier in Proposition 6.1.) But the similarities between the two approaches disappear when we look at players of different types.

When player types are different, I have argued, simple Kantian equilibrium, which corresponds to *Homo kantiensis*, is the wrong way to model cooperation. We must replace it with multiplicative or additive or some other "Kantian variation." Let's write down the definition of Nash equilibrium corresponding to (9.3) and multiplicative Kantian equilibrium in terms of best-response functions or correspondences. For traditional Nash equilibrium, using the notation of Alger and Weibull, the best-response functions are:

$$\beta^1(y) = \arg\max_x \pi^1(x,y)$$
$$\beta^2(x) = \arg\max_y \pi^2(x,y) \tag{9.4}$$

For Alger-Weibull equilibrium (minus the Bayesian part), the best-response functions are:

$$\hat{\beta}^1(y) = \arg\max_x[(1-\kappa)\pi^1(x,y) + \kappa\pi^1(x,x)]$$
$$\hat{\beta}^2(x) = \arg\max_x[(1-\kappa)\pi^2(x,y) + \kappa\pi^2(x,x)] \tag{9.5}$$

For multiplicative Kantian equilibrium, the best-response functions are:

$$\tilde{\beta}^1(x,y) = r^1 x, \text{where } r^1 = \arg\max_r \pi^1(rx,ry)$$
$$\tilde{\beta}^2(x,y) = r^2 x, \text{where } r^2 = \arg\max_r \pi^2(rx,ry) \tag{9.6}$$

For the three cases, an *equilibrium* is a strategy pair (x^*,y^*) such that:

$$(x^*,y^*) \in (\beta^1(y^*),\beta^2(x^*)) \text{ or } (x^*,y^*) \in (\hat{\beta}^1(y^*),\hat{\beta}^2(x^*)) \text{ or}$$
$$(x^*,y^*) \in (\tilde{\beta}^1(x^*,y^*),\tilde{\beta}^2(x^*,y^*)), \tag{9.7}$$

respectively. The key difference between the first two cases and the third is that the first two cases use a best-reply function (or correspondence) that is a mapping $X \to X$, whereas Kantian equilibrium uses a mapping defined $X^2 \to X$. (If there were n players, the best-reply correspondences for Nash equilibrium are mappings $X^{n-1} \to X$, and the best-reply correspondence for Kantian equilibrium is a mapping $X^n \to X$.) This apparently small formal difference, however, is key: for it expresses the idea that a Kantian player thinks of a counterfactual where *all players* vary their strategies in the same way.

In my view, the Alger-Weibull approach is still wedded to the idea that cooperation can be thought of as a noncooperative (Nash) equilibrium, and this is fundamentally different from the view I advocate, that we must conceptualize cooperation as involving a fundamentally different kind of optimization. For a graphical presentation of the difference between (9.4) and (9.6), recall fig. 3.1. Kantian optimizers imagine a counterfactual that lies in the same ray, whereas Nash optimizers think of counterfactuals lying on different rays.

9.6 Surveys and Interviews of Players

In 2014, the Innovation Sample of the German Socio-Economic Panel, known as SOEP-IS, included several questions about recycling. I summarize the responses here.[1] Of the 1,495 people who responded, 96 percent (1,435) said that they recycle plastic and paper. Those who recycle gave the reasons for recycling that are tabulated in table 9.1. The choices were fixed (close-ended question), and respondents could choose more than one reason.

Table 9.1 German social survey: close-ended reasons to recycle

Reason	Number
1. Every little bit counts	811
2. It's what a person should do	1,016
3. I would feel guilty otherwise	461
4. I'd like everyone to recycle	466
5. It keeps the house neater	464
6. People in my neighborhood do	175
7. Waste collection charges are cheaper	374

The clearest Kantian reasons are the second and fourth reasons. The first reason could be thought of as a Nash response, where even the marginal contribution of the individual to a green environment is *greater* than the personal cost of recycling. The fifth reason is Nash. The seventh response could be interpreted either as Kantian, if reducing waste-collection charges is a public good to which everyone should contribute by recycling, or as a confused answer, if the respondent believes that her own recycling will lower her charges. Certainly, the responses are consistent with a large fraction of Kantian optimizers, although there can be many interpretations.

The 4 percent of respondents who do not recycle provided the reasons listed in table 9.2 (again, respondents could give more than one reason).

Table 9.2 German social survey: close-ended reasons to not recycle

Reason	Number
1. Would not make a meaningful difference	21
2. No reason to recycle	13
3. I don't care	11
4. Cost of recycling not worth it	2
5. I don't have the time	12
6. People in my neighborhood don't recycle	17
7. Waste collection charges aren't much higher if I don't	9

Most of these reasons can be explained by Nash optimization.

To the question "How many people do you think recycle in your neighborhood?" 75 percent of respondents answered two-thirds or more, with 48 percent responding 95 percent. Among those who do not currently recycle, one-half said that they would do so if a higher fraction of people recycled. This is consistent with these 28 people being conditional Kantians with high thresholds (or having perceptions of a low participation rate).

In 2014, I conducted a small survey using Amazon's Mechanical Turk. To the open-ended question "Why do you recycle?" I classify the responses as reported in table 9.3. (Several respondents gave more than one reason.)

Table 9.3 Mechanical Turk survey: open-ended reasons to recycle

Reason	Number
1. Help the environment, save the earth, etc.	25
2. It's easy to do	13
3. Dislike of waste	11
4. Save money, lower my trash bill	7
5. Be a part of making a difference	7
6. It's the right thing to do, duty	5
7. Feel guilty if I didn't	2
8. For future generations	1

The first reason is certainly not Nash; it could be Kantian. It is similar to the fifth reason, although "being a part of making a difference" is more clearly Kantian. The fifth reason is also called indicative of an expressive utility from participation. Reason 8 is clearly altruistic, although it is inconsistent with Nash reasoning, if the value I create for future generations (properly discounted?) is less than the cost to me.

To the question "Why do you not recycle?" almost all answers were of the form that recycling is too costly. One person, with the clearest Nash consciousness, wrote "Because my action would not make a meaningful difference."

Close-ended responses to the question "Why do you pay your taxes fairly honestly?" are tabulated in table 9.4.

Table 9.4 Mechanical Turk survey: close-ended
reasons to pay taxes honestly

Reason	Percentage
1. Fear of being caught, paying a fine	52%
2. Country needs the revenue	20%
3. It's what everybody should do	58%
4. Not worth the worry if I didn't	44%
5. What if nobody paid their taxes?	12%

Reason 1 is Nash. (There is a large literature arguing that the probability of being fined and the sizes of fines are far too small to generate the degree of tax compliance that is observed in the United States. See, for example, Frey and Torgler 2007.) Reasons 2, 3, and 5 are consistent with Kantian reasoning.

In some treatments, respondents were given an open-ended question about tax compliance. The responses are given in table 9.5.

Table 9.5 Mechanical Turk survey: open-ended reasons to comply with taxes

Reason	Number
1. It's the right thing to do; duty as citizen; don't want to cheat the government; part of social contract; everyone does their fair share	16
2. Fear of audits; not worth risk	28
3. Support my government; pay for essential services; tax money goes to good use	7
4. Because it's the law	5

Reasons 1 and 3 seem Kantian; reason 2 is Nash.

Answers to the close-ended question "Why do you vote in national elections?" are given in table 9.6.

Table 9.6 Mechanical Turk survey: closed-ended reasons to vote

Reason	Percentage
1. Duty of a citizen	68%
2. Like to participate in choosing	57%
3. My vote could make a difference if close	46%
4. It doesn't take much time	19%
5. If I didn't vote, why should anyone?	8%

Reason 1 is a social norm, which could be interpreted as Kantian. Reason 2 is the expressive reason for voting, in which participation has a value. Reason 3 is Nash. Reason 5 is Kantian.

To the open-ended version of this question, people responded with reasons tabulated in table 9.7.

Table 9.7 Mechanical Turk survey: open-ended reasons to vote

Reason	Number
1. Every vote makes a difference; want my voice to count; have a say	20
2. It's my duty; people died for the right to vote	4
3. Voting gives me a right to complain	3
4. Although one vote may not make a difference, if everyone believed this . . .	1

The vast plurality in table 9.7 seem to view voting as expressive (reason 1). Only reason 4 is clearly Kantian. Both the close-ended and open-ended questions in the Mechanical Turk survey indicate a small fraction of Kantian optimizers in regard to voting.

Stefan Penczynski of the University of Mannheim has conducted laboratory experiments with public-good games where players consist not of single agents but of teams of two. Before the game is played, the members of each team discuss with each other (but not with other teams) how much their team should contribute to the public good. Then one member from each team is randomly chosen to play the game. The purpose of this setup is to elicit from individuals the reasons behind their strategy choice. Here is a summary of the reasons that players gave in their pre-play communication with their team partners.[2]

1. "If everybody contributed the maximum, that would be the most rational and best decision for all. However, I doubt that everybody will do so; that is why, in this case, I would rather keep everything and not be stupid at the end."

2. "I just hope that most people follow the principle of maximizing total welfare. Obviously, we could just all our points [sic] and then hopefully get all the Taler [German dollars] from the other teams. But I am human in my decision."

3. "It makes sense here to think strategically because one's own Taler are not as valuable as the ones the other teams send over. Hopefully the other teams think strategically as well."

4. "Hold everything or pass everything? It would be better to pass everything, if the other teams think this way as well."

5. "I would pass everything as this way the total payout is increased. I assume that the others will pass everything as well."

6. "I think we should rely on the others. Holding Taler leads to much too small an amount. That is the trick: If everybody goes along and passes the Taler, we can leave with more money. And I think we should be optimistic here."

7. "I trust that the other team sends us everything as well—this way everybody gets the maximal amount! We have to trust though; without this a market does not work."

8. "So basically the money amount for everybody will be maximized when everybody passes all Taler. When everybody thinks like that, we would earn 5 Euro. But there will be those that hope to get everything donated without doing something for it themselves. That would not be good, but I hope that we meet nice people that give us everything as well."

9. "I am afraid that few will play cooperatively in order to raise the total profit of all participants. It would be ok for me, however, to pass 40 Taler in order to make the most of the available money for all."

What appears ubiquitous in these discussions is the willingness to play the Kantian strategy. The doubts raised are caused by a lack of trust. None of the players expressed the Nash argument. Several players rationalized the cooperative strategy by referring to the maximization of total profit. As I pointed out in chapter 6, this ambiguity always exists in symmetric games with identical payoff functions: that is, the Kantian equilibrium of the game with self-interested preferences is also a Nash equilibrium of the game that maximizes the total payoff.

9.7 The Bosch-Domènech and Silvestre Experiments

Antoni Bosch-Domènech and Joaquim Silvestre (2017, in press) conducted a series of experiments with students at the University of Pompeu Fabra. In the first experiment, respondents were asked to choose "Circle" or "Square." The results are presented in table 9.8.

Table 9.8 Bosch-Domènech and Silvestre experimental payoffs

	Temperature in Istanbul $\leq 16°C$	Temperature in Istanbul $> 16°C$
You choose Circle	You earn €10	You earn €1
You choose Square	You earn €15	You earn €6

Clearly, Square is a dominant strategy, delivering a higher payoff no matter the temperature in Istanbul. (Payoffs were made after the temperature was checked.)

Next, players were matched randomly to play the one-shot game with a payoff matrix. The results are shown in table 9.9.

Table 9.9 Bosch-Domènech and Silvestre second-game payoffs

	The other player chooses Circle	The other player chooses Square
You choose Circle	You earn €10	You earn €1
You choose Square	You earn €15	You earn €6

The results: in the first game, everyone chose "Square," but in the second game 28 percent chose "Circle." That is, respondents play differently against other human beings than how they play against an impersonal, natural "opponent." Respondents, in a word, do not treat the other player *parametrically* in the second prisoner's dilemma game, while they do treat Nature parametrically. Participants who played Circle in the prisoner's dilemma game were asked to choose from among the following reasons for their choice:

1. I chose at random;
2. It is the choice that I'd like everybody to make in this situation;
3. I like to help others even at a cost to myself;
4. In this manner, our joint earnings are higher; or
5. Taking advantage of others is not right.

The most frequent response was (4); the second most frequent was (2). As I have discussed, it is difficult to distinguish between maximization of total payoff and Kantian optimization in symmetric games. In the Istanbul game, participants universally explained their unanimous choice of Square by its dominant-strategy property, showing that they understood this well. Clearly, for some reason, 28 percent of participants did not focus on this property in the second game. Indeed, one can conjecture that in the second game, participants who chose Circle assumed a degree of joint intentionality among players, for choosing Circle would be pointless (even punishing) if the opponent were to choose the dominant strategy.

The authors propose that participants who chose Circle were motivated by the desire to "do the right thing." I have argued earlier that in symmetric games, doing the right thing means doing what I'd like everyone to do. It must be emphasized that the prisoner's dilemma game in this experiment was one-shot, with no possibility of punishing noncooperators.

TEN

A Generalization to More Complex Production Economies

10.1 Economies with Several Goods

There are generalizations of the efficiency results for Kantian equilibrium to economies that produce several goods.

A. *Economies with a private good and a public good.* A public good, y, is produced with a production function H; a private good, x, is produced with a production function G. Let (E^i, L^i) be the labor vector supplied by agent i to private and public good industries. Individuals have preferences represented by $u^i(x^i, y, E^i + L^i)$. An allocation is feasible if:

$$x^S \leq G(E^S), y \leq H(L^S).$$

One may check that an interior feasible allocation is Pareto efficient if and only if:

$$\forall i \ G'(E^S) = -\frac{u^1_3}{u^i_1} \text{ and } G'(E^S) = H'(L^S)\sum \frac{u^j_2}{u^j_1}, \tag{10.1}$$

where the utility functions are evaluated at $(x^i, y, E^i + L^i)$.

DEFINITION 10.1 A $K^\times$ *equilibrium at an allocation rule* $\mathbf{X}$ for the private good is a feasible allocation $(\mathbf{x}, \mathbf{E}, y, \mathbf{L})$ such that $x^i = X^i(\mathbf{E})$ and $y = H(L^S)$ such that:

(i) given $\mathbf{E}$, no agent would prefer to rescale the vector $\mathbf{L}$, and

(ii) given $\mathbf{L}$, no agent would prefer to rescale the vector $\mathbf{E}$.

PROPOSITION 10.1 *If* $\mathbf{X} = \mathbf{X}^{\mathrm{Pr}}$, *then any interior* $K^\times$ *equilibrium (for this economy) is Pareto efficient.*

PROOF.

1. The argument that condition (ii) implies that $\forall i \ G'(E^S) = -\frac{u^i_3}{u^i_1}$ is just as before.

2. Condition (i) means that:

$$\frac{d}{dr}\Bigg|_{r=1} u^i(\frac{E^i}{E^S}G(E^S),H(rL^s),E^i+rL^i) = u^i_2 H'L^S + u^i_3 L^i = 0, \text{ and therefore:}$$

$$\frac{u^i_2}{u^i_1}H'L^S + \frac{u^i_3}{u^i_1}L^i = 0 \Rightarrow \frac{u^i_2}{u^i_1}H'L^S = G'L^i \Rightarrow H^i\sum\frac{u^i_2}{u^i_1} = G', \qquad (10.2)$$

using step 1. The last step uses the fact that $L^S > 0$. But this is the final (Samuelson) condition for Pareto efficiency from (10.1). ∎

The general approach here is clear. Because Pareto efficiency in this economy has a new condition associated with the public good, there must be two optimization conditions for each agent. This approach can also be applied more generally. For example:

PROPOSITION 10.2 *Suppose that there are m private goods where good i is produced by a production function G^i of labor, and there are q public goods, each produced by a production function H^i of labor. Suppose that the allocation of each private good is proportional to the labor workers expended in its production. Suppose that no worker would like to rescale the labor vector in any industry. Then the allocation (if it is interior) is Pareto efficient.*

We could also have some goods allocated by equal division to those who labored in the industry and some goods allocated proportionally and adjust the definition of Kantian equilibrium accordingly. Of course, private goods must always be allocated using a mixture of equal and proportional division, in order for these generalizations to hold.

Perhaps a somewhat more interesting example is the example of an economy with workplace quality, presented in section 3.10.

10.2 Production with Many Occupations

With a few exceptions, such as those in section 10.1, the strategies that players employ in the games in this part of the book are unidimensional. In particular, in the production economies studied, production is a function of a single kind of efficiency labor or effort. In this section, I show that there are limited generalizations of Kantian optimization to the case where production is a function of several kinds of labor. Thus, I now assume that the production function G maps $\mathfrak{R}^l_+$ into $\mathfrak{R}$: there are l types of labor/

effort, or *occupations*. An aggregate vector of labor supplies will be denoted $\mathbf{E} = (E^1,...,E^l)$; each agent will supply only one kind of labor, but there may be many agents supplying each kind of labor. We denote by $l(i)$ the type of labor that agent i supplies: thus, $l(i) \in \{1,2,...,l\}$ for every i. Although the labor vector is multidimensional, each player's strategy continues to be unidimensional.

Conceptually, it seems clear why we must maintain the restriction of unidimensionality for the individuals' strategies (effort supplies). The idea behind Kantian optimization is that there is a natural conception of what it means to take the same kind of action. If actions were multidimensional, it would be difficult to conceptualize what the "same kind of action" would be. Here, we show that, as long as individuals each have unidimensional effort strategies, even if those strategies are drawn from different sets (in the sense of involving different occupations), players can cooperate by using the familiar multiplicative and additive conceptions of Kantian variation. There will, however, be restrictions on the production functions G required to derive efficiency results.

We now suppose that there are n workers, each with a concave, differentiable utility function $u^i(x,E)$, where x is consumption and E is the amount of the unique type of effort/labor that agent i is capable of supplying. The types of labor that agents can supply are specified by a (single-valued) function $l : \{1,2,...,n\} \to \{1,2,...,l\}$. Thus, a feasible allocation of effort is a vector $(E_1^{l(1)}, E_2^{l(2)},..., E_n^{l(n)})$ in $\mathfrak{R}_+^n$, where the subscript indexes the worker and the superscript indexes the occupation. The associated vector of aggregate labor supplies is $\mathbf{E} = (E^1,...,E^l)$, where $E^j = \sum_{i \, s.t. \, j=l(i)} E_i^{l(i)}$ for $j = 1,2,...,l$. The vector of consumptions $x = (x_1,...,x_n)$ must satisfy $\sum_i x_i \le G(\mathbf{E})$.

DEFINITION 10.2 A production function $G : \mathfrak{R}_+^l \to \mathfrak{R}_+$ is *homothetic* if it is differentiable and for all pairs of components j,k there is a constant γ_{jk} such that, for all positive α and for all vectors $\mathbf{E} \in \mathfrak{R}_+^l$, $G_j(\alpha\mathbf{E}) = \gamma_{jk} G_k(\alpha\mathbf{E})$, where G_j denotes the jth partial derivative of G.

Indeed, we have $\gamma_{jk} = \dfrac{G_j(\mathbf{E})}{G_k(\mathbf{E})}$. If $l = 2$, this is just the familiar condition that along any ray (emanating from the origin), the slopes of the isoquants of G are constant. More generally, the tangent hyperplanes to the isoquants of G are parallel along any ray in $l-$ space.

DEFINITION 10.3[1] A production function $G : \Re_+^2 \to \Re_+$ is C-homothetic along a path $(\theta_1, \theta_2) \in \Re_{++}^2$ if it is differentiable, and for any vector $\mathbf{E} = (E^1, E^2) \in \Re_+^2$, the slopes of isoquants of G are constant along expansion paths $(E^1 + \alpha\theta_1, E^2 + \alpha\theta_2), \alpha \geq 0$. In other words, $G_1(E^1 + \alpha\theta_1, E^2 + \alpha\theta_2) = \gamma G_2(E^1 + \alpha\theta_1, E^2 + \alpha\theta_2)$ for any nonnegative α, and so the constant γ has the value $\dfrac{G_1(\mathbf{E})}{G_2(\mathbf{E})}$.

I denote this property "C-homotheticity" because it was first used by John S. Chipman (1965), but for utility functions.[2] Consider the concave production function $G(E^1, E^2) = 2 - e^{-\theta_2 E^1} - e^{-\theta_1 E^2}$. Note that the slope of the isoquant of this function at (E^1, E^2) is $-\dfrac{\theta_1 e^{-\theta_1 E^2}}{\theta_2 e^{-\theta_2 E^1}}$, which is constant if $\theta_2 E^1 - \theta_1 E^2 = k$, or along expansion paths of slope $\dfrac{\theta_2}{\theta_1}$ in the (E^1, E^2) plane.

PROPOSITION 10.4

a. Let $l = 2$, let G be twice differentiable, and let $\mathbf{H}$ be the Hessian matrix of G. Then G is homothetic if and only if, for all $\mathbf{E} = (E^1, E^2)$:

$$(E^1, E^2)\mathbf{H}\begin{pmatrix} G_2 \\ -G_1 \end{pmatrix} = 0 . \tag{10.3}$$

b. G is C-homothetic along a path (θ_1, θ_2) if and only if, for all $\mathbf{E} = (E^1, E^2)$:

$$(\theta_1, \theta_2)\mathbf{H}\begin{pmatrix} -G_2 \\ G_1 \end{pmatrix} = 0 . \tag{10.4}$$

PROOF. In case a we have $\dfrac{d}{d\alpha}(G_2(\alpha\mathbf{E}) - \gamma G_1(\alpha\mathbf{E})) = 0$. This expands to (10.3), when we substitute for the constant γ its value of $\dfrac{G_2(\mathbf{E})}{G_1(\mathbf{E})}$. A similar argument produces case b, expanding the equation $\dfrac{d}{d\alpha}(G_2(E^1 + \alpha\theta_2) - \gamma G_1(E^1 + \alpha\theta_1, E^2 + \alpha\theta_2)) = 0$. ∎

We next define the conception of a *proportional allocation* for these economies.

DEFINITION 10.4 An allocation is *proportional* if for all players i,
$x_i = \dfrac{G_{l(i)}(\mathbf{E}) E_i^{l(i)}}{\displaystyle\sum_{j=1}^{l} G_j(\mathbf{E}) E^j} G(\mathbf{E})$. That is, each player receives a share of output equal
to the share of the *value* of his effort in the total value of effort, where each
effort is evaluated at its marginal-product "wage." An allocation is a *proportional solution* if it is proportional and Pareto efficient.

This definition is taken from Roemer and Silvestre (1993).

DEFINITION 10.5 An allocation is *generalized equal division* if for all players i, $x_i = \dfrac{G_{l(i)}(\mathbf{E})}{\displaystyle\sum_{j=1}^{l} \lambda^j G_j(\mathbf{E})} G(\mathbf{E})$, where $\lambda^j = \#\{i \mid l(i) = j\}$.

Note that for $l = 1$, proportional allocations are indeed the proportional allocations of chapter 3, and likewise, the generalized equal-division allocation is an equal-division allocation of the earlier type. Note also that the sum over all players of the output shares in Definition 10.2 is one.

To define Kantian allocations, we first write down the game that is induced in these economies when the allocation rule is the proportional rule. The payoff function for player i is given by:

$$V^i(E_1^{l(1)}, E_2^{l(2)}, ..., E_n^{l(n)}) = u^i\left(\frac{G_{l(i)}(\mathbf{E}) E_i^{l(i)}}{\sum_j G_j(\mathbf{E}) E^j} G(\mathbf{E}), E_i^{l(i)}\right). \qquad (10.5)$$

DEFINITION 10.6 An effort vector $(E_1^{l(1)}, E_2^{l(2)}, ..., E_n^{l(n)})$ is a $K^\times$ *equilibrium* for the game $\{V^i\}$ defined by (10.5) if:

$$(\forall i = 1, ..., n)(\arg\max_{r \geq 0} V^i(rE_1^{l(i)}, ..., rE_n^{l(n)}) = 1). \qquad (10.6)$$

Now consider economies that allocate output according to generalized equal division. The induced payoff functions of the game are:

$$\tilde{V}^i(E_1^{l(1)}, ..., E_n^{l(n)}) = u^i\left(\frac{G_{l(i)}(\mathbf{E})}{\sum_{j=1}^{l} \lambda^j G_j(\mathbf{E})} G(\mathbf{E}), E_i^{l(i)}\right). \qquad (10.7)$$

DEFINITION 10.7 An effort vector $(E_1^{l(1)}, E_2^{l(2)}, ..., E_n^{l(n)})$ is *a K^+ equilibrium* for the game $\{\tilde{V}^i\}$ defined by (10.7) if:

$$(\forall i = 1,...,n)(\underset{r \geq -E_i^{l(i)}}{\arg\max}\, \tilde{V}^i(E_1^{l(1)} + r,...,E_n^{l(n)} + r) = 0). \tag{10.8}$$

We can now state the main result:

PROPOSITION 10.5

a. Let G be homothetic. Let $(E_1^{l(1)}, E_2^{l(2)},...,E_n^{l(n)})$ be an effort allocation such that $E_i^{l(i)} > 0$ for all i, that is a $K^\times$ equilibrium for the game $\{V^i\}$. Then the induced allocation is Pareto efficient in the economy $(u^1,...,u^n,G)$.

b. Let G be C-homothetic along the expansion path (λ^1, λ^2). Let $(E_1^{l(1)}, E_2^{l(2)},...,E_n^{l(n)})$ be a K^+ equilibrium for the game $\{\tilde{V}^i\}$. Then the induced allocation is Pareto efficient in the economy $(u^1,...,u^n,G)$.

Thus, under different conceptions of homotheticity on production, if each worker supplies only one kind of labor, then positive multiplicative Kantian equilibria are efficient in proportional economies, and any additive Kantian equilibrium is efficient in an equal-division economy.

The hypothesis on the production function in part *b* seems very restrictive: G must be C-homothetic on an expansion path that depends upon the skills of the workers—since λ^j is the number of workers capable of supplying labor of type j. Let us apply this condition to the Chipman production function stated above, which can be written:

$$G(E^1, E^2) = 1 - \exp(-\lambda^2 \lambda^1 \overline{E}^1) - \exp(-\lambda^1 \lambda^2 \overline{E}^2),$$

where $\overline{E}^j = \dfrac{E^j}{\lambda^j}$, which is the average labor supplied by workers who supply labor of type j. The simplest example would be a production process where each worker supplies his own unique kind of labor: then the values of λ^j are both one, and the expansion path along which the isoquants have constant slope is the 45° line.

PROOF. (we let $l = 2$)

Part a. Let us suppose that worker i supplies labor of type 1. The condition defining $K^\times$ equilibrium is then:

$$(\forall i = 1,...,n)\frac{d}{dr}\bigg|_{r=1} u^i\Big(\frac{G_{l(i)}(r\mathbf{E})E_i^{l(i)}}{G_1(r\mathbf{E})E^1 + G_2(r\mathbf{E})E^2}G(r\mathbf{E}), r\mathbf{E}_i^1\Big) = 0, \tag{10.9}$$

which expands, for a player i who supplies labor of type 1, to:

$$u_1^i \cdot \left(\begin{array}{c} \dfrac{G_1 E_1^1}{G_1 E^1 + G_2 E^2} \nabla G \cdot \mathbf{E} + \\[2mm] G \dfrac{(G_1 E^1 + G_2 E^2) E_i^1 ((\nabla G_1) \cdot \mathbf{E}) - E_i^1 G_1 (E^1 (\nabla G_1 \cdot \mathbf{E}) + E^2 (\nabla G_2 \cdot \mathbf{E}))}{(G_1 E^1 + G_2 E^2)^2} \end{array} \right) + u_2^i E_1^1 = 0,$$

$$(10.10)$$

where G and its derivatives are evaluated at $\mathbf{E}$, and the gradient vector $\nabla G_j = (G_{j1}, G_{j2})$ for $j = 1,2$. (Thus, $\mathbf{H} = (\nabla G_1, \nabla G_2,)$.) The sufficient condition for Pareto efficiency, because the solution is interior, is $u_i^1 G_1 + u_i^2 = 0$, which states that i's marginal rate of substitution equals her marginal productivity. Noting that $\nabla G \cdot \mathbf{E} \equiv G_1 E^1 + G_2 E^2$, and dividing (10.10) through by the positive number E_1^1, we see that (10.10) reduces to the efficiency condition if the second term in the coefficient of u_i^1 is zero; that is, we need to show that:

$$(G_1 E^1 + G_2 E^2)((\nabla G_1) \cdot \mathbf{E}) = G_1 (E^1 (\nabla G_1 \cdot \mathbf{E}) + E^2 (\nabla G_2 . \mathbf{E})),$$

which is equivalent to:

$$\begin{array}{c} (G_1 E^1 + G_2 E^2)(G_{11} E^1 + G_{12} E^2) = \\[2mm] E^1 G_1 (G_{11} E^1 + G_{12} E^2) + E^2 G_2 (G_{21} E^1 + G_{22} E^2) \end{array} \qquad (10.11)$$

The reader can check that condition (10.11) reduces to condition (10.3), which is true by the hypothesis that G is homothetic, and Proposition 10.1. This proves *Part a*.

Part b. The allocation is an additive Kantian equilibrium for the generalized equal-division economy if and only if:

$$(\forall i = 1,...,n)$$

$$\left. \frac{d}{dr} \right|_{r=0} u^i \left(\frac{G_{l(i)}(E^1 + \lambda^1 r, E^2 + \lambda^2 r) \, G(E^1 + \lambda^1 r, E^2 + \lambda^2 r)}{\lambda^1 G_1 (E^1 + \lambda^1 r, E^2 + \lambda^2 r) + \lambda^2 G_2 (E^1 + \lambda^1 r, E^2 + \lambda^2 r)}, E_i^1 + r \right) = 0. \quad (10.12)$$

Verbally, condition (10.12) states that when each player considers the counterfactual "add a constant r to everyone's effort," the optimal constant she would choose is $r = 0$. For a player i for whom $l(i) = 1$, this expands to:

$$u_1^i \cdot \left(\begin{array}{c} \dfrac{G_1}{\lambda^1 G_1 + \lambda^2 G_2}(\lambda^1 G_1 + \lambda^2 G_2) + \\[2mm] G \dfrac{(\lambda^1 G_1 + \lambda^2 G_2)(\lambda^1 G_{11} + \lambda^2 G_{12}) - G_1 ((\lambda^1)^2 G_{11} + 2\lambda^1 \lambda^2 G_{12} + (\lambda^2)^2 G_{22})}{(\lambda^1 G_1 + \lambda^2 G_2)^2} \end{array} \right) + u_i^2 = 0.$$

$$(10.13)$$

Again, the efficiency condition is $u_1^i G_1 + u_2^i = 0$ for worker i. Condition (10.13) reduces to the efficiency condition exactly when the second term in the coefficient of u_1^i is zero—that is, when:

$$(\lambda^1 G_1 + \lambda^2 G_2)(\lambda^1 G_{11} + \lambda^2 G_{12}) = \\ G_1((\lambda^1)^2 G_{11} + 2\lambda^1 \lambda^2 G_{12} + (\lambda^2)^2 G_{22}) \quad (10.14)$$

The reader can check that condition (10.14) is equivalent to condition:

$$(\lambda^1, \lambda^2) H \begin{pmatrix} -G_2 \\ G_1 \end{pmatrix} = 0,$$

which is condition (10.4) for the expansion path (λ^1, λ^2). By the hypothesis of C-homotheticity for this expansion path, *Part b* is proved. ∎

Consider this application of Proposition 10.5a. Suppose that capital is a factor of production: let it be the first factor, so E^1 denotes the input of capital and $E^2, \ldots, E^n$ now denote the contributions of the various kinds of labor. Suppose that there are some individuals who possess capital but no labor, and they, too, have utility functions $u^i(x, E)$ where the provision of capital by them to production involves a disutility (perhaps it reduces security). According to Proposition 10.5a, if G is homothetic, then a positive multiplicative Kantian equilibrium is Pareto efficient. In this case, $G_1(E)$ is the marginal product of capital. In this equilibrium, every individual, whether the provider of capital or the supplier of labor, receives a share of the product proportional to his contribution, evaluated at its marginal-product price. If G exhibits constant returns to scale, then this allocation is identical to the Walrasian equilibrium allocation—that is, each receives a share of the product *equal* to her contribution evaluated at marginal-product prices, because the sum of contributions evaluated at marginal-product prices exhausts the total product. But if G exhibits decreasing returns, then the allocation is not Walrasian, for it allocates the entire product in proportion to contributions, so evaluated. Contrast this with the Arrow-Debreu model, in which pure profits, which exist at Walrasian equilibrium with strictly concave production, are allocated to shareholders, while providers of capital (and labor) each receive a share of the product *equal to* (rather than proportional to) their contributions (always evaluated at marginal-product prices).

10.3 Summary

My tentative inference from these results is that it is difficult to extend the theorems on the efficiency of Kantian equilibrium to games where the efforts of individuals are qualitatively different—meaning that, in production economies, they enter into production in different ways. This is not necessarily a drawback of the Kantian approach, for the mathematics may be telling us something about cooperation as such—namely, that it is difficult to decentralize cooperative behavior in an efficient manner when contributions of individuals are qualitatively different.

PART TWO

Kantian Optimization
in Market Economies

ELEVEN

International Cooperation to Reduce Global Carbon Emissions

This chapter takes a slight detour from Kantian optimization and uses an even simpler concept than simple Kantian equilibrium: the concept of a *unanimity equilibrium*. In the latter, every agent agrees, at equilibrium, on what the value of a public good or bad should be. This idea is familiar from Lindahl equilibrium, and indeed the two models I present in this chapter can be viewed as applications of Lindahl equilibrium. I present them here because they are examples of cooperative economic behavior. (See Erik Lindahl 1919, reprinted in English in Musgrave and Peacock [1958, 168–176].)

The chapter's title refers to the first example, presented in sections 11.1–11.4. The second example, presented in section 11.5, is a familiar one from public economics, of a downstream firm that suffers from the pollution of an upstream firm.

11.1 Introduction

Excessive emission of greenhouse gases may be the most pressing example of a global public bad in our time. The problem cries out for international cooperation. In my view, the main value of the United Nations Climate Change Conference held in Paris in December 2015 was to build trust among nations, for as I have emphasized, trust is a precondition of cooperation. At the conference's end, 196 nations agreed by consensus to the Paris Agreement, informally committing themselves to reductions in carbon emissions.

From the viewpoint of Nash equilibrium, the Paris Agreement is just cheap talk, for there is no enforcement structure with monitoring and penalties to render it the case that the commitment of each nation is a Nash-best response to what other nations have committed to do regarding greenhouse gas emissions reductions.

In this chapter, I present a general equilibrium model that provides a way for countries to decentralize a globally Pareto-efficient solution to the carbon emissions problem. At equilibrium, there is unanimous agreement among countries concerning the level of the global emissions cap. In equilibrium, decentralized choices of country emissions sum up to the global cap, and the allocation of emissions, capital, and consumption is Pareto efficient.

11.2 The Economic Environment and Pareto Efficiency

There are n countries. Country i operates a single firm, whose production function is $G^i(K,E)$, where K is capital and E is the country's carbon emissions. G^i is increasing and concave in its arguments. All firms produce a single consumption good, called x. Labor is implicit in the production function. Capital is purchased on an international capital market, but labor is immobile: hence, the entire labor supply of country i is allocated to the firm of the country. We therefore do not display explicitly the dependence of the technology on labor, nor will we display labor in the utility function of each country.

There is a representative agent in each country i, with utility function $u^i(x^i,E^S)$, where x^i is the consumption of country i's representative agent, E^i is the emission level of country i, and $E^S \equiv \sum E^i$ is global emissions. Utility is increasing in x^i and decreasing in E^S. We assume that these agents care about the future citizens of their country and that they have internalized this in their preferences through the negative dependence of utility on global emissions. Indeed, the form of the utility function permits citizens to care about the welfare of humankind generally, not just their own country's citizens.

Country i has a capital endowment of $\overline{K}^i$. It is easiest to assume that capital does not depreciate. (It also has a labor endowment, but as I remarked, we need not display that explicitly.)

A global allocation $\{(x^i, K^i, E^i) \mid i = 1,...,n\}$ is *feasible* if:

$$\sum x^i \leq \sum G^i(K^i, E^i)$$
$$\sum K^i \leq \bar{K}^S \equiv \sum \bar{K}^i \,. \tag{11.1}$$

By standard methods, one shows the following:[1]

FACT. An interior global allocation is globally Pareto efficient if and only if conditions (11.1) hold with equality and:

(i) for all i, j, $G_1^i = G_1^j$

(ii) for all i, $G_2^i = -\sum_{j=1}^{n} \dfrac{u_2^j}{u_1^j}\,. \tag{11.2}$

Thus, efficiency requires equalization across countries of both marginal products, as well as a Samuelson condition relating the marginal product of emissions to the marginal rates of substitution of the representative agents.

11.3 Unanimity-Walras Equilibrium in Global Emissions

There are three prices (p, r, c), for the good, capital, and a unit of emissions, respectively. Each country's firm will maximize profits, which are given by $pG^i(K, E) - rK - cE$ if the firm "demands" (K, E).[2] Of course, profits include neoclassical profits and labor income. We need not distinguish between these, since workers in each country offer their labor inelastically to the firm and all profits net of capital costs and emissions payments redound to the citizenry.

Capital will be supplied on the global market by the citizenry that owns it.

When a firm emits carbon in amount E^i, it pays cE^i into a global fund and these revenues will be distributed to the global citizenry, according to a share vector $(a^1,...,a^n)$, nonnegative and summing to one. Thus, the value of the global fund will be cE^S, and the income of country i from its demo-grant will be $a^i cE^S$.

Consider the following "game," whose n players are the representative citizens of each country. The strategy space for each player is $\Re_+$. Given a capital and emissions demand by its firm (K^i, E^i), prices, and a vector[3] $a = (a^1,...,a^n) \in \Delta^{n-1}$, the payoff function for player i is:

$$\tilde{V}^i(\hat{E}^S; K^i, E^i, a^i) = u^i\left(\frac{r\bar{K}^i + pG^i(K^i, E^i) - rK^i - cE^i + a^i c\hat{E}^S}{p}, \hat{E}^S\right), \tag{11.3}$$

where $\hat{E}^S$ is a proposal, by county i, for *global* emissions. The specification of the argument of the function $\tilde{V}^i$ reminds us that the *strategy* is a real number $(\hat{E}^S)$—the country's proposal for the global emissions cap—which is conditioned on a particular value of (K^i, E^i, a^i) as well as, of course, on the three prices. This "game" is degenerate, in the sense that agents' payoffs are defined, not on a strategy profile, but on a single number.

Note that the first argument in the utility function on the right-hand side of (11.3) is the amount of the good that country i can purchase given its income, which comes from three sources: its capital income, its profit income, and its demogrant.

DEFINITION 11.1 A *unanimity equilibrium* of the game $\{\tilde{V}^i\}$ defined in (11.3), given the vector $(p, c, r, \mathbf{a}, K^1, E^1, ..., K^n, E^n)$, is a number $\hat{E}^S \in \Re_+$ such that, for all i, $\hat{E}^S$ maximizes $\tilde{V}^i(\cdot)$.

The ethical appeal of the unanimity equilibrium is obvious—if the countries believe that the share vector $\mathbf{a}$ is fair. (I will discuss the fairness issue below.) A unanimity equilibrium can be viewed as both a Kantian equilibrium and a Nash equilibrium, in a trivial sense.

We now define the full equilibrium concept.

DEFINITION 11.2 A *global unanimity-Walras equilibrium with emissions* is a price vector (p, r, c), a share vector $\mathbf{a} = (a^1, ..., a^n) \in \Delta^{n-1}$, demands for capital and emissions (K^i, E^i) by each firm-country i, a vector of consumptions $(x^1, ..., x^n)$, and a *total supply* of global emissions $\hat{E}^S$, such that:

- For each i, $(K^i, E^i) = \arg\max_{K,E} pG^i(K, E) - rK - cE$;
- The number $\hat{E}^S$ is a unanimity equilibrium of the game $\{\tilde{V}^i\}$ defined in (11.3), given prices, $\{K^i, ..., K^n\}$, $(E^i, ..., E^n)$, and $\mathbf{a}$;
- for all i, $x^i = \dfrac{r(\overline{K}^i - K^i) + pG^i(K^i, E^i) - cE^i + a^i cE^S}{p}$); and
- $\sum x^i = \sum G^i(K^i, E^i)$, $\sum K^i = \overline{K}$, and $\hat{E}^S = \sum E^i$.

In words, countries maximize profits taking prices as given, and this involves choosing a net supply of capital to the global capital market, a demand for the consumption good, and a demand for emissions (or, one might say, emissions permits). Countries each choose their desired global level of emissions, given prices, according to their preferences, and in equilibrium all countries agree on the global supply of emissions, and all markets clear, including the market for emissions. Note, especially, that there are no ex ante limits on emissions and no ex ante allocation of emissions credits to countries. The citizens supply the permission to the countries in toto to emit. The *agreement* among countries specifies that firms may not emit until it is verified that total emissions will be no greater (in fact equal to) the citizenry-determined total supply of emissions. It is important to note that the shares in the global fund $(a^1, \ldots, a^n)$ emerge endogenously as part of the equilibrium.

PROPOSITION 11.1 *If utility functions and production functions are differentiable and concave, any global unanimity-Walras equilibrium is Pareto efficient.*

PROOF.

1. By profit maximization, we have:

$$\forall i \quad \frac{r}{p} = G_1^i, \frac{c}{p} = G_2^i. \tag{11.4}$$

2. It follows from the fact (11.2) characterizing Pareto efficiency that condition (*i*) holds. What remains to prove in order to verify condition (*ii*) is that:

$$\frac{c}{p} = -\sum \frac{u_2^i}{u_1^i}.$$

3. A unanimity equilibrium of the game $\{V^i\}$ satisfies:

$$(\forall i) \frac{d}{d\hat{E}^S} u^i \left(\frac{r(\bar{K}^i - K^i) + pG(K^i, E^i) - cE^i + a^i c\hat{E}^S}{p}, \hat{E}^S \right) = 0. \tag{11.5}$$

Compute this says:

$$\text{for all } i, \ u_1^i(x^i, \hat{E}^S)\frac{1}{p}(a^i c) + u_2^i(x^i, \hat{E}^S) = 0,$$

which can be written:

$$\text{for all } i, \frac{a^i c}{p} = -\frac{u_2^i}{u_1^i}. \tag{11.6}$$

Summing the last equations over i proves the claim, by step 2. ∎

11.4 Existence of Unanimity-Walras Global Emissions Equilibrium

I demonstrate existence under an assumption that is simplifying but probably not necessary:

ASSUMPTION QL. All utility functions are quasi-linear of the form $u^i(x, E^S) = x - h^i(E^S)$, h^i convex and increasing, and $-h^i$ satisfies the Inada conditions.

Assumption QL is reasonable in this context: it says that countries wish to maximize national income net of the costs of global warming.

PROPOSITION 11.3 *Under Assumption QL and standard concavity assumptions on the functions G^i including Inada conditions, a unanimity-Walras equilibrium with global emissions exists.*

As a prelude to proving Proposition 11.3, we introduce a correspondence that will be used in all the existence proofs of Part II of the book.[4]

Let Δ^{n-1} be a price simplex of dimension $n - 1$ for an economy with n markets. Let $z : \Delta^{n-1} \to \mathfrak{R}^n$ be the excess demand function of the economy, which obeys Walras's Law: for all $\mathbf{p} \in \Delta^{n-1}$, $\mathbf{p} \cdot z(\mathbf{p}) = 0$. Define the correspondence $\Phi : \Delta^{n-1} \to \Delta^{n-1}$ as follows. On int Δ^{n-1} (the interior of the simplex), define:

$$\Phi(\mathbf{p}) = \{\mathbf{q} \in \Delta^{n-1} \mid z(\mathbf{p}) \cdot \mathbf{q} \geq z(\mathbf{p}) \cdot \mathbf{q}', \text{ for all } \mathbf{q}' \in \Delta^{n-1}\}. \tag{11.8}$$

On $\partial\Delta^{n-1}$ (the boundary of the simplex), define:

$$\Phi(\mathbf{p}) = \{\mathbf{q} \in \Delta^{n-1} \mid \mathbf{p} \cdot \mathbf{q} = 0\}. \tag{11.9}$$

Suppose that $\mathbf{p}^*$ is a fixed point of Φ. It must lie by definition in int Δ^{n-1}. Thus, $z(\mathbf{p}^*) \cdot \mathbf{p}^* = 0$, and the definition of Φ on int Δ^{n-1} tells us that $z(\mathbf{p}^*) \leq 0$. It follows that $z(\mathbf{p}^*) = 0$, for if $z(\mathbf{p}^*)$ had a negative component, Walras's Law would be contradicted.

Therefore, all markets in the economy clear at $\mathbf{p}^*$.

PROOF OF PROPOSITION 11.3.

1. Let $(p, r, c) \in$ int Δ^2. By profit maximization, assuming that the Inada conditions hold for the production functions, we have the demands for capital and emissions in each country, (K^i, E^i) satisfy $pG_2(K^i, E^i) = c$, $pG_1(K^i, E^i) = r$.

2. The *total supply* of emissions by the n countries $\hat{E}^S$ must satisfy:

for all i, $\dfrac{d}{d\hat{E}^S}\left(\dfrac{r(\bar{K}^i - K^i) + pG(K^i, E^i) - cE^i + a^i c\hat{E}^S}{p} - h^i(\hat{E}^S)\right) = 0.$ \quad (11.10)

This says:

$$\frac{a^i c}{p} = h^{i\prime}(\hat{E}^S) \text{ for all } i, \qquad (11.11)$$

where the a^i must sum to one. Define functions $a^i(\cdot)$ by the equations:

$$a^i(X)\frac{c}{p} = h^{i\prime}(X).$$

Obviously, $a^i(X)$ are increasing functions, and since $h^{i\prime}(0) = 0$, and the $h^{i\prime}$ increase without bound, there is a unique value z^* such that $\sum a^i(z^*) = 1$. Let $\hat{E}^S \equiv z^*$. Thus, at these values of $\{a^i\}$ there is unanimity among countries regarding the global supply of emissions.

3. We have now defined the demands and supplies of capital, emissions, and the good at any interior price vector, and the vector **a**. Check that Walras's Law holds:

$$p(\sum x^i - \sum G^i) + r(\sum K^i - \sum \bar{K}^i) + c(\sum E^i - \hat{E}^S) = 0.$$

This uses the fact that $\sum a^i = 1$; the $\{x^i\}$ are defined by $x^i = \dfrac{\Pi^i + r\bar{K}^i + a^i c\hat{E}^S}{p}$, where Π^i are the profits of the country i's firm at the given prices.

Define the excess demand function $z(\mathbf{p}) = (\Delta x(\mathbf{p}), \Delta K(\mathbf{p}), \Delta E^S(\mathbf{p}))$, where $\Delta x(\mathbf{p}) = \sum x^i - \sum G^i$, $\Delta K(\mathbf{p}) = \sum(K^i - \bar{K}^i)$, and $\Delta E^S(\mathbf{p}) = \sum E^i - \hat{E}^S$. Walras's Law holds by step 3.

4. Construct the correspondence Φ as in (11.8) and (11.9) above. At a fixed point of Φ, all markets clear. The shares $\{a^i\}$ are given by step 2 above.

5. It is left to verify that the conditions of Kakutani's Fixed Point Theorem hold. Φ is convex-valued on int Δ^2 and upper hemicontinuous there by the maximum theorem. It is obviously convex valued on $\partial\Delta^2$, and a standard argument, omitted here, shows that it is upper hemicontinuous there. Thus, a fixed point exists. By the discussion before the proof of the theorem, the fixed point is the required equilibrium. ∎

REMARK. Without the assumption of quasi-linearity, the determination of the $\{a^i\}$, in step 2 of the above proof, is not so easy.

I return to the issue whether countries will consider the share vector **a** that emerges as part of the equilibrium to be fair. We can immediately see from equation (11.11) that *the shares of the climate fund received by countries are proportional to their marginal climate damages from global emissions*. Thus, countries more vulnerable to climate change, in the sense that their marginal damages are large at every level of global emissions, receive greater compensation. This reflects a degree of fairness. A more careful discussion of this issue would require understanding how the global emissions level at equilibrium reflects the data of the problem.

The property of the vector **a** just remarked upon, however, is unlikely to suffice as a fully attractive conception of fairness, for that value, like equilibrium prices, will reflect the distribution of endowments, technologies, and damage functions, and it would be difficult to establish the claim that the distribution of these endowments is "fair." Fortunately, there are more degrees of freedom in the allocation of global consumption. The distribution of consumption can be amended by adding fixed transfers of the consumption good T^i for all countries, which sum zero. That is, we can write consumption as:

$$x^i = T^i + \frac{r(\bar{K}^i - K^i) + pG(K^i, E^i) - cE^i + a^i c\hat{E}^S}{p}, \qquad (11.12)$$

where T^i is the net level of the consumption good transferred to country i from the rest of the world. If the utility functions are quasi-linear, these transfers will not alter the equilibrium values of emissions or demands for capital. (Of course, the transfers must be feasible: no country can end up with a negative consumption, and $\sum T^i = 0$.) Thus, by varying the vector of transfers, we produce an $n - 1$ dimensional manifold of efficient equilibria. The political problem presents itself as a conflict over what the transfers should be.

This equilibrium concept decentralizes the problem, once the share vector **a** is announced. There is no need for a centralized decision on the allocation of permits. The scheme is a version of cap and trade, where the global cap on emissions is set by the world's citizenry, by unanimous agreement. The market for emissions permits is replaced by the requirement (agreed to by the community of countries) that total emissions do not exceed the supply of global emissions permits, which is the unanimity equilibrium of the game defined in (11.3).

We have not addressed how the equilibrium is discovered—that is, the dynamics of convergence to equilibrium. This is where the *prescriptive* value of the concept of a global unanimity-Walras equilibrium becomes important. An international team of economists could compute the vector **a**, after consulting with countries and estimating their production and damage functions. The unanimous agreement on the value of the global emissions cap is the selling point. Bargaining and arguing would still enter into negotiations over the vector of country or regional transfers.

11.5 A Model of Unanimity Equilibrium in an Economy with Production Externalities

There are two firms. Concave technology $G(E,B)$ produces both good x as a function of efficiency units of labor and a public bad B that is a production input for the firm. G is increasing in both arguments. Technology H produces a good y as a function of labor and B: $H(E,B)$. Here, H is increasing in its first argument and decreasing in B. Thus, the G firm produces the emissions that negatively affect production in the downstream H firm.

There are n citizens; citizen i owns shares $(\theta^{1i}, \theta^{2i})$ in the two firms. Workers supply labor to the two firms: worker i's firm-specific supplies are (E^{1i}, E^{2i}); we write the total labor supplied by worker i as E^i and denote $E^{1i} = t^i E^i, E^{2i} = (1 - t^i)E^i$. Citizens have concave utility functions $u^i(x^i, y^i, E^i)$, increasing in the first two arguments and decreasing in the third.

Pareto efficiency is characterized by the solution of this program:

$$\max u^1(x^1, y^1, E^1)$$

s.t.

$$u^i(x^i, y^i, E^i) \geq k^i \quad (\lambda^i)$$

$$x^S \leq G(E^{1S}, B) \quad (\alpha)$$

$$y^S \leq H(E^{2S}, B) \quad (\beta)$$

$$E^{1S} = \sum_1^n t^i E^i \quad (\gamma)$$

$$E^{2S} = \sum_1^n (1 - t^i)E^i \quad (\delta)$$

(11.14)

The dual Kuhn-Tucker conditions reduce to the following equations:

(1) $u_1^1 G_2 + u_2^1 H_2 = 0$;

(2) for all i, $\dfrac{u_1^1}{u_1^i} = \dfrac{u_2^1}{u_2^i}$; and

(3) for all i, $\dfrac{u_3^i}{u_1^i} + t^i G_1 + \dfrac{u_2^1}{u_1^1} H_1 (1 - t^i) = 0$.

These conditions, in addition to the material balance conditions stated as constraints in program (11.4), are necessary and sufficient conditions for an interior solution to be Pareto efficient.[5]

We now define an *equilibrium with externalities* for a market economy with these data.

DEFINITION 11.3 An *equilibrium with externalities* is a price vector (p,q,b) for the goods $x, y,$ and $B,$ and nonnegative numbers $(a^1,\dots,a^n)$ summing to one, demands for goods (x^i, y^i) by consumers, supplies of labor (E^{1i}, E^{2i}) by workers, supplies of goods X and Y by the two firms, a demand for the pollutant B^1 by the G firm, demands for labor D^1, D^2 by the two firms, and a (supply) permit to pollute by the citizenry of B^c, such that:

(*i*) Profit maximization of the G firm:

$$(D^1, B^1) \text{ maximizes } pG(D,B) - wD - bB, \text{ and}$$
$$X = G(D^1, B^1) \text{ and } \Pi^1 \equiv pG(D^1, B) - wD^1 - bB^1.$$

(*ii*) Profit maximization of the H firm:

$$D^2 \text{ maximizes over } D, \ qH(D, B^1) - wD, \text{ and}$$
$$Y = H(D^2, B^1), \Pi^2 \equiv qH(D^2, B^1) - wD^2 \qquad .$$

(*iii*) Utility maximization of consumers, who choose (x^i, y^i, E^i) to maximize

$$u^i(x, y, E) \text{ subject to}$$
$$px + qy \le wE^i + \theta^{1i}\Pi^1 + \theta^{2i}\Pi^2 + a^i b B^1.$$

(*iv*) Unanimity of equilibrium among consumers in the choice of the pollutant: Given (D^1, D^2), consumers unanimously choose $B = B^1$ to maximize the function:

$$V^i(B) = \theta^{1i}(pG(D^1, B) - wD^1 - bB) + \theta^{2i}(qH(D^2, B) - wD^2) + a^i bB.$$

(*v*) Market clearing: $X = x^S, Y = y^S, D^1 = E^{1S}, D^2 = E^{2S}$.

Thus, the polluting firm chooses the amount of pollutant B^1 to maximize profits, facing a price for the pollutant inter alia. The revenues collected from the pollution tax are distributed to consumers according to shares a^i that are determined in equilibrium. Condition (iv) states that, given prices and the labor demands of firms, consumers unanimously agree that B^1 is the optimal level of pollution, where optimization maximizes each consumer's income.

Thus, we may think of there being two kinds of regulation of the emissions: through the tax paid by the polluting firm that is returned to consumers as a grant, and by the necessity of unanimous agreement of society that the level of pollution be optimal. We can think of the equilibrium as decentralizing the achievement of Pareto efficiency, once the share vector **a** is specified.

We have:

PROPOSITION 11.4 *Given differentiability, equilibrium with externalities is Pareto efficient.*

PROOF.

1. Profit maximization implies:

$$pG_1(D^1, B^1) = w, \; pG_2(D^2, B^1) = b, \; qH_1(D^2, B^1) = w.$$

2. Utility maximization implies:

$$\frac{u_1^i}{p} = \frac{u_2^i}{q} = -\frac{u_3^i}{w} \text{ for all } i.$$

3. The first-order condition for the maximization of i's payoff function as expressed in condition (iv) of the definition of equilibrium is:

$$\theta^{1i}(pG_2 - b) + \theta^{2i}qH_2 + a^i b = 0.$$

Because $pG_2 = b$, this reduces to $a^i = -\dfrac{\theta^{2i}qH_2}{b}$. Adding up over all i, we have:

$$b = -qH_2.$$

4. Conditions (1) and (2) of Pareto efficiency are immediately implied by the equations in steps 1 and 2 and the last equation in step 3.

5. It remains to verify condition (3) of Pareto efficiency:

$$\frac{u_3^i}{u_1^i} + t^i G_1 + \frac{u_2^1}{u_1^1} H_1(1 - t^i) =^? 0.$$

Substituting $\dfrac{w}{p}$ for H_1 and $\dfrac{p}{q}$ for $\dfrac{u_2^1}{u_1^1}$ shows that this equation is equivalent to:

$$\frac{u_3^i}{u_1^i} + t^i \frac{w}{p} + (1-t^i)\frac{w}{p} = \frac{u_3^i}{u_1^i} + \frac{w}{p} =^? 0.$$

But this is true by step 2, proving the claim. ∎

It might appear that consumers need to know the technology H in order to find the level of B that maximizes V^i—see condition (iv) of the definition of equilibrium. But at equilibrium prices, this is not the case, because the derivative

$$\frac{dV^i}{dB} = \theta^{2i}qH_2 + a^ib = -\theta^{2i}b(\frac{q}{p}\frac{u_1^i}{u_2^i} + a^i),$$

using the fact that the Pareto efficiency holds at equilibrium, and so consumers may compute the individually optimal level of B without knowing the firms' technologies.

PROPOSITION 11.5

a. Under the usual convexity conditions, an equilibrium with externalities exists.

b. The shares a^i are proportional to θ^{2i}. (So owners of the H firm are compensated for the imposition of the pollution on their firm, in proportion to their ownership stakes in the firm.)

PROOF.

1. Denote a price vector by $\mathbf{p} = (p, q, w, b)$. Denote the 3-simplex of prices by Δ^3.

2. We define a mapping $\Phi : \Delta^3 \to \Delta^3$. First, we define the map on $\mathrm{int}\,\Delta^3$. Given $\mathbf{p} \in \mathrm{int}\,\Delta^3$, compute the profit maximizing labor demands D^1, D^2 of the two firms, and the profit maximizing "demand" for the pollutant B^1 by the G firm. These quantities exist and are unique if G, H satisfy the Inada conditions.

3. Define functions $a^i(B) = -\dfrac{\theta^{2i}qH_2(D^2, B)}{b}$ for $i = 1, \ldots, n$. Note that these functions are strictly increasing. By the Inada condition on H, there is a unique value of B such that $\sum a^i(B) = 1$. Denote this value by B^s.

4. Define the income of agent i by:

$$I^i(\mathbf{p}, E^i) = wE^i + \theta^{1i}(pG(D^1, B^1) - wD^1 - bB^1) +$$
$$\theta^{i2}(qH(D^2, B^1) - wD^2) + a^i bB^s \qquad .$$

Now define (x^i, y^i, E^i) as the solution of the consumer's utility maximization program, subject to the income I^i. If u is strictly concave, this solution is unique.

5. Define the following excess demand functions of $\mathbf{p}$:

$$\Delta x(\mathbf{p}) = \sum x^i - G(D^1, B^1), \quad \Delta y(\mathbf{p}) = \sum y^i - H(D^2, B^1),$$
$$\Delta E(\mathbf{p}) = D^1 + D^2 - \sum E^i, \quad \Delta B(\mathbf{p}) = B^1 - B^s.$$

We show that Walras's Law holds. We can write

$$\mathbf{p} \cdot (\Delta x, \Delta y, \Delta E, \Delta B) =$$
$$px^S + qy^S - wE^i - \left(pG(D^1, B^1) - wD^1 - bB^1\right) -$$
$$\left(qH(D^2, B^1) - wD^2\right) - bB^s = 0.$$

using the fact that $\sum a^i = 1$. The sum of the four negative terms in this equation comprises the total income of consumers, which equals the sum of the two positive terms since the budget constraints bind.

6. Denote $\Delta z(\mathbf{p}) = (\Delta x(\mathbf{p}), \Delta y(\mathbf{p}), \Delta E(\mathbf{p}), \Delta B(\mathbf{p}))$. Now define the function (or correspondence) $\Phi : \operatorname{int} \Delta^3 \to \Delta^3$ as in equations (11.8) and (11.9). By the argument given there, any fixed point of Φ must lie in $\operatorname{int} \Delta^3$, and a fixed point is a unanimity equilibrium. The only part of this claim that is not standard is the "unanimity" part. Condition (*iv*) of the definition of unanimity equilibrium holds at a fixed point because, by step 3 above, we have for all i:

$$a^i = -\frac{\theta^{2i} q H_2(D^2, B^1)}{b},$$

which is the first-order condition for B^1 to be the optimal value of the pollutant level for every agent.

Since at equilibrium $\Delta E = 0$, we can allocate the supply of labor between the two firms such that, for each firm, the demand equals the supply of labor.

7. Hence, we need only verify that Φ is upper hemicontinuous, which is standard. ∎

TWELVE

Efficient Provision of a Public and Private Good

A Semimarket Economy

12.1 The Model and Pareto Efficiency

Consider an economy with a private good (x), a public good (y), and labor (E). Citizens have concave, differentiable utility functions $u^i(x,y,E)$ of the usual kind. There is a private firm that produces the private good with production function G using labor as the only input. There is a cooperative firm that produces the public good from labor, using production function H. The private firm is owned by citizens. Each citizen is endowed with $(\bar{E}^i, \theta^i)$, a positive amount of labor in efficiency units and a share of the private firm. The public-good firm will be organized along a cooperative principle.

Let $E^i = (E_1^i, E_2^i)$ be a supply of labor by agent i to Firm 1 (private) and Firm 2 (public), respectively. There are n citizens. A feasible allocation satisfies:

$$G(E_1^S) \geq x^S, H(E_2^S) \geq y,$$
$$(\forall i)(E_1^i + E_2^i \leq \bar{E}^i). \tag{12.1}$$

FACT. An interior[1] allocation in the differentiable case is Pareto efficient if and only if:

$$(A)\ (\forall i)(G'(E_1^S) = -\frac{u_3^i(x^i,y,E^i)}{u_1^i(x^i,y,E^i)}\ \text{ and } (B)\ \frac{G'(E_1^S)}{H'(E_2^S)} = -\sum_i \frac{u_3^i(x^i,y,E^i)}{u_1^i(x^i,y,E^i)}, \tag{12.2}$$

in addition to the feasibility conditions (12.1), where the first two of these hold with equality.

We define a notion of equilibrium that is semi-market. The private firm maximizes profits facing prices for the private good and labor (p, w). Citizens supply labor to both the private firm and the cooperative firm. Workers are paid wages by the private firm but not by the cooperative firm, which operates outside the market. The vector of labor supplies and demands for the private good are conventional. But the vector of labor supplies to the cooperative firm must be an additive Kantian equilibrium of a game to be defined.

Suppose that we are given a vector of labor supplies to the private firm $\hat{E}_1 = (\hat{E}_1^1, ..., \hat{E}_1^n)$ and private-good consumptions $\hat{x} = (\hat{x}^1, ..., \hat{x}^n)$. Define a game among the n players with the following payoff functions:

$$V^i(E_2^1, ..., E_2^n) = u^i(\hat{x}^i, H(E_2^S), \hat{E}_1^i + E_2^i). \tag{12.3}$$

(Recall that $E_2^S = \sum_i E_2^i$.)

We can now define a *Walras-Kant equilibrium with a public and private good* as follows. It consists of a price vector (p, w), an allocation of goods $(\hat{x}^1, ..., \hat{x}^n, \hat{y})$, n effort vectors $\hat{E}^i = (\hat{E}_1^i, \hat{E}_2^i)$, and a supply of the good and demand for labor by the private firm $(\hat{X}, \hat{D})$ such that:

(a) The vector $(\hat{X}, \hat{D})$ maximizes Firm 1's profits, that is, $pX - wD$. Denote these profits by $\Pi(\hat{X}, \hat{D})$;

(b) Given $(\hat{y}, \hat{E}_2^1, ..., \hat{E}_2^n)$, for each i, the choice $(\hat{x}^i, \hat{E}_1^i)$ maximizes $u^i(x^i, \hat{y}, E_1^i + \hat{E}_2^i)$ over the budget set:

$$\{(x^i, E_1^i) \mid px^i \leq wE_1^i + \theta^i \Pi(\hat{X}, \hat{D})\};$$

(c) Given $(\hat{x}^1, ..., \hat{x}^n, \hat{E}_1^1, ..., \hat{E}_1^n)$, the vector $\hat{E}_2 = (\hat{E}_2^1, ..., \hat{E}_2^n)$ is an additive Kantian equilibrium of the game **V** defined in (12.3) above;

(d) Markets clear: $\sum \hat{x}^i = \hat{X}$, $\sum \hat{E}_1^i = D$, and in addition $H(E_2^S) = y$.

In other words, every worker may participate in both the private and cooperative economy; her choices in the private economy are optimal for her, given prices and given the labor she expends in the cooperative firm and the value of the public good, and the levels of participation of workers in the cooperative firm form an additive Kantian equilibrium for them, given the consumption and labor they receive in the private/market sector. So, in the private economy, workers behave as they do under capitalism, but when producing the public good, they optimize in a cooperative fashion.

PROPOSITION 12.1 *Any Walras-Kant equilibrium with a public and private good is Pareto efficient.*

PROOF.

1. We will assume that the equilibrium is interior for simplicity, although the proof extends to corner solutions.

2. By profit maximization, $G'(E_1^S) = \dfrac{w}{p}$. By utility maximization over (x^i, E_1^i), it follows that $\dfrac{w}{p} = -\dfrac{u_3^i}{u_1^i}$, where the argument of u^i is $(\hat{x}^i, \hat{y}, \hat{E}_1^i + \hat{E}_2^i)$. It follows that condition (A) of the characterization of Pareto efficiency in (12.2) holds.

3. By concavity, the following first-order condition characterizes the additive Kantian equilibrium of the game V:

$$\text{for all } i, \left.\frac{d}{dr}\right|_{r=0} V^i(r + E_2^1, \ldots, r + E_2^n) =$$
$$\left.\frac{d}{dr}\right|_{r=0} u^i(\hat{x}^i, H(nr + E_2^S), \hat{E}_1^i + r + E_2^i) = 0.$$

Expanding this condition we have:

$$\text{for all } i, \quad u_2^i H'(E_2^S)n + u_3^i = 0. \tag{12.4}$$

Using the fact that $-G'(E_1^S)u_1^i = u_3^i$, proved in step 2, we can write (12.4) as:

$$u_2^i H'(E_2^S)n - G'(E_1^S)u_1^i = 0. \tag{12.5}$$

Now, since $E_2^S > 0$, by interiority of the equilibrium, $H'(E_2^S)$ is well defined and positive; rewrite equation (12.5) as:

$$\frac{G'(E_1^S)}{H'(E_2^S)n} = \frac{u_2^i}{u_1^i}. \tag{12.6}$$

Add conditions (12.6) over i, giving condition (B) in (12.2) of Pareto efficiency. ∎

What happens if we substitute for condition (c), condition (c^*)?

(c^*) Given $(\hat{x}^1, \ldots, \hat{x}^n, \hat{E}_1^1, \ldots, \hat{E}_1^n)$ the vector $\hat{E}_2 = (\hat{E}_2^1, \ldots, \hat{E}_2^n)$ is a *multiplicative* Kantian equilibrium of the game V defined in (12.3) above.

We have:

PROPOSITION 12.2 *Any Walras-Kant (multiplicative variant) equilibrium in which for all i $E_2^i > 0$ is Pareto efficient.*

PROOF.

1. Same step 2 in Proposition 12.1.

2. We now require:

$$\text{for all } i, \left.\frac{d}{dr}\right|_{r=1} u^i(\hat{x}^i, H(rE_2^S), \hat{E}_1^i + rE_2^i) = 0,$$

$$\text{or: } u_2^i H'(E_2^S)\frac{E_2^S}{E_2^i} + u_3^i = 0.$$

Again, we substitute $-G'(E_1^S)u_1^i$ for u_3^i, giving:

$$\frac{u_2^i}{u_1^i} = \frac{E_2^i}{E_2^S}\frac{G'(E_1^S)}{H'(E_2^S)}.$$

Adding over i gives the required condition (B) for Pareto efficiency. ∎

12.2 Existence of Equilibrium

We have the existence result:

PROPOSITION 12.3 *If G obeys the Inada conditions and is strictly concave, and the utility functions are concave and strictly quasi-concave, then an additive Walras-Kant equilibrium with a public and private good exists.*

PROOF.

1. Denote by Δ the 1-simplex of prices (p,w). Define the compact, convex set:

$$\Omega = \Delta \times \prod_{i=1}^{n}[0, \bar{E}^i].$$

We are given $(p, w, E_2^1, ..., E_2^n) \in \Omega$. Define the supply of the private good and the demand for labor for the private-good firm by profit maximization:

$$(\hat{X}, \hat{D}) = \arg\max_{(X,D)}(pX - wD) \text{ s.t. } X = G(D).$$

Denote the profits by $\Pi(\hat{X}, \hat{D})$.

2. Next, define $\hat{y} = H(E_2^S)$, and define $(\hat{x}^i, \hat{E}_1^i)$ as the solution of:

$$\max_{(x,E)} u^i(x, \hat{y}, E_2^i + E)$$

s.t.

$$px \le wE + \theta^i \Pi(p, w).$$

3. Define:

$$\text{for all } i, \ r^i = \underset{r \in [-\hat{E}_1^i - E_2^i, \bar{E}^i - \hat{E}_1^i - E_2^i]}{\arg\max} \ V^i(r + E_2^1, ..., r + E_2^n). \tag{12.7}$$

Note, by the domain over which the maximization occurs, $r^i + \hat{E}_1^i + E_2^i \in [0, \bar{E}^i]$. By strict quasi-concavity of utility, the solution of (12.7) for a given i is unique.

Now define for all i, $\hat{E}_2^i = r^i + E_2^i$.

4. Note that Walras's Law holds by adding up the budget constraints:

$$p(\sum \hat{x}^i - X) + w(D - \sum \hat{E}_1^i) = 0.$$

Denote the excess demand function by:

$$z(p, w; \hat{y}) = (\Delta x, \Delta E_1),$$

where $\Delta x = \sum \hat{x}^i - X$, $\Delta E_1 = D - \sum \hat{E}_1^i$. Recall that $(\hat{x}^i, \hat{E}_1^i)$ depends on $\hat{y}$. Now define $\Phi^1 : \Omega \to \Delta$ as in equations (11.7) and (11.8). That is, if $\mathbf{p} \equiv (p, w) \in \text{int} \, \Delta$ define:

$$\Phi^1(\mathbf{p}, E_2^1, ..., E_2^n) = \{\mathbf{q} \in \Delta \mid \mathbf{q} \cdot z(\mathbf{p}; H(E_2^S))$$
$$\ge \mathbf{q}' \cdot z(\mathbf{p}; H(E_2^S)), \text{ for all } \mathbf{q}' \in \Delta\} \quad .$$

For $\mathbf{p} \in \partial\Delta$, define $\Phi^1(\mathbf{p}, E_2^1, ..., E_2^n) = \{\mathbf{q} \in \Delta \mid \mathbf{p} \cdot \mathbf{q} = 0\}$.

Define $\Phi^2(\mathbf{p}, E_2^1, ..., E_2^n) = (r^1 + E_2^1, ..., r^n + E_2^n)$, which is single-valued. Last, define $\hat{\Phi} = \Phi^1 \times \Phi^2$, noting that $\hat{\Phi}$ maps Ω into itself.

5. Suppose $(p^*, w^*, E_2^{1*}, ..., E_2^{n*})$ is a fixed point of $\hat{\Phi}$. Then $\Delta x = 0 = \Delta E_1$. Now it also follows from the fixed point property that for all i, $r^i = 0$. Therefore $(E_2^{1*}, ..., E_2^{n*})$ is an additive Kantian equilibrium of the game $\mathbf{V}$ defined in (12.3). This shows that the fixed point is a Walras-Kant equilibrium with a public and private good.

6. It is left only to verify that $\hat{\Phi}$ is upper hemicontinuous and convex-valued. Convex-valuedness is immediate, as is the upper hemicontinuity on

int Δ. The upper hemicontinuity of $\hat{\Phi}$ on $\partial\Delta$ is a standard argument that we skip. ∎

REMARK. The proof of existence of a *multiplicative* Walras-Kant equilibrium should also be true but will be more delicate. This is because the zero vector is always a multiplicative Kantian equilibrium of the game V, but we want to show the existence of a Walras-Kant equilibrium where the vector $\mathbf{E}_2$ is strictly positive (or else we lose Pareto efficiency). Doing this requires cutting out a small piece of the domain $\prod_{i=1}^{n}[0,\bar{E}^i]$ near the origin, and then some conditions on the derivatives of u^i are needed to guarantee that Φ^2 maps this slightly smaller domain into itself. To avoid this complication, I have elected to prove existence for the additive Kantian version, which does not suffer from this problem. See, for example, the proof of Proposition 7.1.

THIRTEEN

Two Designs for Market Socialism

13.1 Introduction

The ethos of socialism is cooperation. Using markets in a socialist economy in a comprehensive way was first proposed in the 1930s by Oscar Lange and Fred Taylor (1938). Since then, many variants have been proposed. Perhaps the latest, at this writing, is that of Giacomo Corneo (2017), who proposes that the government build a sovereign wealth fund that would be invested in international equities, the income from which would be distributed to the population. In addition, a *federal shareholder* would be created, an institution that would purchase large equity positions in many domestic firms, the income from which would redound to the treasury.

What's notable, for the present purpose, is that all designs of market socialism with which I am familiar limit the "socialism" part of their proposals to altering the property rights in firms, with the aim of allocating capital income much more equally than it is allocated in capitalist economies. The two economic foundations of twentieth-century socialist experiments (chiefly, the Soviet Union and its eastern European periphery, and China until 1979) were the replacement of markets by central planning and state ownership of (at least) the major firms of the economy. Market-socialist proposals have replaced planning with markets at least to a considerable extent and have usually replaced state ownership of firms with some alternative form that would putatively give firms the ability to maximize profits without egregious state interference, in order to capture the mechanism of the first theorem of welfare economics. The "socialist" part of these proposals is the socialization of a large part of the nation's capital income.

Although lip service is paid to cooperation, these market-socialist models have not included any precise cooperative protocol in their agents' behavior: to the extent that cooperation might be said to exist in the models of Lange and Taylor, Corneo, and many others, a set that includes my own earlier proposal in Roemer (1994), it must be embodied in the property rights envisaged for firms. In market-socialist models heretofore, agents are presumed to optimize in the same way that Arrow-Debreu agents optimize, maximizing a self-regarding preference order subject to constraints in the autarchic manner. I believe that this approach underplays the importance of the cooperative ethos that must be a key element of socialist design.

One might suppose that socialist citizens would possess preferences with an altruistic element in them. However, I have not seen any market-socialist models with this property—and in any case, if an agent is small in the economy, it is unclear whether his having a preference order with an altruistic character would produce equilibria any different from one in which agents are entirely self-regarding. (See Dufwenberg et al. 2011.) After all, if an agent is small, what difference would her altruistic contribution make, and would this small contribution outweigh the personal cost she sustains by making it? As the reader will by now understand, I prefer to rely on cooperation rather than altruism as the bedrock of a socialist society.

Once again: the lack of a *cooperative behavioral protocol* in market-socialist models is a serious lacuna, since the theory of socialism emphasizes that socialism will replace the ethos of individualism, characteristic of capitalism, with an ethos of cooperation. Cooperation should therefore appear more robustly in our models of socialism and not be limited to a new design of property rights. In this chapter, I embed cooperative behavior in the form of Kantian optimization in two models of market socialism.

In the first of these models, firms, which maximize profits, will be in part privately owned by citizens and in part state-owned. Citizens will choose their commodity consumptions by maximizing utility subject to their budget constraints in the usual manner, but they will choose their labor supplies to firms in a Kantian manner. The state is a passive owner and uses its profit share to finance firms' capital investment. Incomes are redistributed via an affine tax policy. The main result—the "first theory of welfare economics for market socialism"—is that the ensuing equilibrium is Pareto efficient *at any tax rate*. Thus, Kantian optimization in the labor market allows us to separate completely the question of efficiency from that of distribution. The deadweight loss of taxation, so important in discussions of "equity versus efficiency," evaporates.

In the second model, presented in section 13.9, I introduce Kantian optimization among citizens in their investment decisions but not in the labor market.

The first model below is somewhat more complicated than the models in the two previous chapters, for here I assume there are *two* produced private commodities and labor. I have chosen to introduce the complication to show that the usefulness of Kantian optimization is not restricted to economies with a single private commodity. It will be clear that the arguments will hold for economies with any number of private, produced commodities.

13.2 The Economic Environment

There are two produced private goods and a homogeneous kind of labor, measured in efficiency units. There are two firms, each of which produces one of the goods from inputs of labor and capital,[1] using production functions G and H, which map $\mathfrak{R}_+^2 \to \mathfrak{R}_+$. Worker i is endowed with $\bar{E}^i$ units of labor in efficiency units, and receives a profit share θ^{il} from Firm l, for $l = 1,2$. The state owns fractions θ^{0l} of Firm $l = 1,2$ and is endowed with K_0 units of the capital good. Good 1 is used both for consumption and capital, and Good 2 is a pure consumption good. The state uses its capital to finance investment in the two firms, and the private agents spend their incomes on consumption of the two goods. Private agent i has preferences over the two consumption goods and labor expended (in efficiency units) represented by a utility function $\mathfrak{R}_+^2 \times [0, \bar{E}^i] \to \mathfrak{R}_+$. All activity takes place in a single period.

Firms are traditional—they are price takers and demand capital and labor and supply commodities to maximize profits. A linear tax at an exogenous rate $t \in [0,1]$ will be levied on all private incomes, with the tax revenues returned to the population as an equal demogrant. Given their incomes (which consist of after-tax wages, profit income, and the demogrant) and their labor supply, producer-consumers choose the optimal commodity bundle in the classical way. However, the determination of labor supply, and hence of income, is nontraditional—that is to say, the worker does not choose his labor supply in the Nash manner. A vector of labor supplies must be an *additive Kantian equilibrium* of a game to be defined below.

13.3 The Game

Let (p_1, p_2, w, r) be a price vector where p_l is the price of commodity l, for $l = 1,2$, w is the wage rate for labor in efficiency units, and r is the interest rate on capital. Let (E^{i1}, E^{i2}) be a labor supply vector by agent i to Firms 1 and 2. Thus the vector of labors supplied to Firm G is $\mathbf{E}^1 = (E^{11}, ..., E^{n1})$, and the vector of labors supplied to Firm H is $\mathbf{E}^2 = (E^{12}, ..., E^{n2})$. Fix the capital levels K^l, $l = 1,2$, of the two firms. Define the *income* of private agent i at $(\mathbf{E}^1, \mathbf{E}^2)$ under a linear income tax at rate t as:

$$I^i(E^i, E^{S1}, E^{S2}) = (1-t)wE^i + (1-t)(\theta^{i1}\Pi^1(K^1, E^{S1}) +$$

$$\theta^{i2}\Pi^2(K^2, E^{S2})) + \frac{t}{n}(p_1 G(K^1, E^{S1}) + p_2 H(K^2, E^{S2}) - , \qquad (13.1)$$

$$\theta^{01}\Pi^1(K^1, E^{S1}) - \theta^{02}\Pi^2(K^2, E^{S2}) - rK^1 - rK^2)$$

where the profits of the two firms are defined by:

$$\begin{aligned}\Pi^1(K^1, E^{S1}) &\equiv p_1 G(K^1, E^{S1}) - wE^{S1} - rK^1, \\ \Pi^2(K^2, E^{S2}) &\equiv p_2 H(K^2, E^{S2}) - wE^{S2} - rK^2\end{aligned} \qquad (13.2)$$

and E^{Sl} is the labor supplied to Firm l. The last term on the right-hand side of (13.1) is the value of the demogrant, equal to the per capita share of total tax revenues, where taxes are levied on all private incomes but not on the state's income.

The income of the state is:

$$I^0 = \theta^{01}\Pi^1(K^1, E^{S1}) + \theta^{02}\Pi^1(K^2, E^{S2}) + r(K^1 + K^2). \qquad (13.3)$$

That is, the state receives its share of firms' profits plus the return on its investment, but this is not taxed, which explains the specification of the demogrant in (13.1).

Now suppose that every (private) agent were to increase her total labor by a constant ρ, positive or negative. Then i's hypothetical income would be:

$$
\begin{aligned}
&I^i(E^i + \rho, E^{S1} + \lambda n\rho, E^{S2} + (1-\lambda)n\rho) = (1-t)w(E^i + \rho) + \\
&(1-t)(\theta^{i1}\Pi^1(K^1, E^{S1} + \lambda n\rho) + \theta^{i2}\Pi^2(K^2, E^{S2} + (1-\lambda)n\rho)) + \\
&\frac{t}{n}\left(\begin{matrix} p_1 G\left(K^1, E^{S1} + \lambda n\rho\right) + p_2 H(K^2, E^{S2} + (1-\lambda)n\rho) - \\ \theta^{01}\Pi^1(K^1, E^{S1} + \lambda n\rho) - \theta^{02}\Pi^2(K^2, E^{S2} + (1-\lambda)n\rho) - r(K^1 + K^2) \end{matrix} \right)
\end{aligned}, \quad (13.4)
$$

where fraction λ of the total increase in labor nr is allocated to Firm 1, and fraction $(1 - \lambda)$ to Firm 2. We need not adopt a rule for how each agent would allocate her additional labor ρ between the two firms, as this decision (and therefore the value of λ) will turn out not to matter. It is assumed that workers are price takers: in particular, they take the wage w as fixed.

A comment on the logic behind equation (13.4) is in order. A *Nash player*, who chooses his labor supply while assuming that all other labor supplies remain fixed, need not consider the effect of his labor-supply decision on either the profits of firms in which he works or owns equity, or the demogrant, if the economy is large. Hence, our practice in Nash-type analysis is to ignore these effects. But in Kantian optimization, the counterfactual that the worker envisages is that *all* workers change their labor supplies in the same amount as the change he is contemplating, and hence consistency in the thought experiment requires that we alter the labor supplies to firms, and the value of the demogrant, accordingly. By assuming that workers are price takers, we thereby assume that they ignore the macro effect on the wage w of the variation in labor supply ($n\rho$) which they are contemplating. Strictly speaking, this is not rational. Thus, the price-taking assumption has real bite here. The same can be said for traditional models of economic equilibrium, where workers are Nash optimizers, if the number of agents is finite and small.

At this counterfactual labor supply by worker i, $E^{i1} + E^{i2} + \rho$, given her income as specified by (13.4), let the agent compute her commodity demands, which are the solution of the program:

$$\max_{x,y} u^i(x, y, E^i + \rho)$$

subj. to $\qquad\qquad\qquad\qquad\qquad$ (13.5)

$$p_1 x + p_2 y = I^i(E^i + \rho, E^{S1} + \lambda n\rho, E^{S2} + (1-\lambda)n\rho)$$

Denote the solution to this program by $(x^i(I^i[\rho], E^i + \rho), (y^i(I^i[\rho], E^i + \rho))$, where we abbreviate with the notation $I^i[\rho] \equiv I^i(E^i + \rho, E^{S1} + \lambda n\rho, E^{S2} + (1-\lambda)n\rho)$.

We now define the payoff functions of a game. The payoff to agent i is his utility at prices (p_1, p_2, w, r) if the capital invested in the firms is (K^1, K^2) and the vector of labor supplies $(E^1, \ldots, E^n)$ were to determine wage income, profit income, and the value of the demogrant, that is:

$$V_+^i(E^1, \ldots, E^n) = u^i(x^i(I^i[0], E^i), y^i(I^i[0], E^i), E^i) . \qquad (13.6)$$

Incorporated in the payoff function is the assumption that at her personal part of the community effort vector, agent i has chosen her *commodity* demands optimally, given the income generated.

Thus, given a vector of prices $\mathbf{p} = (p_1, p_2, w, r)$ and the ownership shares of firms, a game whose strategies are effort/labor supplies is defined, denoted $\mathbf{V_+}$. We can define its additive Kantian equilibrium, which is a vector of labor supplies $\mathbf{E} = (E^1, \ldots, E^n)$, satisfying:

$$(\forall i)(\arg\max_{\rho} u^i(x^i(I^i[\rho], E^i + \rho), y^i(I^i[\rho], E^i + \rho)) = 0. \qquad (13.7)$$

13.4 Walras-Kant Market-Socialist Equilibrium with Taxation

The data of the economy are $(u^1, \ldots, u^n; G, H; \bar{E}^1, \ldots, \bar{E}^n; \{\theta^{il}, i = 0, \ldots, n; l = 1, 2\}; K_0)$. It is useful, for conceptualizing Pareto efficiency, to define the utility function of the state, which is:

$$u^0(x) = x. \qquad (13.8)$$

That is, the state cares only about Good 1, which it uses for investment.

We now define:

DEFINITION 13.1 A *Walras-Kant (additive) market-socialist equilibrium at tax rate t* consists of:

183

(*i*) a price vector (p_1, p_2, w, r);

(*ii*) labor and capital demands by the two firms of D^1, D^2 and K^1, K^2, respectively;

(*iii*) labor supplies (E^{i1}, E^{i2}) by all workers *i* to Firms 1 and 2; and

(*iv*) for all private agents *i*, commodity demands (x^i, y^i) for the outputs of Firms 1 and 2, respectively, and a demand for the first good by the state of x^0;

such that:

(*v*) at given prices, (K^l, D^l) maximizes profits of Firm *l*, for $l = 1,2$;

(*vi*) the labor supply vector $\mathbf{E} = (E^1, \ldots, E^n)$, where $E^i = E^{i1} + E^{i2}$ constitutes an additive Kantian equilibrium at the given prices of the game $\mathbf{V}_+$, as defined in (13.6);

(*vii*) (x^i, y^i) maximizes the utility of agent *i*, given prices, her labor supply, and her income, given by (13.1);

(*viii*) x^0 maximizes the state's utility u^0 subject to its budget constraint $p_1 x^0 \leq \theta^{01} \Pi^1 + \theta^{02} \Pi^2 + r K_0$; and

(*ix*) all markets clear; that is, $D^l = \sum_i E^{il}$ for $l = 1,2$, $x^S = G(K^1, D^1)$, $y^S = H(K^2, D^2)$, and $K_0 = K^1 + K^2$.

The depreciation rate of capital is set at zero. Thus, at the beginning of the (imaginary) next period, the state's endowment of the capital good would be $K_0 + \dfrac{I^0}{p_1}$ (see equation (13.3)).

13.5 The First Theorem of Welfare Economics
for Market Socialism

The appropriate concept of Pareto efficiency will be called *investment-constrained Pareto efficiency*. An allocation is investment-constrained Pareto efficient if there is no other feasible allocation that makes at least one agent better off without harming any agent, where the state is included as an agent. Since the model is not intertemporal, it is important to qualify the kind of Pareto efficiency that can be realized: citizens cannot trade off present against future consumption in the model, and hence we cannot speak of efficiency in the full sense. To say this more straightforwardly: the state's investment is determined by its endowment of capital, not by any considerations of the population's future welfare. We know that both the Soviet Union and post-1949 China probably invested too much, committing their populations to excessively low consumption. Such can happen in this model, too.

One can show that, with differentiability and the usual convexity assumptions on utility and production functions, an interior allocation[2] is investment-constrained Pareto efficient exactly when:

$$(a)\sum_{i=0}^{n} x^i = G(K^1, E^{1S}) \quad (b)\sum_{i=1}^{n} y^i = H(K^2, E^{2S})$$

$$(c)\sum_{i=1}^{n} E^i = E^{1S} + E^{2S} \quad (d)K^1 + K^2 = K_0$$

$$(e)(\forall i)G_2(K^1, E^{1S}) = -\frac{u_3^i(x^i, y^i, E^i)}{u_1^i(x^i, y^i, E^i)}$$

$$(f)(\forall i)H_2(K^2, E^{2S}) = -\frac{u_3^i(x^i, y^i, E^i)}{u_2^i(x^i, y^i, E^i)} \quad (g)\frac{G_2}{G_1} = \frac{H_2}{H_1}$$

$$\text{, (13.9)}$$

where $G_1 \equiv \dfrac{\partial G}{\partial K}$, and so on.

Conditions (a)–(d) specify feasibility; conditions (e)–(g) specify efficiency.

PROPOSITION 13.1 *Assume differentiability of the production functions and the utility functions. Assume that the production functions are concave and the utility functions are strictly concave. Let $(p_1, p_2, w, r, \mathbf{E}^1, \mathbf{E}^2, \mathbf{D}^1, \mathbf{D}^2, K^1, K^2, \mathbf{x}, \mathbf{y})$ comprise a Walras-Kant (additive) market-socialist equilibrium at any income tax rate $t \in [0,1]$. Then the induced allocation is investment-constrained Pareto efficient.*

PROOF.

1. Although the theorem's statement assumes that the equilibrium is interior, this is easy to relax, with a concomitant alteration of the first-order conditions.

2. At a Walras-Kant equilibrium at tax rate t, profit maximization gives:

$$p_1 G_2(K^1, E^{S1}) = w = p_2 H_2(K^2, E^{S2}) \text{ and } p_1 G_1 = r = p_2 H_1, \quad (13.10)$$

and clearing of the capital market tells us that $K^1 + K^2 = K_0$. Therefore, it follows from (13.9) that an interior equilibrium is investment-constrained Pareto efficient if and only if:

$$(\forall 1 \le i \le n)(-\frac{u_3^i(x^i,y^i,E^i)}{u_1^i(x^i,y^i,E^i)} = \frac{w}{p_1} \ \& -\frac{u_3^i(x^i,y^i,E^i)}{u_2^i(x^i,y^i,E^i)} = \frac{w}{p_2}). \quad (13.11)$$

3. Consider the program:

$$\max_{x,y} u^i(x,y,E)$$

$$\text{subj. to}$$

$$p_1 x + p_2 y = I \ ,$$

where E and I are fixed. Denote the solution $(x^i(I;E), y^i(I;E))$. The first-order conditions for the solution of the program are:

$$p_2 u_1^i(x^i(I;E), y^i(I;E), E) - p_1 u_2^i(x^i(I,E), y^i(I,E), E) = 0$$
$$p_1 x^i(I,E) + p_2 y^i(I;E) - I = 0 \quad (13.12)$$

By the implicit function theorem, the functions (x^i, y^i) are differentiable, and their derivatives are given by:

$$x_1^i(I,E) = \frac{p_1 u_{22}^i - p_2 u_{12}^i}{(p_2, -p_1)U^i(p_2, -p_1)^T}, \quad (13.13)$$

$$y_1^i(I,E) = \frac{p_2 u_{11}^i - p_1 u_{12}^i}{(p_2, -p_1)U^i(p_2, -p_1)^T}, \quad (13.14)$$

$$x_2^i(I,E) = \frac{p_2(p_1 u_{23}^i - p_2 u_{13}^i)}{(p_2, -p_1)U^i(p_2, -p_1)^T}, \text{ and} \quad (13.15)$$

$$y_2^i(I,E) = \frac{p_1(p_1 u_{23}^i - p_1 u_{23}^i)}{(p_2, -p_1)U^i(p_2, -p_1)^T}, \quad (13.16)$$

where U^i is the leading principal submatrix of order two of the Hessian of the function u^i and the superscript ^{T} indicates "transpose." Note that the implicit function theorem indeed applies because U^i is negative definite by the strict concavity of u^i, and so the denominators of equations (13.13)–(13.16) do not vanish.

4. Now the labor-supply vector is an interior additive Kantian equilibrium of the game V_+ if and only if:

for all $i \geq 1$, $\left. \dfrac{d}{d\rho} \right|_{\rho=0} u^i \left(x^i(I^i[\rho], E^i + \rho), y^i(I^i[\rho], E^i + \rho), E^i + \rho \right) = 0$. (13.17)

This statement reduces to:

$$u_1^i \cdot \left(x_1^i I^{i\prime}[0] + x_2^i \right) + u_2^i \cdot \left(y_1^i I^{i\prime}[0] + y_2^i \right) + u_3^i = 0,$$ (13.18)

where $I^{i\prime}[0] \equiv \left. \dfrac{dI^i(E^i + \rho, E^{S1} + \lambda n\rho, E^{S2} + (1-\lambda)n\rho)}{d\rho} \right|_{\rho=0}$.

5. From (13.4), calculate that:

$$I^{i\prime}[0] = (1-t)w + (1-t)(\theta^{i1}\Pi_2^1(K^1, E^{S1})\lambda n +$$
$$\theta^{i2}\Pi_2^2(K^2, E^{S2})(1-\lambda)n +$$
$$\frac{t}{n}\begin{pmatrix} p_1 G_2(K^1, E^{S1})\lambda n + p_2 H_2(K^2, E^{S2})(1-\lambda)n - \\ (\theta^{01}\Pi_2^1(K^1, E^{S1})\lambda n - \theta^{02}\Pi_2^2(K^2, E^{S2})(1-\lambda)n) \end{pmatrix}.$$ (13.19)

Since the four partial derivatives $(\Pi_1^1, \Pi_2^1, \Pi_1^2, \Pi_2^2)$ of the firms' profit functions are zero, by profit maximization, and $p_1 G_2 = p_1 H_2 = w$, (13.19) reduces to:

$$I^{i\prime}[0] = (1-t)w + tw = w,$$ (13.20)

for any t. It is now evident why we did not have to specify how workers allocate the increment r in labor between the two firms: the parameter λ does not appear in condition (13.20).

We therefore write the condition for Kantian equilibrium of labor supplies, equation (13.18), as:

$$u_1^i \cdot (x_1^i w + x_2^i) + u_2^i \cdot \left(y_1^i w + y_2^i \right) + u_3^i = 0.$$ (13.21)

6. We now expand equation (13.21) by making a sequence of substitutions: (i) substitute the expressions for the four derivatives of the x^i and y^i functions from (13.13) through (13.16), and (ii) eliminate p_1 via the substitution $p_1 = \dfrac{p_2 u_1^i}{u_2^i}$, the first-order condition from (13.12). So doing reduces (13.21) to:

$$\frac{u_1^i}{d}\left(w \frac{p_2 u_1^i}{u_2^i} u_{22}^i - w p_2 u_{12}^i + p_2(\frac{p_2 u_1^i}{u_2^i} u_{23}^i - p_2 u_{13}^i) \right) +$$
$$\frac{u_2^i}{d}\left(w p_2 u_{11}^i - w p_2 \frac{u_1^i}{u_2^i} u_{12}^i + \frac{p_2 u_1^i}{u_2^i}(p_2 u_{13}^i - \frac{p_2 u_1^i}{u_2^i} u_{13}^i) \right) +$$ (13.22)
$$u_3^i = 0,$$

where $d = (p_2, -p_1)U^i(p_2, -p_1)^T = p_2^2\left(\dfrac{u_1^i}{u_2^i}, -1\right)U^i\left(\dfrac{u_1^i}{u_2^i}, -1\right)^T$, which is a negative number. Last, divide both sides of equation (13.22) by the positive number u_2^i, simplify, and calculate that that equation reduces to:

$$\frac{w}{p_2} = -\frac{u_3^i}{u_2^i},\tag{13.23}$$

which is one of the two required efficiency conditions for agent i.

7. Now substitute for p_2 in the last equation using $p_2 = \dfrac{p_1 u_2^i}{u_1^i}$, yielding:

$$\frac{w}{p_1} = -\frac{u_3^i}{u_1^i}.\tag{13.24}$$

By equations (13.23), (13.24), and (13.11), the proposition is proved. ■

The key move in the proof is to show that, regardless of the tax rate, when a worker thinks of all workers as varying their labor supplies in the amount that she is contemplating varying her own, she internalizes the externality generated by her labor-supply choice—a choice that affects firm profits and tax revenues. Her own action causes a negligible change in these magnitudes, but of course the aggregate effect of many small changes is significant. The *additive counterfactual* in the universal change in labor supplies and *linear income taxation* combine in such a way as to exactly cancel the deadweight loss of taxation that afflicts Nash optimization in the labor-supply decision. (This is the meaning of equation (13.20), the key to the proof.) This kind of pairing—associating a specific cooperative optimization protocol with a particular allocation rule, where the two together deliver Pareto efficiency—is a feature of Kantian equilibrium in simpler (nonmarket) environments, as we have seen in Part I. What's new here is combining additive Kantian optimization with markets.

A remark on why the incentive problem, causing deadweight losses in the standard model, does not bite here. Consider, for dramatic effect, an income tax rate of one, and suppose that every worker is supplying zero labor (as he would in the standard Nash-type model at this tax rate). But here, by using the Kantian optimization protocol, a worker balances his share of an increase of the demogrant that would occur if *all* workers increased their labor supply from zero to some small positive ρ against his (very small) disutility of labor at zero. The trade-off is usually worth it, even though his after-tax wage is zero. Consequently, at the Kantian equilibrium, even at a tax rate of unity, (most) workers will supply a positive amount of labor.

13.6 An Example of Walras-Kant (Additive) Market-Socialist Equilibrium

Because capital allocation is passive in this model, let's simplify by studying an economic environment where the capital inputs are fixed, there is no state, and we model production as a function of labor only:

$$G(E) = E - \frac{a}{2}E^2, H(E) = E - \frac{b}{2}E^2$$

$$u^i(x, y, E) = x^{1/3} y^{1/3} (\bar{E}^i - E)^{1/3}, \text{for } i = 1, \ldots, n \tag{13.25}$$

There are n agents, and the total endowment of labor is $\bar{E}^S = \sum_{i=1}^{n} \bar{E}^i$. We let $\theta^{i1} = \theta^{i2} = \frac{1}{n}$ for all $1 \leq i \leq n$. We set $\theta^{01} = \theta^{02} = 0$. We normalize the price vector by choosing $w = 1$. There is no market for capital and hence no interest rate.

An interior allocation is a Walras-Kant market-socialist equilibrium at income tax rate t when the allocation is Pareto efficient, the income of i is given by (13.1), and markets clear. (The critical condition that the labor supplies comprise a Kantian equilibrium of the game $\mathbf{V}_+$ is embedded in the efficiency conditions, as the proof of Proposition 1 shows.) We write these conditions as:

$$1 - aE^{S1} = \frac{1}{p_1}, 1 - bE^{S2} = \frac{1}{p_2} \quad (\text{MRT}^l = w / p_l)$$

$$\frac{x^i}{\bar{E}^i - E^i} = \frac{1}{p_1}, \frac{y^i}{\bar{E}^i - E^i} = \frac{1}{p_2} \quad (\text{MRT}^l = \text{MRS}) \tag{13.26}$$

and (13.1) holds for all i. By (13.26), the post-fisc income of agent i is given by $I^i = p_1 x^i + p_2 y^i = 2(\bar{E}^i - E_i)$. Hence, (13.1) can be written:

$$2(\bar{E}^i - E^i) = (1 - t)E^i + \frac{1-t}{n}(\Pi^1 + \Pi^2) + \frac{t}{n}(G(E^{S1}) + H(E^{S2})) =$$

$$(1-t)E^i + \frac{p_1 G(E^{S1}) + p_2 H(E^{S2})}{n} - \frac{(1-t)}{n}(E^{S1} + E^{S2}) \tag{13.27}$$

By adding up the equations over all i in (13.26), we have:

$$p_1 x^S = p_1 G(E^{S1}) = \bar{E}^S - (E^{S1} + E^{S2}),$$
$$p_2 y^S = p_2 H(E^{S2}) = \bar{E}^S - (E^{S1} + E^{S2}) \qquad (13.28)$$

Now using the expressions for commodity prices in (13.26), we write these equations as:

$$\frac{G(E^{S1})}{1 - aE^{S1}} = \bar{E}^S - (E^{S1} + E^{S2}), \frac{H(E^{S2})}{1 - bE^{S2}} = \bar{E}^S - (E^{S1} + E^{S2}). \qquad (13.29)$$

System (13.29) comprises two equations in the two unknowns E^{S1} and E^{S2}; the solution must be a vector $(E^{S1}, E^{S2}) \in (0, \frac{1}{a}) \times (0, \frac{1}{b})$. Thus total production at Walras-Kant equilibrium for this economy, if such exists, is independent of the tax rate t. Profits are also independent of t. Taxation simply redistributes an invariant output vector of commodities.

Parameterize the example with $(a, b) = (0.1, 0.2)$, $\bar{E}^S = 10, n = 100$. We have not yet specified the individual endowments $\bar{E}^i$. We solve (13.29):

$$E^{S1} = 3.28, E^{S2} = 2.63. \qquad (13.30)$$

Profits are positive for both firms and comprise 28 percent of national income.

To complete the analysis, we must specify the $\{\bar{E}^i\}$ and solve for $\{E^i\}$. Rewrite equation (13.27) as:

$$2\bar{E}^i + E^i(t - 3) = \frac{\Pi^1 + \Pi^2}{n} + \frac{t}{n}(E^{S1} + E^{S2}). \qquad (13.31)$$

Examination shows that equation (13.31) possesses an interior solution in which $E^i \in (0, \bar{E}^i)$ for all i exactly when:

$$\text{for all } i, \quad \bar{E}^i > \frac{1}{2n}(\Pi^1 + \Pi^2 + t(E^{S1} + E^{S2})). \qquad (13.32)$$

If, on the other hand, (13.32) is false for some i, then there is no interior equilibrium.

It is of interest to compute the lower bound on the labor endowment that will guarantee an interior Walras-Kant equilibrium at tax rate t. From (13.32), this depends on the tax rate. We compute this lower bound for various tax rates for our example as in table 13.1.

Table 13.1 The minimum value of $\bar{E}^i$ supporting an interior
Walras-Kant equilibrium as a function of the tax rate

Tax rate t	min $\bar{E}^i$
0	0
0.1	0
0.2	0
0.3	0
0.4	0
0.5	0.003
0.6	0.011
0.7	0.018
0.8	0.026
0.9	0.033
1.0	0.041

Recall that the average labor endowment with our parameterization is $\dfrac{\bar{E}^S}{n} = 0.1$. From the table, a Walras-Kant market-socialist equilibrium exists where all agents work regardless of the distribution of individual labor endowments, as long as $t \leq 0.4$. But as the tax rate rises, the restriction on the distribution of labor endowments bites.

For tax rates larger than 40 percent, equilibrium still exists, but workers who are insufficiently skilled do not work. We illustrate with a second paramaterization. The utility functions and production parameters are as before, but we examine an economy with two agents ($n = 2$), where $\bar{E}^1 = 9, \bar{E}^2 = 1$. If both agents work, then E^{S1} and E^{S2} are given by (13.30). Let us look for an equilibrium where $t = 1$. Both agents must then have the same after-tax income. Inequality (13.32) is false for agent 1, so there is no equilibrium at $t = 1$ where both agents work. We therefore set agent 2's labor supply to zero: $E^2 = 0$. The other equations characterizing a Walras-Kant market-socialist equilibrium are:

$$\frac{x^1}{\overline{E}^1 - (E^{11} + E^{12})} = \frac{1}{p_1}, \frac{y^1}{\overline{E}^1 - (E^{11} + E^{12})} = \frac{1}{p_2},$$

$$G'(E^{11}) = \frac{1}{p_1}, \ H'(E^{12}) = \frac{1}{p_2}$$

$$x^1 = x^2, \ y^1 = y^2,$$

$$G(E^{11}) = x^1 + x^2, H(E^{12}) = y^1 + y^2,$$

$$\frac{x^2}{\overline{E}^2} \geq \frac{1}{p_1}, \frac{y^2}{\overline{E}^2} \geq \frac{1}{p_2}.$$

(13.33)

The two equations in the first line say that the marginal rates of substitution for the agent with positive labor supply equal the correct price ratios; the second line says that the marginal rates of transformation equal the correct price ratios; the third line is true because when the tax rate is 1, both agents have the same (post-fisc) income, and so consume the two commodities identically; the fourth line expresses market clearing for the two commodities; and the fifth line expresses the efficiency condition for the agent who supplies zero labor. The solution is given by:

$$x^1 = x^2 = 1.513, y^1 = y^2 = 1.024,$$

$$p^1 = 1.592, p^2 = 2.352, E^{11} = 3.717, E^{12} = 2.874$$

(13.34)

13.7 Existence of Walras-Kant Market-Socialist Equilibrium

We first note:

PROPOSITION 13.2 *Let* $(p_1, p_2, w, r, \mathbf{E}^1, \mathbf{E}^2, \mathbf{D}^1, \mathbf{D}^2, K^1, K^2, \mathbf{x}, \mathbf{y})$ *be a Walrasian equilibrium at* $t = 0$. (The state is simply another agent that desires to consume only the first good and possesses no labor endowment.) *Then it is also an additive Walras-Kant market-socialist equilibrium at* $t = 0$.

PROOF. We know that the allocation is investment-constrained Pareto efficient by the usual first welfare theorem for private-ownership economies. The income equation (13.1) holds by definition of Walrasian equilibrium. We need only show that the labor supplies comprise a Kantian equilibrium, which is to say that equation (13.21) holds. But we have shown that this is equivalent to the efficiency conditions that $MRS^i = MRT$. These conditions hold by hypothesis, since the allocation is Walrasian and therefore Pareto efficient, and the claim is proved. ∎

We assume:

ASSUMPTION A.

(i) G,H are unbounded, concave, and homothetic, and the Inada conditions hold; and

(ii) all consumer preferences are representable by strictly concave, differentiable utility functions, and both commodities are normal goods for all consumers.

Let Δ^3 be the 3-simplex of price vectors $\mathbf{p} = (p_1, p_2, w, r)$. We define a correspondence on the domain $\operatorname{int}\Delta^3$. Let Q be any real number and $Q^{i^*}(\cdot)$ be positive continuous functions on $\operatorname{int}\Delta^3$. Let:

$$A^i(p_1, p_2, w; Q) = \arg\max_{x,y,E}\{u^i(x,y,E) \mid p_1 x + p_2 y = wE + Q\}$$

$$B^i(p_1, p_2, w; Q^t) = \{(x,y,E) \in \Re_+^2 \times \qquad\qquad (13.35)$$
$$[0, \bar{E}^i] \mid p_1 x + p_2 y = (1-t)wE + Q^t(\mathbf{p})\}$$

Now define $\Gamma^i : \operatorname{int}\Delta^3 \rightarrow\rightarrow \Re_+^3$ by:

$$\Gamma^i(p_1, p_2, w; Q^*(\mathbf{p})) = \bigcup_{\infty > Q \geq \tilde{Q}} A^i(p_1, p_2, w; Q) \bigcap B^i(p_1, p_2, w; Q^{i^*}(\mathbf{p})), \qquad (13.36)$$

where $\tilde{Q} = Q^{i^*}(\mathbf{p}) - tw\bar{E}^i$. $\tilde{Q}$ may be positive, zero, or negative. Last, define:

$$\Gamma(p_1, p_2, w; Q^*(\mathbf{p})) = \Gamma^1(p_1, p_2, w; Q^{1^*}(\mathbf{p})) \times \ldots$$
$$\times \Gamma^n(p_1, p_2, w; Q^{n^*}(\mathbf{p})) \qquad\qquad (13.37)$$

LEMMA 13.3 Let $t \in (0,1]$ and $(p_1, p_2, w, r) \in \operatorname{int}\Delta$. Let $Q^{i^*} : \operatorname{int}\Delta \to \Re_{++}$ be continuous functions for all i. If Assumption A(ii) holds, then Γ is a (nonempty) continuous function mapping $\operatorname{int}\Delta \to \prod_{i=1}^{n}(\Re_+^2 \times [0, \bar{E}^i])$.

PROOF.

1. It suffices to show that Γ^i is single-valued and continuous for any i. By strict concavity of preferences, the correspondence A^i is single-valued and continuous on $\operatorname{int}\Delta$. Suppose that Γ^i contains two elements—that is, there are allocations $(x_\nu, y_\nu, E_\nu) \in A^i(p_1, p_2, w; Q_\nu) \bigcap B^i(p_1, p_2, w; Q^*(\mathbf{p}))$, for $\nu = 1,2$, with $Q_2 > Q_1$. It follows that:

$$p_1(\delta x) + p_2(\delta y) = w(\delta E) + (\delta Q)$$
$$p_1(\delta x) + p_2(\delta y) = (1 - t)w(\delta E) \qquad (13.38)$$

where $\delta x \equiv x_2 - x_1$, and so on. Therefore, the quantities on the right-hand sides of the two equations in (13.38) are equal, implying that:

$$\delta Q = -tw\delta E, \qquad (13.39)$$

and so $\delta E < 0$ (note $t > 0$ by assumption). Therefore:

$$p_1 x_2 + p_2 y_2 = (1 - t)wE_2 + Q^*(\mathbf{p}) < (1 - t)wE_1$$
$$+ Q^*(\mathbf{p}) = p_1 x_1 + p_2 y_1 \qquad (13.40)$$

and so either $x_2 < x_1$ or $y_2 < y_1$. But since $(x_\nu, y_\nu, E_\nu) \in A^i(p_1, p_2, w; Q_\nu)$ for $\nu = 1,2$, it must be that $x_2 > x_1$ and $y_2 > y_1$ because both commodities are normal goods, and the consumer's wealth (check the definition of A^i) is greater at $\nu = 2$ than at $\nu = 1$. This contradiction proves that Γ^i contains at most one element.

2. Next we show that Γ^i contains at least one element. $B^i(p_1, p_2, w; Q^{i^*})$ is a *planar segment*. We say that a point (x, y, E) lies *above* (respectively, *below*) the planar segment $B^i(p_1, p_2, w; Q^{i^*})$ if it lies in the positive orthant and $p_1 x + p_2 y < (1 - t)wE + Q^{i^*}$ (respectively, $p_1 x + p_2 y > (1 - t)wE + Q^{i^*}$). Note that the points on planar segment

$$p_1 x + p_2 y = wE + \tilde{Q}, \quad (x, y, E) \in \Re_+^2 \times [0, \bar{E}^i]$$

lie entirely below (or, at one point, on) the planar segment $B^i(p_1, p_2, w; Q^{i^*})$ because:

$$wE + \tilde{Q} = wE + Q^{i^*} - tw\bar{E}^i \leq wE + Q^{i^*}$$
$$-twE = (1 - t)wE + Q^{i^*} \qquad (13.41)$$

It therefore follows that $A^i(p_1, p_2, w; \tilde{Q})$ lies below (or possibly on) the planar segment $B^i(p_1, p_2, w; Q^{i^*})$. On the other hand, for large values of Q, the points of

$$p_1 x + p_2 y = wE + Q, \quad (x, y, E) \in \Re_+^2 \times [0, \bar{E}^i]$$

must lie entirely above B^i. Since $A^i(p_1, p_2, w; Q)$ is a continuous function of Q, by the Berge maximum theorem, it follows that there exists at least one value of Q such that $A^i(p_1, p_2, w; Q) \cap B^i(p_1, p_2, w; Q^{i^*}) \neq \varnothing$. Thus, Γ^i is a well-defined function.

3. Continuity of Γ^i follows from Berge's maximum theorem. ∎

PROPOSITION 13.4 *Let an economic environment* $\{u, \theta, G, H, \bar{E}, K_0\}$ *be given, and let Assumption A hold. Suppose that* $\bar{E}^i > 0$ *for all (private) agents and that* $\theta^{01} + \theta^{02} < 2$. *Then a Walras-Kant equilibrium exists for any* $0 \leq t < 1$.

PROOF.

1. The theorem is true for $t = 0$ by Proposition 13.2, since a Walrasian equilibrium exists at $t = 0$ under the stated premises. Henceforth, we assume $0 < t < 1$.

2. Given a price vector $(p_1, p_2, w, r) \in \text{int } \Delta^3$, define (D^1, D^2, K^1, K^2) to be the solution of:

$$
\begin{aligned}
(K^1, D^1) &= \underset{(K,E)}{\arg\max}(p_1 G(K, E) - wE - rK) \\
(K^2, D^2) &= \underset{(K,E)}{\arg\max}(p_2 H(K, E) - wE - rK)
\end{aligned}
\tag{13.42}
$$

Note that, by Assumption A(i), the solution exists and satisfies:

$$
G_2(K^1, D^1) = \frac{w}{p_1}, \quad H_2(K^2, D^2) = \frac{w}{p_2},
$$

$$
G_1(K^1, D^1) = \frac{r}{p_1}, \quad H_1(K^2, D^2) = \frac{r}{p_2}
$$

3. The profits of the two firms and the value of the demogrant are defined at (D^1, D^2, K^1, K^2). Profits are positive for any price vector $(p_1, p_2, w, r) \in \text{int } \Delta^3$. We now consider the budget constraints of individuals:

$$
\begin{aligned}
p_1 x + p_2 y ={}& (1-t)wE + (1-t)\big(\theta^{i1}\Pi^1(K^1, D^1) + \theta^{i2}\Pi^2(K^2, D^2)\big) + \\
& \frac{t}{n}(p_1 G(K^1, D^1) + p_2 H(K^2, D^2) - \theta^{01}\Pi^1(K^1, D^1) - \\
& \theta^{02}\Pi^2(K^2, D^2) - r(K^1 + K^2))
\end{aligned}
\tag{13.43}
$$

and the budget constraint of the state at the firms' demands:

$$
p_1 x^0 = \theta^{01}\Pi^1(K^1, D^1) + \theta^{02}\Pi^2(K^2, D^2) + r(K^1 + K^2).
\tag{13.44}
$$

Let $Q^{i^*}(\mathbf{p})$ equal the sum of the last two terms on the right-hand side of equation (13.43). By the theorem's premise, all private agents have positive income at any $(p_1, p_2, w, r) \in \text{int } \Delta^3$, because the state does not receive all the firms' profits by assumption, and the tax rate is positive. $Q^{i^*}(\cdot)$ are positive continuous functions, and so the premises of Lemma 13.3 hold; therefore, the functions $\Gamma^i(p_1, p_2, w; Q^{i^*}(\mathbf{p}))$ are defined and continuous. Henceforth, we write $\Gamma^i(p_1, p_2, w; Q^{i^*}) \equiv \Gamma^i(\mathbf{p})$. Let $(x^i, y^i, E^i) = \Gamma^i(\mathbf{p})$ for $i \geq 1$.

4. Define the excess demand functions at a vector $\mathbf{p} = (p_1, p_2, w, r) \in \text{int } \Delta$:

$$\Delta E = D^1 + D^2 - \sum E^i, \quad \Delta x = \sum_{i=0}^{n} x^i - G(K^1, D^1),$$

$$\Delta y = \sum_{i=1}^{n} y^i - H(K^2, D^2), \quad \Delta K = K^1 + K^2 - K_0$$

(13.45)

Define the excess demand function for the economy by:

$$z(\mathbf{p}) = (\Delta x, \Delta y, (1-t)\Delta E, (1-t)\Delta K).$$

(13.46)

Next, define the correspondence Φ on Δ as in equations (11.8) and (11.9), above.

5. By summing the budget constraints in (13.43) and (13.44) we verify Walras's Law for this economy, defined on $\text{int } \Delta^3$:

$$p_1 \Delta x + p_2 \Delta y + (1-t)w\Delta E + (1-t)r\Delta K = z(\mathbf{p}) \cdot \mathbf{p} = 0.$$

(13.47)

6. At a fixed point $\mathbf{p}$ of Φ, $z(\mathbf{p}) = 0$. Consequently, $\Delta x = \Delta y = (1-t)\Delta E = (1-t)\Delta K = 0$, and all markets clear. We deduce $\Delta E = \Delta K = 0$ from the premise that $1 - t > 0$.

7. Associated with these prices is an allocation $(\mathbf{x}, \mathbf{y}, \mathbf{E})$, with $(x^i, y^i, E^i) \in \Gamma^i(\mathbf{p})$ for all $1 \leq i \leq n$. We must show that $(E^1, \ldots, E^n)$ is a K^+ equilibrium at prices $\mathbf{p}$. This follows immediately from the definition of the functions Γ^i, because the first-order conditions for Kantian equilibrium, which were derived in the proof of Proposition 13.1 and are stated in equations (13.23) and (13.24) follow from the fact that $(x^i, y^i, E^i) \in A^i(p_1, p_2, w; Q)$ for some constant Q. And the fact that $(x^i, y^i, E^i) \in B^i(p_1, p_2, w; Q^*(\mathbf{p}))$ means that (x^i, y^i, E^i) satisfies i's budget constraint, so the commodity demands are optimal for i, given her income.

8. Thus, a fixed point of Φ is a Walras-Kant market-socialist equilibrium at tax rate t. To show the existence of a fixed point, we need to check that

the premises of Kakutani's fixed point theorem hold. Φ is obviously convex-valued. Upper hemicontinuity of Φ at any point in $\mathrm{int}\,\Delta$ follows quickly.

Last, we examine the upper hemicontinuity of Φ at points on the boundary of the simplex. Suppose that $\mathbf{p}^j = (p_1^j, p_2^j, w^j, r^j) \to \mathbf{p} \in \partial\Delta^3$. Suppose that the sign pattern of $\mathbf{p}$ is $(+,+,0,+)$. We have $\Phi(p_1, p_2, w, r) = \{(0,0,1,0)\}$. Eventually p_1^j, p_2^j, r^j are positive and bounded away from zero, and $w^j \to 0$.

We must show that $\lim_{j \to \infty} \Phi(\mathbf{p}^j) = (0,0,1,0)$. Without loss of generality, we may assume that $\mathbf{p}^j \in \mathrm{int}\,\Delta^3$ for all j. Denote the excess demands at $\mathbf{p}^j$ by $\Delta x(j), \Delta y(j), \Delta E(j)$, and $\Delta K(j)$. We will show that, for j sufficiently large,

$$\Delta E(j) > \max[\Delta x(j), \Delta y(j), \Delta K(j)], \qquad (13.48)$$

and this will imply that, for sufficiently large j, $\Phi(\mathbf{p}^j) = (0,0,1,0)$. To show (13.48), we will show that $\dfrac{\Delta z(j)}{\Delta E(j)} \to 0$, for $z \in \{x, y, K\}$.

We show that $\dfrac{\Delta K(j)}{\Delta E(j)} \to 0$. We know that $\Delta E(j) \to \infty$, because $w^j \to 0$, and so the firms will demand unbounded amounts of labor, while the supply of labor is bounded. If $\Delta K(j)$ were bounded above, we would be done. So we suppose that $\Delta K(j)$ is unbounded. It follows that for at least one firm — say, the G firm — $K^{1j} \to \infty$ and $D^{1j} \to \infty$. But by profit maximization, $\dfrac{G_2(K^{1j}, D^{1j})}{G_1(K^{1j}, D^{1j})} = \dfrac{w^j}{r^j} \to 0$. By homotheticity of G (Assumption A(i)), the points (K^{1j}, D^{1j}) must eventually lie below any ray in the positive quadrant of (K,D) space. This implies that $\dfrac{\Delta K(j)}{\Delta E(j)} \to 0$, as required.

The other cases of points on $\partial\Delta^3$ yield to similar analysis. Hence, the premises of Kakutani's theorem hold, and a fixed point in $\mathrm{int}\,\Delta^3$, which is a Walras-Kant market-socialist equilibrium, exists. ■

13.8 A Market-Socialist Design Where Investors Are Kantian Cooperators

Note that in the model just presented, Kantian optimization in one market, the labor market, suffices to guarantee Pareto efficiency at the equilibrium, for any tax rate in the unit interval. In this section, I present a model where, again, Kantian optimization occurs in only one market, but this time it is the capital market. Private investors make their investment decisions using the additive Kantian protocol, and again we can completely separate efficiency from "equity."

I propose here a two-period model, so that investors face the usual decision in which they must trade off consumption in different periods by investing. Investment, that is to say, is not passive as it is in the model presented in the above sections. In the market-socialist literature, capital investment in firms has almost always been relegated to a public institution—either the state treasury or publicly owned banks. Pranab Bardhan (1993) and Bardhan and Roemer (1992) advocate a system of main banks, modeled after the Japanese practice, each of which is responsible for monitoring firms in its orbit and raising investment funds for them. Leland Stauber (1987) recommends that investment be handled by nonprofit institutions of various kinds, including ones owned by local governmental bodies. Roemer (1994) suggests that investment be carried out by the state treasury but that the value of firms be determined by a stock market in which individuals can trade stock denominated in a special "coupon" currency.

Here, I propose how investment can be decentralized completely, with investment decisions made by individuals who own capital, and no intermediary institutions. This immediately raises two problems: first, it would seem that capital income would then naturally become unequal, contradicting the main distributional goal of socialism, which is to equalize the distribution of capital income in a country. Second, there would be no natural monitors of firm behavior, because no investor would have a large enough position in any firm to have the incentive to monitor its management. I deal with the first problem through redistributive income taxation. I do not address the second problem here: this proposal should be viewed as exactly analogous to the general equilibrium model of Arrow and Debreu, where individuals own capital goods and decide how much to invest in firms based on the utility-maximization calculus. The firm-monitoring problem is ignored there as well. To deal with it, intermediary institutions between individuals and firms, such as banks, would have to exist to channel investments by individuals to firms. Describing the governance of such institutions is another question.

Why is this exercise worthwhile, given my decision to ignore the institutional structure that must intermediate between investors and firms? Because the theory I present addresses a major issue—perhaps *the* major issue—in socialist finance, which is this: in a market economy, individuals (households) will accumulate savings at different rates, based on their differential rates of time preference and differential skills, the latter leading to differential wage incomes. The socialist mechanism must channel these savings into capital investment, and in a way that does not lead to massively differential capital incomes among the citizenry. How to accomplish this is perhaps the most important conceptual problem for market socialism, and the problem is addressed in its starkest form in the general equilibrium model of Arrow and Debreu.

To summarize, I propose how a precise formulation of cooperative investment behavior can achieve equilibria in a market economy that are:

- decentralized;
- Pareto efficient; and
- egalitarian.

This leaves us to ponder whether the foundation on which the theory rests, Kantian optimization, is a psychologically realistic protocol that humans might be able to achieve or whether it is simply a mathematical trick whose achievement, given human nature and cognitive capacity, would be utopian.

13.9 The Economic Environment

I wish to propose the simplest possible model in which to present these ideas. There will be one firm, which produces a single good from capital and labor, whose production function is a concave, increasing function G. With capital and labor inputs K and L, where L is measured in efficiency units, the output of the good is $G(K,L)$. The good can be either consumed or used as capital.

The economy will last for two periods. Production occurs only in period one. There are n citizens; citizen i has a utility function $u^i(x_1^i) + \beta^i u^i(x_2^i)$, where u^i is a concave function and x_j^i is the consumption of individual i in period j, for $j = 1,2$. β^i is the subjective time discount factor for agent i. At the beginning of period one, citizen i possesses an endowment of the good in amount W_0^i, and this endowment may be used either for consumption or for investment in the firm. When invested and used by the firm, capital depreciates at a rate d. The total capital K that is invested in period one will be returned to the economy in amount $(1-d)K$ in period two and will then be consumed.

Citizens are also endowed with different amounts of labor in efficiency units: let the efficiency units of labor possessed by citizen i be denoted L^i. Leisure does not enter the utility function of workers, so all labor will be used in production in period one.

A feasible allocation for the economy can be denoted by $(K, \{x_1^i, x_2^i, \hat{x}_1^i, \hat{x}_2^i\})$, where K is the total capital investment in period one, x_j^i is the consumption of individual i in period $j = 1,2$, and $\hat{x}_1^i$ and $\hat{x}_2^i$ are the consumptions of the good by individual i in the two periods supplied from the output of the firm in period one, where the following inequalities must hold:

$$x_1^S \leq W_0^S - K + \hat{x}_1^S, \tag{13.49}$$

$$x_2^S \leq (1-d)K + \hat{x}_2^S, \tag{13.50}$$

$$\hat{x}_1^S + \hat{x}_2^S \leq G(K, L^S). \tag{13.51}$$

The first inequality says that total consumption in period one cannot exceed the endowment that was not invested plus what is produced by the firm in period one and consumed; the second inequality says total consumption in period two cannot exceed the depreciated capital stock that was invested in the firm in period one plus what was produced in period one for consumption in period two; and the third inequality says that what is produced with the capital and labor supplied to the firm in period one suffices to satisfy the consumption plan of the economy in the two periods.

A *Pareto-efficient allocation* is a feasible allocation with the property that any other feasible allocation must reduce the utility of at least one citizen. An *interior allocation* is a feasible allocation at which:

$$\text{for all } i, \, x_1^i > 0, \, x_2^i > 0 \text{ and } 0 < K < W_0^S$$
$$\text{and } \hat{x}_1^S > 0, \hat{x}_2^S > 0. \tag{13.52}$$

We can characterize interior Pareto-efficient allocations as follows. Let

$$G_1(K,L) = \frac{\partial G(K,L)}{\partial K} \text{ and, similarly, } u^{i\prime}(x) = \frac{du^i(x)}{dx}.$$

PROPOSITION 13.5 *Assume that* $G_1(W_0^S, L^S) < d$. *An interior allocation is Pareto efficient if and only if:*

$$G_1(K,L^S) = d \text{ and } (\forall i)(u^{i\prime}(x_1^i) = \beta^i u^{i\prime}(x_2^i)).$$

PROOF.[3]

A feasible allocation is Pareto efficient if it solves the following program:

$$\max u(x_1^1) + \beta^1 u(x_2^1)$$
$$\text{subj. to}$$
$$(\forall j > 1)(u(x_1^j) + \beta u(x_2^j) \geq k^j) \quad (\lambda^j) \tag{13.53}$$
$$x_1^S \leq W_0^S - K + \hat{x}_1^S \quad (\alpha)$$
$$x_2^S \leq (1-d)K + \hat{x}_2^S \quad (\beta)$$
$$\hat{x}_1^S + \hat{x}_2^S \leq G(K,L^S) \quad (\gamma)$$

The Kuhn-Tucker conditions for an interior solution are:

- $G_1(K,L^S) = d$;
- for all j, $u'(x_1^i) = \beta^i u'(x_2^i)$; and
- the last three constraints in program (13.53) hold with equality.

In particular, there exists a (unique) value $K < W_0^S$ such that $G_1(K,L^S) = d$ if and only if $G_1(W_0^S, L^S) < d$, if G is strictly concave. ∎

In words, an interior Pareto-efficient allocation must use just that amount of capital that sets the marginal product of capital equal to the rate of depreciation, given full employment of labor, and it must equalize the ratio of the marginal utilities in the two periods to the discount factor, for each consumer. In particular, all interior Pareto-efficient allocations employ the same amount of capital in production, since the first equation in Proposition 13.5 uniquely determines K, since L^S is fixed. So total production is a constant in such allocations. All that changes across Pareto-efficient allocations is how the output is allocated among citizens.

We now assume the economy is that described above. As well as their endowments of labor and the good, citizens own the firm, in shares θ^i, where $\sum_{i=1}^{n} \theta^i = 1$. (We need not discuss how the shares come to be distributed.) We introduce three markets, for investment, labor, and the good as consumption. At the beginning of period one, a market for capital (the investment good) opens, with a rental rate for capital (r), and a labor market opens, with a wage (w) for one efficiency unit of labor. At the end of period one, a market for the firm's output opens, with a price (p) for the good. All purchases of the good at this point are used for consumption, in either period one or period two. The firm maximizes profits at these prices, demanding an amount of capital K and an amount of labor L in efficiency units at the beginning of period one and selling its output at the end of period one. The profit of the firm at an allocation (K,L) of capital and labor and prices (p,r,w) is $\Pi(K,L)$ = $pG(K,L) - rK - wL$.

Furthermore, there is an income tax rate t in $[0,1]$. If the (pretax) income of agent i is y^i, her after-tax income will be $(1-t)y^i + t\dfrac{y^S}{n}$.

Consumer-worker-investors supply capital and labor to the firm at the beginning of period one. All capital is supplied from the endowments W_0^i. Given the amount of capital the agent is supplying to the firm, he chooses how to spend his income on the consumption good, which the agent allocates to periods one and two. The agent's investment decision—how much of its endowment of the good to supply as capital to the firm—must be an additive Kantian equilibrium of a "game" played among investors, which we now describe.

1. Citizen i supplies L^i, its entire labor endowment, to the firm. Suppose it supplies an amount of capital K^i to the firm, where $K^i \leq W_0^i$. Then its budget constraint is:

$$p(x_1^i + \hat{x}_2^i) \leq p(W_0^i - K^i) +$$
$$(1-t)\left(\theta^i \Pi(K,L) + rK^i + wL^i\right) + \frac{t}{n} pG(K,L) \tag{13.54}$$

Constraint (13.54) states that the value of the good the agent consumes in period one plus the amount of the good it purchases for consumption in period two must not exceed the value of the good it saves from its endowment in period one plus its after-tax income plus the value of its demogrant. Note that the market income of the consumer comes from three sources—its share of firm profits, its capital income from the rental of the capital good to the firm, and its wage income. Note that the entire output of the economy is taxed in period one, which explains the form of the demogrant.

In addition, its period two consumption must satisfy:

$$x_2^i \leq (1-d)K^i + \hat{x}_2^i. \tag{13.55}$$

Inequality (13.55) says that the agent's period two consumption must not exceed the depreciated capital stock that it receives back from the firm and what it purchased from the firm at the end of period one as for consumption good in period two.[4]

2. Suppose that we fix the capital investment profile of the economy, $(K^1,\ldots,K^n)$, and so $K = K^S$ and $L = L^S$. The agent now determines its consumption demands in order to maximize $u^i(x_1^i) + \beta^i u^i(x_2^i)$ subject to budget constraints (13.54) and (13.55). This is a conventional utility-maximization problem. Of course, the solution depends on the investment profile $(K^1,\ldots,K^n)$.

3. Now suppose that each agent imagines adding a constant ρ—zero, positive or negative—to the profile of investments, producing a new total investment of $K^S + n\rho$. This will of course change the utility-maximizing demands of consumers for the consumption commodity in the two periods. Denote the new demands of the commodity by $x_1^i(\rho), x_2^i(\rho)$. We can now define the utility of agent i at the investment deviation ρ as:

$$V^i(K^1 + \rho,\ldots,K^n + \rho) = u^i(x_1^i(\rho)) + \beta^i u^i(x_2^i(\rho)). \tag{13.56}$$

To say that $(K^1,\ldots,K^n)$ is an additive Kantian equilibrium of the game $\{V^i\}$ means that the functions $\{V^i\}$ are maximized at $\rho = 0$ for every player i.

That is, no citizen would like to translate the investment vector by any constant.

We can now state:

DEFINITION 13.2 A *Walras-Kant market-socialist equilibrium at a tax rate* t is a feasible allocation for the economy, and a vector of prices (p,r,w), such that:

(i) the firm demands (K,L) to maximize $pG(K,L) - rK - wL$, yielding profits Π and total output $Y = G(K,L)$;

(ii) given Π, Y, and K^i citizen i demands $(x_1^i, x_2^i, \hat{x}_1^i, \hat{x}_2^i)$ to maximize $u(x_1^i) + \beta^i u(x_2^i)$ subject to constraints (13.54) and (13.55);

(iii) the vector of investments $(K^1, ..., K^n)$ is an additive Kantian equilibrium of the game $\{V^i\}$ defined in (13.56); and

(iv) all markets clear, that is:

$$K^S = K, L^S = L, G(K,L) = \hat{x}_1^S + \hat{x}_2^S.$$

This is a private ownership economy (the firm is owned by consumers); all choices are decentralized, including the investment decision. It differs from the conventional Arrow-Debreu model of a private ownership economy only in the investment decision, which is cooperative. In the original Arrow-Debreu formulation, the investment vector is a *Nash* equilibrium of the game $\{V^i\}$, where $\rho = 0$. To put this more simply, the agent's utility-maximization problem has her choosing not only her consumptions but her investment at the same time. In contrast, here the investment choice is a Kantian equilibrium, which has ramifications for the consumer's choice of consumptions, which are chosen in the Nash manner.

We have:

PROPOSITION 13.6 *For any* $t \in [0,1]$, *any interior Walras-Kant market-socialist equilibrium is Pareto efficient.*[5]

PROOF.

1. Let an equilibrium at tax rate t be given: the allocation is $(K^S, L^S; K^1, ..., K^n; \{x_1^i, x_2^i, \hat{x}_1^i, \hat{x}_2^i \mid i = 1, ..., n\})$, and the prices are (p,r,w). By profit maximization, we have $pG_1(K^S, L^S) = r$ and $pG_2(K^S, L^S) = w$.

2. Because the consumption choices maximize the agents' utilities given their investment choices, a conventional analysis shows that:

$$u^{i\prime}(x_1^i) = \beta^i u^{i\prime}(x_2^i)$$

$$p(x_1^i + \hat{x}_2^i) = p(W_0^i - K^i) + (1-t)(\theta^i \Pi + rK^i + wL^i) + \frac{t}{n} pY,$$

$$x_2^i = \hat{x}_2^i + (1-d)K^i$$

$$K^i < W_0^i$$

where the last inequality comes from the interiority assumption.

3. Now consider the Kantian deviation on investment: if we add a constant ρ to the investment profile $(K^1, \ldots, K^n)$, the new consumption variables will satisfy these equations:

$$u^{i\prime}(x_1^i(\rho)) = \beta^i u^{i\prime}(x_2^i(\rho)) \tag{13.57}$$

$$\begin{aligned} p(x_1^i(\rho) + \hat{x}_2^i(\rho)) = {} & p(W_0^i - (K^i + \rho)) + \\ & (1-t)(\theta^i(G(K^S + n\rho) - r(K^S + n\rho) - wL^S) + \\ & r(K^i + \rho) + wL^i) + \frac{t}{n} pG(K^S + n\rho, L^S) \end{aligned} \tag{13.58}$$

$$x_2^i = \hat{x}_2^i + (1-d)(K^i + \rho) \tag{13.59}$$

$$K^i + \rho \leq W_0^i \tag{13.60}$$

Invoking the Implicit Function Theorem, we can calculate the derivatives of the functions $\{x_1^i(\cdot), x_2^i(\cdot), \hat{x}_2^i(\cdot)\}$. Differentiating the above system with respect to ρ and setting $\rho = 0$ gives:

$$u^{i\prime\prime}(x_1^i)x_1^{i\prime}(0) - \beta^i u^{i\prime\prime}(x_2^i)x_2^{i\prime}(0) = 0$$

$$x_2^{i\prime}(0) = \hat{x}_2^{i\prime}(0) + 1 - d \tag{13.61}$$

$$px_1^{i\prime}(0) + p\hat{x}_2^{i\prime}(0) = r - p$$

(The interesting calculation is the one leading to the third equation; the reader is invited to check it.) Using Cramer's Rule, we can solve for the numbers $\{x_1^{i\prime}(0), x_2^{i\prime}(0)\}$ as follows:

$$x_1^{i\prime}(0) = \frac{u^{i\prime\prime}(x_2^i)\beta^i(r - pd)}{D}, \tag{13.62}$$

$$x_2^{i\prime}(0) = \frac{u^{i\prime\prime}(x_2^i)(r - pd)}{D}$$

$$\text{where } D = \det \begin{pmatrix} u^{i\prime\prime}(x_1^i) & -\beta^i u^{i\prime\prime}(x_2^i) & 0 \\ 0 & 1 & -1 \\ p & 0 & p \end{pmatrix}.$$

4. Now, since $(K^1,\ldots,K^n)$ is a Kantian equilibrium of the game $\{V^i\}$, we must have, from (13.56):

$$(\forall i) \frac{d}{d\rho}\bigg|_{\rho=0} \left(u^i(x_1^i(\rho)) + \beta^i u^i(x_2^i(\rho)) \right) =$$

$$u^{i\prime}(x_1^i)x_1^{i\prime}(0) + \beta^i u^{i\prime}(x_2^i)x_2^{i\prime}(0) = \tag{13.63}$$

$$u^{i\prime}(x_1^i)\frac{u^{i\prime\prime}(x_2^i)\beta^i(r-pd)}{D} + \beta^i u^{i\prime}(x_2^i)\frac{u^{i\prime\prime}(x_2^i)(r-pd)}{D} = 0,$$

where the last inequality is achieved by substituting from (13.62). Now, using the fact that $u^{i\prime}(x_1^i) = \beta^i u^{i\prime}(x_2^i)$, the last expression in (13.63) implies that:

$$r = pd.$$

Hence, invoking step 1 of the proof, we have:

$$G_1(K^S, L^S) = d.$$

This proves that the allocation is Pareto efficient, by Proposition 13.5. ∎

13.10 Summary

We have shown that by embedding Kantian optimization by citizens in either their labor supply decision or their investment decision in general equilibrium models that are otherwise quite conventional, equilibria exist that are Pareto efficient at any rate of income taxation. Thus, cooperation in the Kantian manner suffices to dissolve the "equity-efficiency trade-off." Voters may choose a redistributive tax rate from purely distributional considerations, without having to worry about economic costs.

It is important to remark that, unlike previous market-socialist models, this one relies not on equality in the distribution of profit shares in the population but rather on the income taxation as the mechanism of equalizing income. For this reason, these models conceptualize a "social democratic" vision of socialism rather than a Marxist one. What's new here in the social-democratic design is the inclusion of a cooperative ethos in the form of Kantian optimization by citizens. Historically, cooperation in the (social-democratic) Nordic economies occurred not through Kantian optimization (as far as we know) but through centralized bargaining among a national trade union federation, the state, and an employers' association, and the "solidaristic wage" policy: for economic analysis of that mechanism, the reader should consult the many articles of Karl Moene with coauthor Michael Wallerstein and other coauthors (for example, Moene and Wallerstein 1997, 2001; and Barth, Moene and Willumsen 2014). In the Nordic economies, firms remain, in the main, privately and unequally owned, and income equality is achieved through income taxation and the solidaristic wage.

FOURTEEN

An Economy of
Worker-Owned Firms

14.1 Introduction

In the market-socialist models of chapter 13, firms were owned by citizens and the state. In the model of this chapter firms continue to maximize profits, but these are distributed to the firms' workers in proportion to their labor contributions. In addition, workers are paid market wages for their labor contributions. We also introduce two occupations, where each worker supplies one kind of occupational labor to the firm. Multiplicative Kantian optimization by workers in their labor supply decisions, along with price-taking behavior and profit-maximizing firms, delivers a one parameter family of Pareto-efficient equilibria.

The model contrasts with the usual conception of the worker-owned firm, in which firms are supposed to maximize value added per worker, which is distributed to workers according to some formula but workers are not paid wages (see Drèze 1993).

14.2 The Model and the Game

There is an economy with one good. There are two kinds of labor—two occupations. The good is produced by a concave production function $G(E,D)$, where E and D are the levels of the two occupational labor supplies. We simplify here by ignoring the capital input.

There are n citizen workers, partitioned into two elements:

$$I_1 = \{i \mid \bar{E}^i > 0 \text{ and } \bar{D}^i = 0\}, n_1 = \# I_1$$
$$I_2 = \{j \mid \bar{D}^{n_1+j} > 0 \text{ and } \bar{E}^{n_1+j} = 0\}, n_2 = \# I_2,$$

where $\bar{E}^i$ (or $\bar{D}^i$) is the endowment of labor the agent has in the E (or D) occupation. We index the workers in the first occupation by $i = 1,\dots,n_1$ and workers in the second occupation by $i = n_1 + j$, $j = 1,\dots,n_2$. Individuals have utility functions of the form $u^i(x,E)$ (for $i = 1,\dots,n_1$) or $u^i(x,D)$ (for $i = n_1 + 1,\dots, n_1 + n_2$), depending upon the kind of labor they possess.

The economy uses markets, with three prices, (p,w,d), p being the price of the good, w the wage of E labor, and d the wage of D labor. There is one firm, using the production function G. The firm maximizes profits. The profits accrue to workers in proportion to their labor supplies, as follows. A fraction λ of profits will be divided among the E workers in proportion to their labor contributions, while fraction $1 - \lambda$ of the profits are divided among the D workers in proportion to their labor contributions. λ is an *exogenous* parameter of the model. Thus, for instance, the income of a worker of type 1 (that is, $i \in I_1$) will be:

$$wE^i + \frac{E^i}{E^S}\lambda\Pi , \qquad (14.1)$$

where Π is the firm's profits and $E^S \equiv \sum_{i \in I_1} E^i$. The analogous expression holds for workers of type 2.

Given prices, consider a game $\mathbf{V}^1$ whose players are the E-*type* workers. We are *given* a total labor supply $\hat{D}^S$ by the D-*type* workers. The payoff function for the ith worker of the E-*type* is:

$$V^{1,i}(E^1,\dots,E^n;\hat{D}^S)$$

$$= u^{1i}\left(\frac{wE^i + \dfrac{E^i}{E^S}\lambda(pG(E^S,\hat{D}^S) - wE^S - d\hat{D}^S)}{p}, E^i \right), \text{ for } i = 1,\dots, n_1. \ (14.2)$$

Analogously, given a total labor supply by the E-*type* workers of $\hat{E}^S$, consider a game $\mathbf{V}^2$ among the D workers whose payoff functions are:

$$V^{2,n_1+j}(D^{n_1+1},\dots,D^{n_1+n_2};\hat{E}^S)$$

$$= u^{2i}\left(\frac{dD^{n_1+j} + \dfrac{D^{n_1+j}}{D^S}(1-\lambda)(pG(\hat{E}^S,D^S) - w\hat{E}^S - dD^S)}{p}, D^{n_1+j} \right),$$

for $j = 1,\dots,n_2$. $\qquad (14.3)$

DEFINITION 14.1 A *Walras-Kant worker-ownership equilibrium with profit-share parameter* $\lambda \in [0,1]$ is:

- a price vector (p,w,d)
- consumption bundles (x^i, E^i) for all $i \in I_1$ and (x^{n_1+j}, D^{n_1+j}) for all $j = 1,\ldots,n_2$, such that:
- the vector (x^S, E^S, D^S) solves the firm's profit maximization problem:

$$\max_{x,E,D} px - wE - dD$$

$$s.t. \quad x = G(E,D)$$

- given D^S, $(E^1,\ldots,E^{n_1})$ is a multiplicative Kantian equilibrium of the game $\mathbf{V}^1(\cdot; D^S)$ defined in (14.2) for the type 1 workers,
- given E^S, $(D^{n_1+1},\ldots,D^{n_1+n_2})$ is a multiplicative Kantian equilibrium of the game $\mathbf{V}^2(\cdot; E^S)$ defined in (14.3) for the type 2 workers,
- for worker $i \in I_1$ and $j \in I_2$ we have:

$$x^i = \frac{wE^i + \dfrac{E^i}{E^S}\lambda(pG(E^S,\hat{D}^S) - wE^S - d\hat{D}^S)}{p},$$

$$x^{n_1+j} = \frac{dD^{n_1+j} + \dfrac{D^{n_1+j}}{D^S}(1-\lambda)(pG(\hat{E}^S,D^S) - w\hat{E}^S - dD^S)}{p}$$

$$x^S = \sum_{i=1}^{n} x^i, \ E^S = \sum_{i\in I_1} E^i, \ D^S = \sum_{j\in I_2} D^{n_1+j} \quad .$$

Conceptually, the main difference between this model of an economy with worker-owned firms and Jacques H. Drèze's (1993) model is that here workers receive a wage and then a share of profits, whereas in Drèze's model workers do not receive wages but divide up value-added net of the cost of capital. In the present economic environment, since there is no payment to capital, this means that total firm revenues would be divided up among workers. Drèze's model also has weights by which the labor contribution of different occupations are multiplied, determining the shares of value added that workers of different occupations receive, but the weights emerge endogenously, whereas in my model, the weights $(\lambda, 1 - \lambda)$ are exogenous—a policy variable. The endogenous weighting of the labor of different occupations in my model is accomplished with occupational wages, which emerge as part of the equilibrium.

14.3 The First Welfare Theorem for Worker-Owned Economies

PROPOSITION 14.1 *Any Walras-Kant worker-ownership equilibrium such that the two occupational labor vectors are strictly positive is Pareto efficient.*

PROOF.

1. By profit-maximization, we have:

$$\frac{w}{p} = G_1(E^S, D^S), \quad \frac{d}{p} = G_2(E^S, D^S). \tag{14.4}$$

2. The condition that the vector $\mathbf{E} = (E^1, ..., E^{m_1})$ be a multiplicative Kantian equilibrium of the game V^1 is:

$$(\forall i \in I_1) \quad u_1^i \cdot \frac{1}{p}(wE^i + \frac{E^i}{E^S}\lambda\Pi_1 E^S) + u_2^i E^i = 0, \tag{14.5}$$

where Π_1 is the derivative of the profit function with respect to the labor supply of type 1. By profit maximization, at the equilibrium allocation, $\Pi_1 = 0$, and so (14.5) reduces to:

$$u_1^i \frac{w}{p} E^i + u_2^i E^i = 0 ; \tag{14.6}$$

invoking the fact that $E^i > 0$, we have:

$$\frac{w}{p} = -\frac{u_2^i}{u_1^i} \text{ for all } i \in I_1 . \tag{14.7}$$

3. In like manner, we have:

$$\frac{d}{p} = -\frac{u_2^{n_1+j}}{u_1^{n_1+j}} \text{ for all } j \in I_2 . \tag{14.8}$$

4. By (14.4), (14.7), and (14.8), the allocation is Pareto efficient. ∎

14.4 Existence of a One-Parameter Family of Walras-Kant Worker Ownership Equilibria

PROPOSITION 14.2 *Under standard conditions,*[1] *there exists a Walras-Kant worker ownership (WKWO) equilibrium for any* $\lambda \in [0,1]$.

PROOF.

1. Let Δ^2 be the 2-simplex. Let $\mathbf{p} = (p, w, d) \in \text{int } \Delta^2$. Let (X, A, B) be the profit-maximizing supply of output, demand for labor of occupation 1 by the firm, and demand for labor of occupation 2 by the firm. This exists and is unique if G is strictly concave, differentiable, and satisfies the Inada conditions, since the first-order conditions are then:

$$\frac{w}{p} = G_1, \quad \frac{d}{p} = G_2.$$

2. Given B, we show the existence of a unique vector $((x^1, E^1), , ..., (x^{n_1}, E^{n_1}))$ such that:

(i) for each $i \in I_1$, $\dfrac{w}{p} = -\dfrac{u_2^i(x^i, E^i)}{u_1^i(x^i, E^i)}$, and

(ii) for each $i \in I_1$, $px^i = wE^i + \dfrac{E^i}{A} \lambda \Pi(A, B)$.

It is easiest to see this claim if we define worker i's utility function over consumption and *leisure* (measured in efficiency units):

$$U^i(x^i, \bar{E}^i - E^i) \equiv u^i(x^i, E^i), i = 1, ..., n_1.$$

Write $\ell^i \equiv \bar{E}^i - E^i$. Conditions (i) and (ii) above now become:

$$(i') \quad \frac{w}{p} = \frac{U_2^i(x^i, \ell^i)}{U_1^i(x^i, \ell^i)} \text{ and}$$

$$(ii') \quad px^i + \ell^i(w + \frac{\lambda \Pi(A, B)}{A}) = w\bar{E}^i + \frac{\bar{E}^i}{A} \lambda \Pi(A, B).$$

The locus of points (x^i, ℓ^i) described by (i') is an expansion path for the utility function U^i in the nonnegative quadrant of the (x^i, ℓ^i) plane, and the locus of points (x^i, ℓ^i) described by (ii') intersects the positive quadrant of that plane in a nonempty straight-line segment of negative slope. The intersection of these two loci exists and is a unique point if consumption and leisure are both normal goods, for this guarantees that the expansion path begins at the origin, is a monotone increasing path, and eventually lies entirely above the line segment of (ii'), so it intersects that line segment in a single point.

Hence, the point defined by (i) and (ii) exists and is unique.

3. In like manner, given A, there exists a unique vector $((x^{n_1+1}, D^{n_1+1}), ..., (x^{n_1+n_2}, D^{n_1+n_2}))$ such that:

(*i*) for each $j \in I_2$, $\dfrac{d}{p} = -\dfrac{u_2^{n_1+j}(x^{n_1+j}, D^{n_1+j})}{u_1^{n_1+j}(x^{n_1+j}, D^{n_1+j})}$, and

(*ii*) for each $j \in I_2$, $px^{n_1+j} = dD^{n_1+j} + \dfrac{D^{n_1+j}}{B}(1-\lambda)\Pi(A,B)$.

4. We now define an excess demand function for this economy on int Δ^2. Denote:

$$\Delta x(\mathbf{p}) = \sum_{i \in I} x^i - X, \quad \Delta E(\mathbf{p}) = A - \sum_{i \in I_1} E^i, \quad \Delta D(\mathbf{p}) = B - \sum_{j \in I_2} D^{n_1+j}, \quad (14.9)$$

where x^i, E^i, D^i are the quantities defined in steps 2 and 3.

5. Define the excess demand function on int Δ:

$$z(\mathbf{p}) = (\Delta x(\mathbf{p}), \Delta E(\mathbf{p}), \Delta D(\mathbf{p})) \qquad (14.10)$$

6. The reader may now verify that Walras's Law holds:

$$p\Delta x + w\Delta E + d\Delta D = 0 . \qquad (14.11)$$

7. We note that z is single valued. From here on, we proceed as in earlier sections.

Define the correspondence $\Phi : \Delta \rightarrow \Delta$ as in equations (11.8) and (11.9) above.

8. If $\mathbf{p}^*$ is a fixed point of Φ, then $z(\mathbf{p}^*) = 0$. All three markets clear at $\mathbf{p}^*$. It is left only to observe that the conditions (*i*) and (*ii*) in steps 2 and 3, which define the supplies of the two occupational labor vectors, and the demand for the consumption good, exactly characterize what it means for those vectors to be multiplicative Kantian equilibria of the games $\mathbf{V}^1$ and $\mathbf{V}^2$. This is true, because condition (*i*) is the first-order condition for the vector $\mathbf{E}$'s being a multiplicative Kantian equilibrium of the game $\mathbf{V}^1$, and condition (*ii*) is the budget constraint of the worker (and likewise for the game $\mathbf{V}^2$). This shows that the allocation is indeed a WKWO equilibrium and $\mathbf{p}^*$ is an equilibrium price vector.

9. It is left to verify the premises of the Kakutani theorem for Φ. On int Δ^2, upper hemicontinuity follows from Berge's maximum theorem. The correspondence is single valued on the interior, so it is convex valued. We skip the verification of these properties on the boundary of the simplex. ∎

REMARK. Society is free to choose the share λ. More generally, suppose there are m occupations, and $G : \Re_+^m \to \Re_+$. Then *there will exist equilibria for any profit-share vector* $\Lambda = (\lambda^1, \ldots, \lambda^m)$ *in the* $(m - 1)$ *unit simplex*. For instance, one could choose Λ so as to divide profits equally among all occupations by letting λ^j be proportional to the number of workers of occupational type j. (Within each occupation, the profits will be divided in proportion to effort.) Thus, in this economy, we can achieve an approximation to equality of distribution of capital income.

Of course, we have avoided the question of capital inputs and so have not had to worry about paying interest to investors. I do not think there would be any problem adding capital to the model; however, workers would then have to pay interest to investors before dividing the remaining profits among themselves.

FIFTEEN

Conclusion

Positive or Normative?

In this short conclusion, I attempt to evaluate the purpose and use of the ideas that I have presented. Are the concepts of Kantian optimization and equilibrium intended to be positive (descriptive) or normative (ethical)?

My references to Michael Tomasello's work suggest that my intention is positive. How can we formalize our understanding of cooperative behavior, in the sense that Nash equilibrium and general equilibrium theory have formalized our understanding of competitive behavior? I rely upon Tomasello to establish the claim that cooperation is essentially unique in humans (or at least, it is far more highly developed) in the class of great apes and, moreover, that our failure to give it proper attention in economic theory is serious.

I intend the concept of simple Kantian equilibrium to be both a positive and a normative concept: positive because I believe it is a good model of many real instances of cooperation, and normative because I believe that the observation "we must all hang together, or . . . we shall all hang separately" makes good sense as a recommendation for action in such situations. (Recall the definition of solidarity from chapter 1.) That good sense is formalized by the proposition that in monotonic games, simple Kantian equilibria are Pareto efficient, whereas noncooperative (Nash) equilibria are not (Proposition 3.3). And the class of monotonic games includes the two great problems with which noncooperative theory deals ineffectively: the tragedy of the commons, or the case of congestion externalities, and the free-rider problem, or the case of the provision of public goods. So the observation that simple Kantian optimization solves both types of problem efficiently, although restricted to the simple case of essentially symmetric games (see Proposition 2.1), is of massive importance.

However, most of this book is concerned with generalizations of simple Kantian equilibrium to cover the case when individuals are heterogeneous in their preferences. Here, the central concepts are those of multiplicative and additive Kantian equilibrium (though there are variations on these; see chapter 4). I have recounted some just-so stories of how tribes of fishers may have learned to optimize in the way proposed in multiplicative Kantian optimization: expand your fishing time only if you would have all other fishers do likewise (by the same factor). But I have no evidence that this ever happened. I cannot argue that additive and multiplicative Kantian equilibrium are intended as descriptions of reality. They are, as far as I know, mainly normative concepts. They are prescriptions for behavior.

Evidence that they are *natural* prescriptions for cooperative behavior is that in simple production economies, the equilibria associated with these two ways of optimizing deliver Pareto efficiency for the two most venerable allocation rules in cooperative societies: division of the product in proportion to labor expended, and equal division of the product. Moreover, a somewhat deeper result (Corollary 4.5) is that the only allocation rules that can be efficiently implemented in production economies with *some kind* of Kantian reasoning are mixtures of these two venerable allocation rules. This mathematical fact reinforces my conjecture that Kantian optimization, as here defined, is a natural way of modeling cooperation.

To say that the concepts of additive and multiplicative Kantian equilibria are prescriptions for behavior is to propose them as a way of organizing cooperation among a group of individuals who desire to cooperate. They are ethically convincing prescriptions, if the characterization of equilibrium, that "nobody desires to alter the vector of efforts by rescaling [or translation]," appeals as a property of fairness to the individuals in the society. Or, in the emissions problem of chapter 11, an even simpler characterization of cooperation may have normative appeal: that countries unanimously agree on what the cap on global emissions should be and view the shares $\{a^i\}$ as fair.

Despite my viewing these more complex forms of Kantian optimization as prescriptive, let me give several historical examples which suggest that their descriptive power may be useful. In his interesting book *Trust*, Francis Fukuyama (1995) argues that different national cultures have varying levels of trust, which has important consequences for industrial organization. According to Fukuyama, trust is most highly developed in Japanese culture, where people extend trust far beyond the family orbit. In contrast, in Sinitic cultures (China, Hong Kong, Singapore, Taiwan), trust typically does not extend beyond the family. In both Japan and Sinitic societies, firms begin as family firms. In Chinese firms, the (male) founder of the firm eventually passes the firm down to his son, and he to his grandson, but there is significant resistance to drawing in outside management when the firm becomes large or when the relevant generation of male descendants does not contain a competent manager. When such a point is reached, Chinese firms tend to fail, according to Fukuyama. In Japan, there is no such reluctance: outside management is brought in, as are outside investors. Consequently, we observe large private firms in Japan that evolved from family firms, but not so in Sinitic societies. Large firms in Chinese cultures, so Fukuyama claims, must be formed by the state.[1] He also argues that, in France, the monarchy effectively destroyed civic associations, which have never recovered, and, in the process, destroyed trust beyond the family; consequently, in France, too, the state must form large firms, which will not evolve naturally from family firms. It is not a coincidence that the Japanese developed a kind of industrial relations that depends upon trust among workers and between workers and managers. Executives of American automobile firms were astonished when they learned that, on Japanese auto assembly lines, every worker has a switch with which he or she can stop the line, emblematic of the more cooperative relationship between workers and management in Japan than in the United States. American auto firms have since adopted many of the practices of Japanese auto firms.

A second example comes from American history. Jon Elster (2017) analyzes the effort to build cooperation among merchants and farmers in the American colonies in the decade 1766–1776 to refuse importing and exporting goods from and to Britain. (Farmers made up 90 percent of the free population.) According to Elster, the free-rider problem among merchants was solved through ostracism of violaters, triggered by the reporting of violations in the press. (This, then, was effectively a Nash equilibrium with punishments—or, at least, the fraction of Nash players was nontrivial.) The main problem for farmers, however, was apparently not self-interested Nash behavior but ignorance of the rate of participation of other farmers in the boycott. Elster quotes historian Thomas Breen (2004), who writes: "Until the colonists forged a greater sense of confidence that other colonists living in other places could be trusted to forgo British imports, they found it hard to translate rhetoric about the renunciation of the market into genuine self-denial and seriously to *join utter strangers* throughout America in resisting a powerful military adversary" (200; the italics are Elster's). Here, the press was vital in providing the necessary information to the farmers dispersed around the colonies. If Breen's observation is correct, we have here conditional Kantian behavior (or, in Elster's terminology, a quasi-moral norm).

Having the concept of Kantian optimization will help us, I believe, to see more examples of cooperation in real life. Showing that cooperative equilibrium can be modeled in a parsimonious way—that is, without introducing what many economists consider to be exotic arguments in preferences—and demonstrating the strong formal similarity of Kantian equilibrium to our central model of noncooperative equilibrium will, I hope, elevate the significance of cooperative behavior in our economic life to the august status that competitive behavior now occupies. Moreover, as I have said, the psychological foundations of cooperation may be weakened: they need not include altruism but rather should include what I think is a more universal human belief, the conception of fairness as symmetry. My hope that the more complicated versions of Kantian optimization can be used prescriptively exploits this view of fairness that is deeply embedded in our minds.

1 Introduction

1. Tomasello's view is extreme. Others, such as Frans de Waal (1996) and Philip Kitcher (2011), argue that limited cooperation exists in chimpanzees and other great apes.
2. See Kobayoshi and Koshima (2001).
3. Tomasello disagrees with some who argue that chimpanzees do cooperate in hunting smaller monkeys.
4. Formally, the game being played here is the game of chicken. The issue is whether to share the captured food peacefully or to fight over it. In chapter 2, we show that the cooperative solution to the game of chicken is often to share peacefully, but this depends upon the precise values of the payoffs.
5. The Walrasian model is to be contrasted with the general equilibrium model of Makowski and Ostroy (2001), who formalize the nineteenth-century Austrian tradition in which equilibrium is produced by many bargaining games, where each attempts to extract as much surplus as she can from her opponents. Prices, for these authors, are what one sees after the "dust of the competitive brawl clears" and do not decentralize economic activity, as with the Walrasian auctioneer. Their model cannot be accused of being asocial, although it is hypercompetitive.
6. Symmetry of the game is clearly sufficient for the existence of a simple Kantian equilibrium. It is, however, not necessary. Consider a prisoner's dilemma, which is asymmetric (the off-diagonal payoffs are not symmetric across the two players). It remains the case that both players prefer (Cooperate, Cooperate) to (Defect, Defect). If the strategy space consists of only these two strategies, then (Cooperate, Cooperate) is a simple Kantian equilibrium. If, however, the game is one with mixed strategies, a simple Kantian equilibrium may not exist.

7. "Act always in accordance with that maxim whose universality as law you can at the same time will" (Kant 2002, 55). It may be more textually accurate to justify the Kantian nomenclature by invoking Kant's hypothetical imperative. I use the term for its suggestive meaning and do not wish to imply that there is a deeper, Kantian justification of my proposal.

8. Readers should not be distracted by the fact that Rawls called himself a Kantian. He was referring to his attempt to construct justice as a corollary to rationality, not to the specific use of the hypothetical imperative in daily decisions.

2 Simple Kantian Equilibrium

1. A clip of the scene can be viewed at: https://www.youtube.com/watch?v =LJS7Igvk6ZM.

2. In chapter 3, it will be established that, in contrast, Nash equilibria are typically Pareto inefficient in strictly monotone games.

3. Since the payoffs are von Neumann–Morgenstern utilities, we are free to pick one payoff to be 0 and one to be 1 for each player. Thus, the prisoner's dilemma game in mixed strategies is a two-parameter game — here (b,c).

3 Heterogeneous Preferences

1. We can, more generally, assume the strategy sets are real intervals $[a^i, b^i]$ or even more general sets of real numbers. (Discrete sets are used to model games with a finite number of strategies.) Simplicity of presentation is purchased by the assumption that strategy sets are the nonnegative real numbers.

2. In particular, we have computed the unique K^x equilibrium for this economy.

3. See Abramitzky (2018).

4. I thank Luis Corchon for this example.

5. I thank Andreu Mas-Colell for suggesting this application.

6. We prove (3.67) in the usual fashion, by deriving the Kuhn-Tucker conditions for the maximization of one agent's utility subject to feasibility and lower bounds on the utilities of the other agents.

4 Other Forms of Kantian Optimization

1. It is in fact true that as $\beta \to 0$, the K_β equilibrium approaches the K^+ equilibrium. To demonstrate this, let $X^i(\mathbf{E}) = \theta^i(\mathbf{E})G(E^S)$ be any allocation rule. Compute that the first-order condition characterizing K_β equilibrium is:

for all i, $u_1^i\big(\theta^i(\mathbf{E})G'(E^S)(E^S + n\beta) + \nabla\theta^i(\mathbf{E}) \cdot (\mathbf{E} + \beta)\big)G(E^S) + u_2^i \cdot (E^i + \beta) = 0.$

As $\beta \to \infty$, this expression approaches:

$u_1^i\big(\theta^i(\mathbf{E})G'(E^S)(n\beta) + \beta\nabla\theta^i(\mathbf{E}) \cdot 1\big)G(E^S) + u_2^i\beta = 0,$ or

$u_1^i\big(n\theta^i(\mathbf{E})G'(E^S) + \nabla\theta^i(\mathbf{E}) \cdot 1\big)G(E^S) + u_2^i = 0.$

220

Calculation shows this is exactly the first-order condition characterizing K^+ equilibrium.

2. The existence of K_β solutions in these production economies is studied in chapter 7.

3. Some important allocation rules are excluded by the assumption that the shares θ^i do not depend on the function G. For instance, we can characterize the Walrasian rule using share functions (see equation (7.7) below), but the shares depend on G. For a discussion of what allocation rules can be implemented efficiently with Kantian variations, when the shares depend upon G as well as the effort vector, see Roemer (2015).

5 Altruism

1. See Dufwenberg et al. (2011) for a thorough study of Pareto efficiency when preferences are other-regarding. We are concerned here with the special case of our simple production economies.

2. An anonymous social welfare function takes the same value for any permutation of its arguments. Informally, it ignores the names of individuals.

3. The same method extends the proposition to any of the efficient Kantian pairs (X_β, φ_β).

6 Is Kantian Optimization Really Nash Optimization under Another Guise?

1. There is a further way in which the replacement of the two utility functions (u^1, u^2) by the social welfare function V is more convincing in Proposition 6.1 than in the example given at the beginning of this section, using the supporting tangent to the utility possibilities set. In the case of Proposition 6.1, the function V depends only on the utility functions (u^1, u^2), while the value of a in the earlier example depends upon G as well. This makes the Nash representation of the Kantian equilibrium in the latter case more natural. We build this requirement into the Nash challenge henceforth.

2. Kitcher (2011, 4) writes: "This ability to form coalitions, and ultimately to constitute a stable social group, expresses a further expansion of those fundamentally psychologically altruistic tendencies attributed in the case of maternal care."

3. V_j^1 is the derivative of V^1 with respect to the utility of the jth player.

4. *Theorem* (Hadamard) Let $F : M_1 \rightarrow M_2$ be a continuous function between two smooth, connected manifolds of $\Re_+^n$. Suppose that: (1) F is proper; (2) the Jacobian is everywhere invertible; and (3) M_2 is simply connected. Then F is a homeomorphism (and hence globally bijective).

5. I am grateful to Burak Ünveren for the last paragraph in this proof.

6. Computed with *Mathematica*.

7. From the quasi-linear example, it is easy to see that given *any* separable function $V(a,b)$, there exist self-regarding preferences u^1, u^2 such that the social welfare function that "rationalizes" the Kantian equilibrium of the economy (u^1, u^2) for any concave G is V. If $V(a,b) = q(a) + t(b)$, just let $u^1 = q^{-1}(x - h^1(E))$, $u^2 = t^{-1}(x - h^2(E))$. I do not know whether any nonseparable social-welfare function V has this property.

7 Existence and Dynamics of Kantian Equilibrium

1. Notice the difference between these best-reply correspondences, which are defined on the entire effort vector, and the Nash-best-reply correspondences, which are defined on the vectors E^{-i}. The difference is illustrated graphically in fig. 3.1.
2. It is understood that the argument of the function G in (7.6) should, more precisely, be written as $\min(\rho E^s + n(\rho - 1), nM)$.
3. The introduction of the Walrasian rule, in which the share functions θ^i depend on G as well as E, raises the question whether there are other such rules that can be efficiently implemented in the Kantian manner. Indeed there are, but I have not presented them in this book. For details, see Roemer (2015).
4. It is a well-known mathematical fact that a contraction mapping possesses a unique fixed point and that iterated application of the mapping from any initial point converges to the fixed point.

8 Evolutionary Considerations

1. I thank Burak Ünveren for this result.
2. We define Region V to exclude N_1, to avoid its overlapping with Region VII.
3. In N_4, $(1,1)$ is also a Nash equilibrium strategy, which coincides with the Kantian equilibrium. If Nashers play 1, of course they are indistinguishable from Kantians. If Nashers randomize among their equilibrium strategies, Kantians drive them to extinction.
4. Punishment, in environments such as the one in this chapter, is biologically altruistic because the individual receives no return for punishing his opponent, an act that is presumed to be costly to him.

9 Alternative Approaches to Cooperation

1. The responses were sent to me by Carsten Schröder of SOEP in DIW, Berlin. I am grateful to Carsten for including these questions on the survey.
2. Personal communication with Stefan Penczynski.

10 A Generalization to More Complex Production Economies

1. I state the definition for $l = 2$, to avoid discussion of tangent planes to iso-level surfaces of G, which would be needed for higher dimensions.
2. The citation to Chipman (1965) is thanks to Joaquim Silvestre.

11 International Cooperation to Reduce Global Carbon Emissions

1. The "standard method" is to maximize the utility of one country subject to feasibility constraints and to lower bounds on the utilities of all other countries. The Kuhn-Tucker conditions for the solution characterize Pareto efficiency.
2. To say that the firm "demands" emissions E^i means that it proposes to emit that many tons of carbon.
3. The unit simplex in $\mathfrak{R}^n_+$ is denoted Δ^{n-1}.
4. This correspondence is introduced in Mas-Colell, Whinston, and Green (1995), Proposition 17.C.1, and the derivation of the next several paragraphs is from that source.
5. It is possible to eliminate the $\{t^i\}$ from these conditions, using the fact that workers are indifferent as to the amount of labor they supply for each firm. But characterizations (1)–(3) will suffice for our needs.

12 Efficient Provision of a Public and Private Good

1. An *interior* allocation is one where (x^i, y, E^i) is positive for all i and $E^i < \bar{E}^i$. It is not necessary that both E^i_1 and E^i_2 be positive for every i.

13 Two Designs for Market Socialism

1. Each firm could produce both goods, at the cost of some additional notation.
2. An allocation is called *interior* if all private agents consume positive amounts of both commodities and leisure and if all supply positive amounts of labor (but it is not necessary that any agent supplies labor to both firms).
3. The assumption $G_1(W^S_0, L^S) < d$ is needed for interior Pareto-efficient allocations to exist. If this inequality were violated, then all efficient allocations require that $K = W^S_0$.
4. Alternatively, the firm may return the full capital K^i to the investor and subtract depreciation from profits. This leads to a different distribution of income, but the propositions below are unaffected.
5. The theorem is also true for noninterior equilibria. The restriction to interiority simplifies the characterization of Pareto efficiency, and so it is appropriate for pedagogical purposes.

14 An Economy of Worker-Owned Firms

1. The main assumption that deserves mention is that leisure and consumption are normal goods for all preference orders.

15 Conclusion

1. Fukuyama was writing in the 1990s; I do not know whether his characterization of Chinese firms continues to hold today.

REFERENCES

Abramitzky, R. 2018. *The mystery of the kibbutz*. Princeton, NJ: Princeton University Press.

Akerlof, G. 1982. "Labor contracts as partial gift exchange." *Q. J. Econ.* 97, 543–569.

Alger, I., and J. Weibull. 2013. "*Homo moralis*: Preference evolution under incomplete information and assortative matching." *Econometrica* 81, 2269–2302.

Andreoni, J. 1990. "Impure altruism and donations to public goods: A theory of warm-glow giving." *Econ. J.* 100, 464–477.

Barberà, S., and M. Jackson. 2016. "A model of protests, revolution, and information." https://dx.doi.org/10.2139/ssrn.2732864.

Bardhan, P. 1993. "On tackling the soft budget constraint in market socialism." In P. Bardhan and J. Roemer, eds., *Market socialism: The current debate*. New York: Oxford University Press.

Bardhan, P., and J. Roemer. 1992. "Market socialism: A case for rejuvenation." *J. Econ. Persp.* 6, 101–116.

Barth E., K. Moene, and F. Willumsen. 2014. "The Scandinavian model: An interpretation." *J. Pub. Econ.* 117, 60–72.

Bergstrom, T. 1995. "On the evolution of altruistic ethical rules for siblings." *Am. Econ. Rev.* 85, 58–81.

Boehm, C. 2012. *Moral origins*. New York: Basic Books.

Bosch-Domènech, A., and J. Silvestre. 2017. "The role of frames, numbers and risk in the frequency of cooperation." *Int'l Rev. Econ.* 64, 245–267.

———. In press. "Experiment-inspired comments on John Roemer's theory of cooperation." *Rev. Soc. Econ.*

Bowles, S., and H. Gintis. 2004. *Microeconomics*. New York: Russell Sage Foundation.

———. 2011. *A cooperative species: Human reciprocity and its evolution*. Princeton, NJ: Princeton University Press.

Boyd, R., H. Gintis, S. Bowles, and P. Richerson. 2003. "The evolution of altruistic punishment." *PNAS* 100, 3531–3535.

Bratman, M. 1992. "Shared cooperative activity." *Phil. Rev.* 101, 327–421.

Breen, T. 2004. *The marketplace of revolution.* Oxford: Oxford University Press.

Brekke, K. A., S. Kverndokk, and K. Nyborg. 2003. "An economic model of moral motivation." *J. Pub. Econ.* 87, 1967–1983.

Brennan, G., and L. Lomasky. 1993. *Democracy and decision: The pure theory of electoral preference.* New York: Cambridge University Press.

Chambers, C. P., and J. D. Moreno-Ternero. 2017. "Taxation and poverty." *Soc. Choice & Welfare* 48, 153–175.

Chipman, J. S. 1965. "A survey of the theory of international trade: Part 2, The neoclassical theory." *Econometrica* 33, 685–760.

Corneo, G. 2017. *Is capitalism obsolete?* Cambridge, MA: Harvard University Press.

Cox, J., et al. 2009. "Trust in private and common property experiments." *S. Econ. J.* 75, 957–975.

Darwall, S. 2009. *The second-person standpoint.* Cambridge, MA: Harvard University Press.

Drèze, J. 1993. *Labour management, contracts and capital markets.* Oxford: Basil Blackwell.

Dufwenberg, M., et al. 2011. "Other-regarding preferences in general equilibrium." *Rev. Econ. Stud.* 78, 613–639.

Dunbar, R. I. M. 2009. "The social brain hypothesis and its implications for social evolution." *Ann. Hum. Biol.* 36, 562–572.

Elster, J. 1989a. *The cement of society.* New York: Cambridge University Press.

———. 1989b. "Social norms and economic theory." *J. Econ. Persp.* 3, 99–117.

———. 2017. "On seeing and being seen." *Soc. Choice & Welfare* 49, 721–734.

Feddersen, T. 2004. "Rational choice theory and the paradox of not voting." *J. Econ. Persp.* 18, 99–112.

Fehr, E., and H. Gintis. 2007. "Human motivation and social cooperation: Experimental and analytical foundations." *Ann. Rev. Soc.* 33, 43–64.

Fehr, E., and K. M. Schmidt. 1999. "A theory of fairness, competition and cooperation." *Q. J. Econ.* 114, 817–868.

Frey, B., and B. Torgler. 2007. "Tax morale and conditional cooperation." *J. Comp. Econ.* 35, 136–159.

Fukuyama, F. 1995. *Trust: The social virtues and the creation of prosperity.* New York: Free Press.

Gambetta, D. 2015. "What makes people tip?" In C. Lopéz-Guerra and J. Maskiver, eds., *Rationality, democracy and justice: The legacy of Jon Elster.* New York: Cambridge University Press.

Gilbert, M. 1990. "Walking together, a paradigmatic social phenomenon." *Midwest Stud. Phil.* 15, 1–14.

Gintis, H. 2000. "Strong reciprocity and human sociality." *J. Theor. Biol.* 206, 169–179.

Hardin, G. 1968. "The tragedy of the commons." *Sci.* 162, 1243–1248.

Ju, B.-G., E. Miyagama, and T. Sakai. 2007. "Non-manipulable division rules in claims problems and generalizations." *J. Econ. Theory* 132, 1–26.

Kandori, M. 1992. "Social norms and community enforcement." *Rev. Econ. Stud.* 59, 63–80.

Kant, I. 2002. *Groundworks for the metaphysics of morals.* Ed. and trans. A. Wood. New Haven: Yale University Press.

Kitcher, P. 2011. *The ethical project.* Cambridge, MA: Harvard University Press.

Kobayashi, H., and S. Koshima. 2001. "Unique morphology of the human eye and its adaptive meaning: Comparative studies on external morphology of the primate eye." *J. Hum. Evol.* 52, 314–320.

Laffont, J.-J. 1975. "Macroeconomic constraints, economic efficiency, and ethics: An introduction to Kantian economics." *Economica* 42, 430–437.

Lange, O., and F. Taylor. 1938. *On the economic theory of socialism.* Minneapolis: University of Minnesota Press.

Lindahl, E. 1919. *Die Gerechtigkeit der Besteuerung.* Lund: Gleerup.

Makowski, L., and J. Ostroy. 2001. "Perfect competition and the creativity of the market." *J. Econ. Lit.* 39, 479–535.

Mas-Colell, A. 1987. "Cooperative equilibrium." In J. Eatwell, M. Milgate, and P. Newman, *The Palgrave dictionary of economics,* vol. 1. London: Macmillan.

Mas-Colell, A., and J. Silvestre. 1989. "Cost share equilibria: A Lindahlian approach." *J. Econ. Theory* 47, 239–256.

Mas-Colell, A., M. D. Whinston, and J. R. Green. 1995. *Macroeconomic theory.* New York: Oxford University Press.

Mirrlees, J. 1971. "An exploration of the theory of optimum income taxation." *Rev. Econ. Stud.* 38, 175–208.

Moene, K., and M. Wallerstein. 1997. "Full employment as a worker disciplining device." In J. Roemer, ed., *Property relations, incentives, and welfare.* New York: St. Martin's Press.

———. 2001. "Inequality, social insurance and redistribution." *Am. Pol. Sci. Rev.* 95, 859–874.

Moulin, H. 1987. "Equal or proportional division of a surplus, and other methods." *Int'l J. Game Theory* 16, 161–186.

Musgrave, R. A., and A. T. Peacock, eds. 1958. *Classics in the theory of public finance.* London: Macmillan.

Olson, M. 1965. *The logic of collective action.* Cambridge, MA: Harvard University Press.

Rabin, M. 2003. "Incorporating fairness into game theory and economics." In C. F. Camerer, G. Loewenstein, and M. Rabin, eds., *Advances in behavioral economics.* Princeton, NJ: Princeton University Press.

Richter, A., and J. Grasman, 2013. "The transmission of sustainable harvesting norms when agents are traditionally cooperative." *Ecological Econ.* 93, 202–209.

Roemer, J. 1994. *A future for socialism.* Cambridge, MA: Harvard University Press.

——. 1996. *Theories of distributive justice.* Cambridge, MA: Harvard University Press.

——. 2006. "Party competition under private and public financing: A comparison of institutions." *Advances Theoretical Econ.* https://doi.org/10.2202/1534-5963.1229.

Roemer, J., and J. Silvestre. 1993. "The proportional solution for economies with both private and public ownership." *J. Econ. Theory* 59, 426–444.

Skyrms, B. 2004. *The stag hunt and the evolution of social structure.* New York: Cambridge University Press.

Stauber, L. 1987. *A new program for democratic socialism.* Carbondale, IL: Four Willows Press.

Stern, T. D. 2016. "Challenges for US climate policy." Speech, Council on Foreign Relations, January 15. https://www.cfr.org/event/challenges-us-climate-policy.

Sugden, R. 1982. "On the economics of philanthropy." *Econ. J.* 92, 341–350.

Thomson, W. 2015. "For claims problems, compromising between the proportional and constrained equal awards rules." *Econ. Theory* 60, 495–520.

Tomasello, M. 2014a. *A natural history of human thinking.* Cambridge, MA: Harvard University Press.

——. 2014b. "The ultra-social animal." *Eur. J. Soc. Psychol.* 44, 187–194.

——. 2016. *A natural history of human morality.* Cambridge, MA: Harvard University Press.

Von Neumann, J., and O. Morgenstern. 1944. *Theory of games and economic behavior.* Princeton, NJ: Princeton University Press.

Waal, Frans de. 1996. *Good natured: The origins of right and wrong in humans and other animals.* Cambridge, MA: Harvard University Press.

Walker, J., and E. Ostrom. 2009. "Trust and reciprocity as foundations for cooperation." In K. Cook, M. Levi, and R. Hardin, eds., *Whom can we trust?* New York: Russell Sage Foundation.

An *italic* page number indicates a figure.